CONTENTS

W9-BTR-641

Illustrations appear as a group following p. 112

Library of Congress Cataloging in Publication Data
Friess, Horace L., 1900–1975
Felix Adler and ethical culture.

Includes index.
1. Adler, Felix, 1851–1933.   2. Ethical culture movement—
Biography.   I. Weingartner, Fannia.
II. Title.
BP605.E84A343   170'.92'4 [B]   80-27742
ISBN 0-231-05184-0   AACR1
ISBN 0-231-05185-9 (pbk.)

Columbia University Press
New York   Guildford, Surrey

Copyright © 1981 The Ethical Culture Society
All rights reserved
Printed in the United States of America

HORACE L. FRIESS

FELIX ADLER AND ETHICAL CULTURE

MEMORIES AND STUDIES

EDITED BY
FANNIA WEINGARTNER

1981
COLUMBIA UNIVERSITY PRESS
NEW YORK

FELIX ADLER C.1920.

FELIX ADLER AND ETHICAL CULTURE

$7.50

FOREWORD

A gifted student is fortunate when he finds an outstanding teacher who helps him to develop his own distinctive capacities. Such a teacher is fully rewarded when his student is able to record and interpret his teacher's wisdom and achievement. This book is the outcome of such influence and reflection in the relation of Felix Adler and Horace Friess.

In chapter 1 the author recounts his meeting with Adler and their increasingly close personal and intellectual association. At the time of their meeting Professor Adler was in his sixty-sixth year, nearing his retirement from Columbia University, and Horace Friess was seventeen years old and in his junior year in Columbia College. Friess gives a vivid description of Adler—his "interesting and memorable appearance" with "distinctive and sensitive features. . . . his smooth-rounded and high-domed head" with eyes "intensely blue and brilliant without being hard." The author also remarks that he had previously been ignorant about Adler's "prominence in the world of social reform, education, and distinctive religious teaching."

Horace Friess at seventeen was a strikingly handsome young man with beautiful deep-set brown eyes and an expression of thoughtfulness unusual in one so young. He was slender and notably graceful and, though not an athlete, was skillful at tennis and swimming. There was indeed a certain grace in his youthful attitude toward other people and his outlook on the world which distinguished him from his fellow students. He had achieved an excellent record both in New York City's Mount Morris High School and in his first two college years. Moreover in the Dutch Reformed Church in which his family—his parents, two sisters and he himself—were communicants, his qualities had led to early appointment as Sunday School teacher and, indeed, superintendent. He had, in fact, entered college with some expectation of becoming a clergyman, but by the time he met Professor Adler had decided to pursue a career as a teacher of philosophy.

This career was destined to be that of a deeply devoted teacher and scholar in Columbia University's department of philosophy from 1919 on and also in its department of religion, established in 1962, of which he became the first chairman. Friess was greatly influential in the organization and development of this new department and of related work, such as the university seminar on religion on which he published a monograph in *The Review of Religion*, a journal he edited. Among his other publications were his doctoral dissertation including his translation and critical edition of *Schleiermacher's Soliloquies (Monologen)*, *Religion in Various Cultures* (with Herbert W. Schneider), *The Bible of the World* (with Robert O. Ballou and Friedrich Spiegelberg), and a volume of selections from Dr. Adler's writings which he called *Our Part in This World*. Taking an active part in the Ethical Culture Movement from 1926 on, he was a Leader of the New York Society for Ethical Culture from 1952 until his death at the age of seventy-five in 1975. In some ways the nature of Horace Friess's teaching and influence is well indicated by the full title of the Buttenwieser chair at Columbia—the Professorship in Human Relations, of which he became the first incumbent in 1964. Friess retired in 1966.

As already noted, when Friess first met Felix Adler, the former was still a college student while the latter was at the height of his career as teacher and thinker. Adler had recently published *An Ethical Philosophy of Life*, a comprehensive account of how he had arrived at his mature convictions in philosophy and religion, and a full statement of his teaching.

To Felix Adler the greatest good for human beings is to be found in their relation to and interaction with other humans. Every such relationship, every social institution offers in different ways and in various degrees the setting in which the highest good may be realized. Thus in the family the relation of husband and wife, of parents and children, provides the intimate opportunities for such experience. In the vocations other relationships are to be found, both between individuals and between different vocational groups. Indeed in all social and political connections, in racial and

national interrelations, further development of the greatest good
for humankind are to be sought.

These greatest societal values are to be sought not in the simi-
larities of various capacities but precisely in differing excellences
which may supplement one another. As in the family and in vocational relations the growth and development of unlike qualities,
so contrasting national and racial endowments constitute the supreme human good. When these relations are envisaged in terms
of their ultimate possibilities, ethical spiritual ideals may be described in religious terms—the ethical manifold constituting godhead, not as an individual person but as an infinite plurality of
persons in productive and creative relation to one another.

Adler's ethical and ethico-religious ideal expressed itself con-
cretely and practically in the efforts of each individual in all his
and her personal relationships to elicit from others the latent
worth ideally ascribed to the other and in so doing to evoke the
best in himself or herself.

In no relationship, whether of individuals or groups, it seems
to the present writer, is the application of Felix Adler's ethical
philosophy clearer than in the relation of teachers and students.
What might become all too artificial and self-conscious in parent-
child or wife-husband relationships in attempts to discover and
evoke distinctive excellence, and what might well be utopian with
regard to actual vocational, international, and interracial contacts,
is precisely what the relation of student and teacher presupposes.

As was suggested above, when a truly great teacher encounters
an outstandingly promising student the ideal of eliciting the distinctive, potential worth of the latter is clearly a joyous challenge
to the teacher. And in seeking to advance the education of the
student, the teacher inevitably develops his own excellence. Such
an experience is a central interest in Horace Friess's memories and
studies of Felix Adler. In this book, recollections of their first
meeting and of the ripening of their relation to one another are
detailed. The philosophic education which Friess owed to Adler,
supplementing the influence of other fine teachers—notably John
Dewey, Wendell T. Bush, and Frederick J. E. Woodbridge—is set
forth in the following pages as is the inception and history of this
book. The care with which teacher and student alike sought to

avoid domination and subservience recalls the dictum of Friedrich
Nietzsche that a student only becomes a worthy follower of his
master when he ceases to be a mere follower.

The nature of the studies which Adler suggested and which
Friess undertook in the early 1930s is explained in chapter 1. It is
significant that the model for these studies which he suggested
were found by Adler in a series of papers which Friess had written in the late twenties: a number of articles on the German philosopher of culture, Wilhelm Dilthey, and an essay on the philos-
opher-theologian Hamann, for example. The studies which Adler
proposed were carried out through the planning and writing of
this book, on which Horace Friess was engaged for more than
forty years.

Inevitably as the author worked out and reworked his plans, he
himself changed and grew, and so his perspective was also modified and altered. Among other things the extent to which his
interpretation of Adler's thought and activities involved a biographical presentation was reconsidered. Though this book is not
a conventional biography, the inner structure provides a rich and
comprehensive record of Adler's life and work. And however
many versions of some chapters were written and other revisions
were made as the author lived from relatively young manhood to
relatively old age, a consistency of outlook marks the final version
here presented.

Horace Friess completed this book only a few days before his
death at the age of seventy-five. He had devoted the last years of
his life to this work, often with heroic effort against increasing
trials of fatal illness. He himself felt that though completed his
book required finishing in the sense in which a craftsman provides "finish" to his product. This finishing has been accomplished
by masterly editing, which achieves the author's explicit inten-
tions. Though everything in the text was written by Horace Friess
except for the addition, always indicated, of some quotations primarily from Adler's writings, it is the result of the skill in selection
and reorganization for which the editor, Fannia Weingartner,
deserves credit and the reader's gratitude. Thanks are also due to
Anne Friess Kirschner for editorial assistance. It should be noted
that shortly before his death Horace Friess wrote a letter

asking Edward L. Ericson to be his literary executor and requesting him to seek the advice and assistance of two of Friess's lifelong friends and Columbia University colleagues, John Hermann Randall, Jr., and the present writer.

James Gutmann
Professor of Philosophy Emeritus
Columbia University

EDITOR'S NOTE

In the various reworkings of this book by the author some of the citations for quotations from the works of Felix Adler were lost. Since Adler, in the course of his long career, gave literally hundreds of addresses and wrote numerous articles on such key topics as religion, education, the family, labor, and public affairs, it proved impossible to recover these citations. Principal statements of Felix Adler's views on all of these topics appear in his books, listed in the bibliography. However, substituting passages drawn from these books for the particular quotations chosen by Horace Friess seemed to us unwarranted editorial intrusion. The engagement of one mind and life with another has seemed to us of primary importance; and this is Horace Friess's book. Researchers' attention is drawn to the substantial collection of Felix Adler's papers, described in the bibliography and now permanently housed in the Rare Book and Manuscript Library of Columbia University.

F.W.

ACKNOWLEDGMENT

The following have given assistance and encouragement for the publication of this book:

George Beauchamp
Algernon D. Black
Dorothy Borg
Rose Elbert
Edward L. Ericson
Eileen and Mike Franch
Constance Friess, M.D.
William Gellin
Elliott and Ruth Gruenberg
James Gutmann
Ruth Friess Gutmann
Marion Helbing
Mark Huber
Helen and Steven Jacobs
Frank Karelsen
Anne Kirschner
Mr. and Mrs. Sol Kornbluh
William Kulok
Arnold and Lee Lewis
John Morris
Roy Neuberger
New York Society for Ethical Culture
John and Mercedes Randall
Herbert and Nanette Rothschild Fund
Louis Sapir
Sidney Scheuer Fund
Ivan Schapiro
Joy Stephens
Hugh Stern

FELIX ADLER AND ETHICAL CULTURE

[1]

THE MEETING:
1917–1933

IT WAS DURING the spring of 1917 that I first met Felix Adler, by
visiting his graduate seminar in ethical philosophy at Columbia
University. He was in his sixty-sixth year, a leading citizen of notable accomplishment, and he had just finished writing a major
book, entitled *An Ethical Philosophy of Life*. I was seventeen and a
junior in Columbia College.

In April 1917 the United States entered the war against Germany. In the fall the Russian Revolution ended tsarist rule and
ushered in the Marxist-Leninist dictatorship. The war in Europe
had already been raging for three years. The battle of Verdun,
which had been fought from August to December of 1916, typi-
fied the horrifying deadlock on the Western Front. We students
in college, who were still too young for battle, were nevertheless
caught up in the fever of events and of high-pitched feelings. In
the summer of 1916 many of us worked on farms or in factories.

I was introduced to Felix Adler by a fellow student, James Gutmann, one of a group of six who were becoming steady friends.*
Beginning in 1916 we dined or took lunch together at least once
a week during the academic year, and five of us continued to do
so for more than fifty years. At first, in 1916, confronted by the
great war in Europe, we read and discussed Bertrand Russell's
Why Men Fight, a book of important insights, especially in the
opening chapters. We did not solve the problem of war, but our
friendship lasted.

*The others were John Herman Randall, Jr., who, like James Gutmann and
myself, became professor of philosophy at Columbia University; Frank Tannen-
baum, who became professor of history at Columbia University; and Albert Red-
path, who became a trustee of the university. The sixth was Edward Gluck, who
embarked on a career in the U.S. Army, retiring as General Gluck from the Judge
Advocate's office. He spent much of his life abroad.

1

James Gutmann had long known Felix Adler through having attended the Ethical Culture School, his parents and many of their circle being members of the New York Society for Ethical Culture. I had never met Adler before this, and was in fact quite ignorant of his prominence in the world of social reform, education, and distinctive religious teaching.

Felix Adler's appearance was interesting and memorable. He had at that time rather sparse wisps of greyish beard on his chin, but his smooth, rounded, high-domed head was quite bald. His face had a delicate creamy skin that flushed easily, especially when he was amused or excited by feelings of indignation. His eyes were intensely blue and brilliant, without being hard. His figure was short, not muscular but agreeably proportioned, compact and energetically mobile. Others beside myself have remarked that his appearance in late life seemed in some ways like that of a Chinese sage. Yet his visage clearly was of a Western, Jewish type with distinctive individual and sensitive features.

The terms of Adler's appointment at Columbia as Professor of Social and Political Ethics in 1902 permitted him to offer a seminar for graduate students, usually in each semester though sometimes only in one. The rest of his time was left free for his work as leader in the Ethical Culture movement (which he had founded in 1876). For by the time Adler joined the Columbia faculty in 1902 he was a man of fifty, with a very active career of social reform and teaching behind him. From 1903 to 1917 he regularly held his seminars at Columbia, except in 1908–09, when he was the Roosevelt Exchange Professor in the University of Berlin.

There were two main themes that Professor Adler repeatedly treated in his seminars. One he characterized as "an ethical theory of society," and under this head he expounded a view of social institutions which was critical both of classic individualism and of the chief forms of socialism then current. This first theme most obviously related to his title at Columbia, Professor of Social and Political Ethics. But in his own view a second theme of his seminars was equally germane, namely, a reconstruction of religious thought, of what Adler called "the spiritual ideal."

In pursuit of this second theme he criticized usual theological assumptions in both their classic and their revised, modernist forms. He maintained that "a social conception of Godhead," that is, a vision of the spiritual universe as an infinite life of interaction between uniquely diverse members, should replace the traditional monotheist idea of God as a single individual Being. He viewed the latter idea as belonging with kingship to an outmoded stage of social authority, and as not congruent with ideals of a freer society.

Social theory and religious philosophy both interested me greatly and the question of their relation was of live moment in the face of the challenge offered by the Russian Revolution. So after my meeting with him I enrolled in Professor Adler's seminar for the subsequent two years. I recall two papers he asked of me: one, in the field of social theory, was to report on Grant Robertson's then recently published book on Bismarck; the other, in the sphere of religion, was to make an analysis of the Roman Catholic breviary, the missal, as a handbook of religious thought and observance. In these tasks I was directed to consider both the might of the State and the cultus of the Church.

In the wake of the war with Germany, the moral relevance of reviewing Bismarck must be apparent to everyone. For Felix Adler's generation, and for him personally, because in 1870 he had been an American student at the University of Berlin, the career and policies of Bismarck symbolized the tangle of might and right, and the dubious claim that might can make right in statecraft. This age-old challenge for public morals was being presented on an immense scale in the war-freighted world that my own generation was experiencing. The hope that civil dealing would increase and force diminish in the conduct of international affairs was widely cherished and was to have considerable consequences.

For one brought up in a Protestant home with an active religious interest, as I had been, to explore the Roman missal for the first time was a sheer gain for my education. The definite provision in the Roman system for so many of life's different contingencies made it possible to learn abundantly from the Church, without my being drawn to conversion. I was to find that Dr. Adler himself continually studied the classic forms of religion with a profound respect and a desire to profit from a better understanding of them. This attitude impressed and attracted me.

The two assignments for his seminar, given to me as a fledgling not quite twenty, were obviously not designed to accrue to the benefit of scholarship. But they had the value of getting me to probe into life more deeply, and of indicating certain directions of thought that remained compelling in future years. By imparting this kind of impetus, Felix Adler became known to me, first, as a vital and wise teacher. But presently he came to be something more as well—a searcher of men.

After the armistice in November 1918 young men flocked back to the colleges from the army camps in this country and for a time there was a shortage of teachers, because many older men were still overseas. This circumstance led to my beginning to teach Introduction to Philosophy courses to Columbia undergraduates as early as 1919. It has sometimes seemed to me a mixed blessing that I began to teach so soon after graduating from college. But, on the positive side, it led to my coming into further touch with Adler and his associates. My friend James Gutmann had begun teaching at that time in the Ethical Culture School, while another of our circle, John Herman Randall, Jr., was also beginning to teach at Columbia.

Adler was accustomed to meet with his associates in the leadership of the Ethical Culture Societies at least once in the spring and once in the fall. He would often invite some interested students to attend such meetings as guests. My first experience of this kind was in the spring of 1919, at a conference held at Buck Hill Falls; Gutmann and Randall also came. Here I first met the group of fifteen or so men who were then leaders of the Ethical Culture Societies in America.

In that year, and on several later occasions, there were dramatic clashes over issues of the recent war and the current treaty making. Felix Adler's misgivings about British imperialism clashed with the feelings and outlook on world politics of several Anglophile colleagues, among them particularly (though not solely)

Horace Bridges, at that time the leader of the Chicago Ethical Society. Beside his estimate of Britain's role, Adler's inability to share Woodrow Wilson's idealistic interpretation of the war and his refusal to approve a League of Nations on conditions of the Versailles Treaty and the exclusion of Germany caused considerable regret among many of his followers.

My own interest at these gatherings of the Ethical Culture leaders centered upon getting to know their religious outlook. Though Adler rejected Hebrew and Christian monotheism, his thinking was still in many ways linked to the classic theological tradition, in contrast to that of some of his colleagues. It was important to me to understand this, both then and afterward. Until my sophomore year in college, 1916, I had given some serious consideration to the Protestant ministry as a vocation. But even before I met Felix Adler, philosophical studies and other influences had diverted me from pursuing this calling. Yet a very strong interest in religious questions remained.

My friend Randall and I together enjoyed the splendid lectures on the History of Christian Thought given by Arthur Cushman McGiffert, then president of the Union Theological Seminary, just across the street from Columbia. The intellectual climate at Columbia University has often been regarded, in conventional circles, as cool or even unfriendly to religion. Yet, in the philosophy department, at the time of which I write, it was a vital and active interest of many of the teachers and students to explore and to interpret religion in its many forms and functions. The teachers were not engaged in an apology for any set religious system, but religion was not a dead issue for any of them; each had something to say, and not perfunctorily, about its nature and role amid the world's changes. To evaluate Adler's ideas on religion and ethics in this atmosphere required my casting them into a philosophical crucible together with the distinctly varying views of other exciting teachers.

As an institution of teaching and learning Columbia did not fail us students in those years of the war and after. President Nicholas Murray Butler was aggressively pro-Ally, and indeed he managed to alienate some important men (among them the historians Charles Beard and James Harvey Robinson) by policies in support of the war, which they saw as restrictive of academic freedom. The atmosphere on the campus in the war years had characteristics of electric storm; it was heavy-laden with the sense of world suffering and danger.

At the same time these momentous events were being illuminated by critical thought and a high level of teaching in many branches. The graduate faculties, especially those of political science and law, had for several decades been building up to a level of worldwide repute. In history and in the social sciences the long-term issues of development for industrial society were being examined and discussed by many eminent scholars. And I hope I will be pardoned if I emphasize the extraordinary stimulus we received from teachers in the field of philosophy and in the humanities. In the light of today it does seem strange that only fifty years ago study of the nonwestern peoples was still a rather rare specialty and not in the mainstream of general education. But the Western heritage—in literature, thought, institutions, and problems—was studied with a fresh comprehensiveness at Columbia under the impact of World War I.

In those years the philosophy department, with F. J. E. Woodbridge, John Dewey, W. T. Bush, William P. Montague, and Felix Adler, had reached a high standard of excellence both for historical understanding and contemporary reconstruction of ideas. We students in that department were much drawn to and molded by the living intelligence and constructive purpose that it forwarded. It gave us not only lasting intellectual resources, but in view of the tragic events of the period it also performed a truly spiritual function. For one could feel that, were we to be cut down in youth by war, we had yet been fortunate to see some of the very best possibilities and fruits that life can offer. It was for me an experience both inciting and reconciling.

The summer months, when he was not abroad, Felix Adler spent mostly at a site he had bought as early as 1882 in the Adirondack Mountains at Keene Valley. In the city, during three-fourths of the year, there was virtually no letup in the stream of activities that occupied him. The summer months in the mountains offered him a much prized change. Amid the fir trees on top of a cliff just back of his house, he hid a cool little study that was not to be visited except on invitation. Each morning and afternoon he took the steep path, spending many hours there, and most of his close associates, at one time or other, were invited to share his reflections.

For several decades this region's summer population included many interesting professional people. Within half a mile from Adler's cottage was the unique retreat of some Boston families, known as Putnam Camp, to which William James at times repaired. About ten miles north, at Glenmore, Thomas Davidson, a remarkable Scotsman of "open heart and striving mind" established an informal school, which drew a group of philosophers and which continued to be a lively meeting place well after Davidson's early death in 1900. At his own place Adler now and again arranged to have a student with him in the summer, either as a secretary or perhaps just as a good listener who could supplement his regular secretary through note-taking and conversation on some special subjects.

My turn for service in this capacity came during the summer of 1921. And my closer acquaintance with Dr. Adler's mind really began then in his private study on the woodland cliff. It was a trimly appointed, one-room building with a high-pitched roof from which winter snows would slide off. This gave the space inside a pleasant height and airiness too. Mr. Ernest Jacques, an estimable Englishman who served as Adler's secretary for many years, would be there ahead of him to fire the small iron stove if it was a cool mountain day, or to open windows and the glass doors on the porch if the weather was warm. When Adler came in he lit up a cigar and sat himself down in a canvas-backed chair. So settled, he never seemed in a hurry while dictating; there were often long pauses. Yet I was struck by the amount of manuscript that resulted from spending several hours daily in this way.

Up on that cliff one sat amid the evergreen treetops and through them there was a long view down the valley. Dr. Adler's discourse also had elevation and vision beyond the day. His theme centered on human dignity, personal uniqueness and essential relationships, the nature of freedom and obligation. For years he had been weaving together his views on social ethics and his religious outlook in an ethical philosophy of life. He wanted me to grasp the connections of his thought with exactness.

Adler had rejected classic individualism, but at the same time he also opposed various forms of socialism for treating only one aspect of society whether economic, ethnic, or religious. He favored instead a pluralistic view of what he called "organized democracy." The essential organs of society—family, occupation, state, school, and religion—each have their different spheres of inviolable right and responsibility. Adler opposed placing an absolute or total authority in any one locus, such as the state's sovereignty, or in the leadership of any party or elite class. He viewed all the essential human relations, the basic social institutions, as both means and ends of humanity. He criticized those liberals who granted importance to institutions only as instruments for the development and happiness of individuals. Individuals and groups, he held, can claim and acquire freedom, not by their self-sufficiency, but by their responsive and originating powers in relation to others. Because a person becomes himself within the web of his relationships, it does not follow that he has any less dignity as an end-in-himself or as an unduplicable member of mankind.

I listened readily and with relish to this ethical theory of society, both for its social and its pluralistic accent. Perhaps I too easily took this side of Adler's thought as valid, because it agreed rather well with views advanced by other teachers for whom I also had high regard, among them John Dewey. Individual self-sufficiency might make sense on an open frontier, but a more functional approach to freedom, as depending on how one's powers operated in specific relations, seemed needed in the context of industrial society.

Dr. Adler was especially concerned to bring together his social ethics and his religious outlook. In this effort his thought diverged both from Dewey's and from traditional theology. Like the theologians he sought a universal vision of perfection, but he wanted it to be more fully relevant to the new actualities of a freer society than he felt the classic theologies could be. He gave the latter frequent study, especially Augustine and Calvin. But what is central to ethical life, namely the interaction of many different selves, inevitably becomes a secondary consideration, he said, if perfection is vested in a single Divine Being, whether in a theistic or a pantheistic sense. Ethical vision, in contrast, must find Divine Life in the interplay of members, infinitely differentiated yet also united in that each is indispensable to all the rest. Felix Adler was thus bent on putting the idea of ethical relationship between unique selves into the very center of divinity. The transcendent reach of his vision resembled the *visio Dei* of classic theology and of sublime poetry such as Dante's. But instead of the beatific vision culminating in the light of a Super-Sun, an infinite stellar firmament seemed to Adler a more valid image or symbol of Universal Divine Life.

He set forth this view repeatedly in those hours with me at his cliff study in the summer of 1921. He wanted so much to impart his matured religious thought precisely and fully to someone he felt might consider it carefully with a somewhat trained understanding. If I was welcome company then, despite my youth, I am sure it was because at that time I was more interested in religious philosophy and theology than most of his older associates.

For me there was more than learning at stake. I felt that my heart and mind were being searched, or rather that I was pressed, by what Adler said, to search them myself. For I did not feel that he was pushing me to agree with him; my freedom was fully honored. Still, a sister of Mrs. Adler thought to give me a hint about him. "You know he is a weigher of souls," she said.

Some responses I then ventured to make from my Protestant upbringing now strike me as quite callow. For instance, I suggested that the Lord's Prayer, the "Our Father," might not be subject to the reservations felt toward certain articles in the historic creeds. Upon this Adler went to some length to show the divergence in the spirit of this prayer from the sense of human responsibility which he thought modern ethics must assume. From what he said I learned, but only slowly, that the vital issue in religion is not whether a historic position can be acceptably interpreted, but how it bears upon the spiritual path one finds decisive.

From this angle the appropriateness of Adler's distinctive religious vision to his practical mission in active life seemed transparently clear and impressive. I was listening to a man with a long productive and unusually examined experience. His views had been wrought out with strong conviction in a heated forge of constant effort. Considered only as a theory, his idea of a social Godhead, as I pondered it, seemed to me in its own way beset with problems no less than are all attempts to theologize about limitless, transcendent perfection. The thought of an infinitely differentiated Divine Life "at the heart of the world" seemed no less metaphorical than other views of divinity. But as such I found it far from devoid of serious meaning.

The personal need I sensed at the time was less for a conversion in outlook than for a correction of habits toward stronger engagement in matters of human moment. The piety in which I had been reared began to seem too sentimental, perhaps sweetly penetrating yet indulgent to a kindly somnolence. Although I was still too inexperienced and uninformed to estimate Adler's way in life, my sequestered mind found an immediate quickening in this singular brush with the spirit of it.

In that year, 1921, I had my twenty-first birthday. On August 13, Felix Adler reached his seventieth, a day on which he received a good many congratulatory messages and a party of friends visited him at his Adirondack summer home. Amid the company who had long been close to him I felt very new and young indeed. A distance of forty-nine years rich in events and associations lay between Dr. Adler's age and mine. Happily a pleasant mediation was offered us by the Adirondack scene, through the delight afforded by forest and mountain walks. In his own youth, while a student in Europe, Adler had developed a keen taste for mountain country, and this had led him to acquire his own strikingly beautiful site at St. Huberts above Keene Valley.

Dr. and Mrs. Adler had five children, two sons and three daughters. The daughters were at St. Huberts during a large part of each summer. My walks there came to be not always with Professor Adler, quite often they were with Ruth, his youngest daughter. She regarded the place as her true home, having loved the long summers there since her infancy. We climbed Noonmark together and, in a second summer, took a longer, more serious walk through Avalanche Pass, camping out with a party at Lake Colden. Our conversations on such walks became more and more warmly personal. Some members of the family doubtless noticed this, yet I think there was still considerable surprise when we became engaged at the end of the second summer. Ruth and I were married, with Dr. Adler conducting the ceremony, in June 1923.

The relations I entered into at St. Huberts included something more. Mrs. Adler, Nellie (as she was called in the family), was like an exquisite, rare wildflower. She was as free and spirited *au fond* as she was outwardly shy and delicate. Her spontaneous feelings were strong and her expressions had an unassuming vigor. She was the second oldest in the large and interesting family of Joseph and Regina Goldmark. Her three brothers and six sisters were each markedly individual, and most of them achieved a distinction in their own right. Soon after their mother, Regina, became a widow in the early 1880s, Felix Adler persuaded her to come with the children to Beede's, a guest house at St. Huberts, and in 1889 they built their own house in the woods of Noonmark just above his. Some of the Goldmark family, especially Charles, Pauline, and Josephine, excelled in camping and climbing and in love of the woods generally. Theirs was a special and dear place in the affections of my wife and myself.

In his seventieth and seventy-first summers Dr. Adler also still enjoyed a little climbing. I well remember going up Noonmark with him. It took a long while to reach the top, not so much because of his age, but rather because of the abundant talk by which the steep walk was interrupted. One could keep moving and talking more easily on the beautiful and more level Ausable River trails, favorite walks that we often did together, at least as far as "the great pine" with its view into a high-walled gorge of the river at that point. When it was not events of the day, or ideas of moral philosophy, Adler might like to expound a view of natural beauty, or perhaps to explain a preferred gait in climbing which he had learned from Swiss guides. It seemed to me somewhat odd to have the beauty of the woods attributed to the constitution of the mind. Yet this idealistic interpretation may seem less forced when one reflects on what beauty the forest may have for animals, whose experience of it is but sensuous and practical.

Discourse on esthetics was sometimes concluded by Adler's drawing out of early memory long passages from Schiller and other poets, which it amused him to recite in German with an impressive resonance as we continued along the trail. I recall, as one example, these lines from Schiller's *Das Ideal und das Leben:*

> Wollt ihr hoch auf ihren Flügeln schweben,
> Werft die Angst des Irdischen von euch,
> Fliehet aus dem engen dumpfen Leben
> In des Ideales Reich.
>
> Bis der Gott, des Irdischen entkleidet,
> Flammend sich vom Menschen scheidet
> Und des Aethers leichte Lüfte trinkt.
> Froh des neuen ungewohnten Schwebens,
> Fliesst er aufwärts, und des Erdenlebens
> Schweres Traumbild sinkt und sinkt und sinkt.*

By his summer neighbors at St. Huberts, many of whom were conservative in outlook, Adler was highly respected. Yet they also sensed their unfamiliarity and their distance from many of his assumptions. On one Sunday in the summer he would address them. There were those neighbors who had a closer feeling for him, such as the Reverend Henry Sloane Coffin, who enjoyed counting Adler among "the most Christian men I know." Yet I

---

*Would'st thou soar heavenward on its joyous wing
Cast from thee, earth, the bitter and the real,
High from this cramp'd and dungeon being, spring
Into the realm of the ideal!

Until the god cast down his garb of clay,
And rent in halloweing flame away
The mortal part from the divine—to soar
To the empyreal air! Behold him spring
Blithe in the pride of the unwonted wing,
And the dull matter that confined before
Sinks downward, downward, downward as a dream!
Translation by Sir Bulwer-Lytton, Bart. *The Poems and Ballads of Schiller* (New York, 1844).

remember also how controversy penetrated the peace of the woods during the summer when the possible commutation of the death sentence for Sacco and Vanzetti was being debated with other neighbors.

At table with family and close friends Adler's conversation had lively variety and much playfulness. He was fond of analyzing styles of writing and he delighted in all word-play, including puns. He could relish reading in four or five languages at least. In amusement over some of his own jests Adler's face flushed rosily from top to bottom, and tears sometimes rolled down his cheeks in laughter. Often a neighbor or cousin joined in the convivial mealtimes. When dear companions like Robert and Estelle Kohn and John Elliott were visiting, there was great lingering at breakfast with both serious talk and witty merriment. On Sundays, before dinner, there was usually a simple family ritual in the course of which Adler held forth. In the late evening, after games or reading aloud at the fireside, an intruder into the living room might see the glow of a cigar in the darkened corner where Dr. Adler sat alone and gathered the day's thoughts, or perhaps those for the morrow.

How and why I saw Felix Adler rather closely during the last twelve years of his life, from 1921 to 1933, has now been told. But some of the consequences require a further word.

Like many girls who marry young college teachers, Ruth Adler discovered that along with me she was wedded to a Ph.D. dissertation-still-in-process. This complication lasted three years. The year 1926 was triple-starred for us, by a completion of the doctorate, by my Columbia appointment as assistant professor of philosophy, and above all by the birth of our daughter, Anne, that December.

My doctoral dissertation included, as one part, a translation of Friedrich Schleiermacher's *Monologen,* a rather effusive work on the conduct of life, written in 1800, at the height of the author's involvement with the German Romantic circle in Berlin. This appealed to my father-in-law's interest in literary style and expression and led him to spend hours going over the florid German text and my first draft as he showed me what the art of translation really involves.

In the course of these hours our philosophical understanding of one another advanced enormously. Adler found the naturalistic and esthetic leanings of my thought "not ethical enough," but from his point of view there was indeed no other possible judgment. Neither of us could then tell whether his influence might work some future change in me. There was always a virile energy in Adler's statement of his views. But I felt no undue attempt on his part to tug me into his philosophical camp, or to enlist me in his work. Once I heard him say to a colleague, apropos of recruiting leaders for the Ethical Culture movement, that if a man is spiritually undecided in his twenties, it is rarely the case that he will set his life's course later with enough singleness of mind to give effective leadership. Very probably he had given me up on that score. At the same time, it is clear that Dr. Adler chose to spend time with me because he hoped to leave behind a fuller understanding of his matured philosophical and religious thought.

Some critical essays and reviews that I wrote during the late 1920s, chiefly of German thinkers, may have increased his confidence in my ability to appraise receptively. In any case, by around 1929 he suggested that I might some day do a critique of his thought in a like spirit. That is now more than forty-five years ago, and nothing truly answering to his suggestion is yet available! After his death in 1933 I did several memorial pieces, and later in the 1930s and 1940s some occasional editing of selected papers of his.* But my readiness to do anything larger advanced very slowly indeed.

I long felt a danger of writing in too great subservience to the impress of a man fifty years older than myself, who was both a powerful father figure and a searcher of men. It was, I am sure, a philosophical examination of his thought, and not a biography, that Adler hoped I might some day offer. Still the whole course of his life and ideas more and more asserted its fascination and its difficulties for me. My own training was not that of a historian.

*Our Part in This World (New York: Columbia University Press, 1946).

But as my judgment grew more independent, the many-sided active career of Felix Adler during the greater part of his life, before ever I met him, did appear decisively important for any just view of him and his thought.

The studies that follow in this book represent a compromise. They have much biographical content and they are placed so as to give my view of a sequence in the development of Felix Adler's personality and aims. Yet they are far indeed from offering a complete biography. The chapters that deal with main concerns of Adler in the second half of his life, 1892–1933, seem to me to be about a man and a mind of whom I had knowledge by direct acquaintance. For though I did not meet him until he was in his sixties, I judge that in his forties he had become much the man who later spoke to me face to face. By contrast, the account I give of Adler and his work in the first half of his life, 1851–91, has had to be reconstructed from documents and some oral testimonies.

It both startles and rouses me to find that I am now almost a decade older than Dr. Adler was when I first met him in that Columbia University seminar of 1917. Through all tumults and changes since then, many of the issues that filled his life continue to move in the value-conflicts and confrontations of our epoch.

[2]

UNDER THE PARENTAL ROOF:
1851–1870

ELIX ADLER WAS not quite six years old when he first came to America from Germany in 1857. He traveled with his parents and his brother Isaac, who was eight. The crossing from Le Havre to New York took seventeen days because of a ten-days' gale and an engine breakdown off the Banks. In retrospect, Felix recalled that he had crossed the Atlantic some thirty-three times, but that this first voyage was the only one on which he had been seasick. There was "delight in romping on the deck," he says, "until it began to heave underneath, and there was an answering heave. My first sea-sickness and my last."

The family was coming from Alzey, a town not far from Worms in Rhine-Hesse. Dr. Samuel Adler, then forty-eight, was already a man of repute for his Judaic learning and his work in the Reform movement of German Judaism. In a memoir, *Years in Germany*, written in New York to acquaint his family with the prior course of his life, Samuel Adler gave a moving account of his earlier life.* It is a story of progress through hard circumstances by persistent determination and self-discipline.

Born in Worms, in 1809, Samuel was the son of Sinig, later called Jacob, Adler. Jacob had five children, three boys and two girls, and he died in 1822, when Samuel, the second son, was only in his thirteenth year, leaving the family with little money. Still Jacob's "last wishes" were that the boys should all study for the rabbinate; "God would be helpful," he believed. Having himself studied in the Frankfurt yeshiva under a well-known cousin, Nathan Adler, Jacob had assumed responsibility for the early education of his own sons. Samuel observed that, under his father's

*Samuel Adler, *Years in Germany*, Agnes Goldman Sanborn, tr. Typescript, Adler Papers.

16

teaching, "the Bible and the Talmud were the sphere in which our intellects moved; everything else was excluded." And he added, "an impulse towards wider knowledge was not in me, nor was it stimulated."

During his teens and after, Samuel worked at odd jobs, often days and nights, to help support his mother and the family." Inadequate nourishment and insufficient clothing" caused him "periodic illness over many years," he says, which "did not come to a complete stop until the spring of 1843." Meanwhile, his older brother, whose scholarship was regarded as outstanding, succumbed to tuberculosis at the age of seventeen in 1824. Yet Samuel not only continued his Talmudic studies at the yeshiva in Frankfurt and in Worms, but was eventually persuaded by his younger brother, Abraham, to broaden his studies. Of this he wrote:

Finally my brother after all prevailed. With inner resistance I submitted, received from him instruction, inadequate enough, in Latin, German, and geography, and miserably prepared, went in the spring of 1831 to Bonn where at this time a number of competent young men were devoting themselves to Jewish theology. There I remained two and a half years, attended lectures on philosophy, philology, and history, but profited little from all this, partly because deeply embedded in orthodoxy, I regarded these matters merely as a necessary evil, my heart and my zeal belonging to rabbinical literature to which were devoted a part of the day and the larger share of the night.

In the fall of 1833 Samuel moved to Giessen, the university of his province, where he found "teachers extraordinarily valuable for my level of culture and future education." He studied "Arabic, Syrian, and Persian. . . . wrote many little reviews" and "gradually in a fundamental transformation . . . felt myself liberated from the shackles of blind tradition" and possessed of higher intellectual interest. In February 1836, he received a doctorate from Giessen. From 1836 to 1842 he preached in Worms as assistant to the rabbi, then took on a newly formed district rabbinate, including a number of congregations in and about Alzey.

Though he had become engaged in 1838 to Henrietta Frankfurter, daughter of a rabbinical family at Friedberg, they were not married until February 21, 1843, presumably because of financial uncertainties. The letters between Samuel and Henrietta through the intervening five years go far to filling a small trunk.

During his district rabbinate at Alzey Samuel Adler attended the three big conferences of German Reformed Judaism at Brunswick in 1844, Frankfurt-am-Main in 1845, and Breslau in 1846. He also turned many of his own practical efforts in the direction of the Reform program, laboring for Jewish civil equality and doing away with the special "Jewish oath" required to qualify Jews in the courts. His attainments, against local opposition in places where the "so-called religious service was wild and repulsive," led to more intelligible worship as against mere sticking to custom. He built up religious instruction of the young from virtually nothing; and his efforts eventually resulted in a ruling by "the district school administration . . . that Jewish religious teaching was declared compulsory on a par with the two Christian confessions, and was given an equal place and voice in all conferences concerning schools as a whole."

In the congregations he served, Samuel Adler also managed to get "the rampart removed from that part of the gallery where the women sat"; at Pentecost he conducted a confirmation for "both boys and girls of the religious school"; and managed "omission of all outdated views and hopes in prayers" as recommended in the big Reform conferences. The opposition to be overcome was often furious, but at last only "three in number no longer attended the synagogue, and their spokesman whenever he met me on the street, spat in front of me to the accompaniment of abusive language."

By the early 1850s Samuel's zeal for Judaic learning, his diligence in native reforms, and his doctorate from Giessen all marked him as qualified for some major rabbinical post. An offer came from a synagogue in Lemberg, which Samuel, after a visit there, accepted with enthusiasm. But first the Austrian government wished to inquire of the Hessian government as to the candidate's political record. The answer was that, although no specific charges had been brought against Samuel Adler during the political upheavals of 1848, he was well known to be an advocate of democratic reforms. His brother, Abraham, moreover, had been imprisoned and deprived of his post as rabbi in Worms because of his efforts for political change. Nevertheless, sanction for Samuel's appointment in Lemberg came from the Austrian authorities during the summer of 1854.

But the illness of his brother, as an aftermath of his imprisonment, and the consequent necessity for their mother to live with Samuel's household, led him to decline the invitation to Lemberg in order to remain and care for his relatives in the familiar environment in Hesse. In 1856 both his brother and mother died.

Then, as Samuel concludes in this memoir, "what followed thereafter is extraordinary." On the very day of his mother's burial he received news of a call coming from the Temple Emanu-El in New York City to succeed to the rabbinate of Dr. Mertzbacher there. Samuel and his wife promptly agreed to accept this opportunity. He closes his memoir saying:

It was a satisfaction to realize that I had accomplished numerous worthwhile things in Alzey and that my name will long survive there in honored and affectionate remembrance.

On the 21st of February (our wedding anniversary) I gave my farewell address, and on the next morning (Washington's birthday), I left Alzey accompanied by the good wishes of the whole parish.

Members of Temple Emanu-El had selected a residence for the Adler family at 15th Street and Second Avenue, next to Stuyvesant Square. This was close to the Temple, which was then located on East 12th Street. It was a pleasant neighborhood of substantial homes, the quiet tree-shaded square being surrounded by three-story, red brick houses with high-ceilinged rooms. The Old Friends Meeting House was there with its school next door. The Academy of Music, center of the city's artistic and musical events, stood around the corner. A new meeting place for lectures and a library was the Cooper Union Institute at 8th Street. Here also was the center of the city's shopping district. And so the Adlers began their new life.

Samuel, of course, wanted his sons to have excellent general schooling and after a brief trial of the then poor public schools, both Isaac and Felix were sent to the Columbia Grammar School. There the curriculum consisted largely of Latin, Greek, English, and Mathematics. Felix recalled the mental discipline as "severe: five hours of lessons in school, and at least four hours of home preparation, often five or six." Substantial language study, especially in Latin and Greek, gave a foundation in humanities and in expression which Felix enjoyed through life and which proved important in his future career. But on the emotional side these school years fell short of being happy ones. The emergence into a community largely gentile was to be sure an important step but not an easy one. Looking back Felix wrote of it: "A Jewish boy from a family largely German among typically American boys of the wealthy class, I found I was forced back upon myself by lack of companionship."

Samuel Adler devoted much personal care to the religious education of his sons. His private library was considered to be among the best in the city for Jewish studies. So the boys' instruction in Hebrew, in Bible, in Jewish history and in elements of Judaic learning (from a Reformed standpoint) took place mostly at home. But they also attended the Jewish school of the Temple Emanu-El and as teenagers did some teaching there. Felix's performance in this was uniquely honored with a medal and citations.

Felix's mother, Henrietta, brought much of the needed emotional warmth to the Adler household. Sensible and with a pleasant quick humor, she was devoted and even indulgent in caring for her children's wants and comforts. She was at one with her husband in the principles of their piety and active faith. To shield his scholarly pursuits she became the agent in many of the family's daily contacts with the outside world. Felix, to whom his mother's companionship was particularly important, remembered her love as outgoing rather than narrowly possessive. He often went with her on visitations to neighbors and on errands of helpfulness into homes of the poor. These excursions, a constant part of the parents' ministry, were not only lessons in charity, but gave the child an early and visible impression of the existence and meaning of poverty.

In the nation at large the storm of civil war was gathering when the Adlers arrived, and in a few years more it broke upon the country. It was indeed a fire-baptism into American nationality, and remained basic to their personal consciousness of American social and political ideals. The nation's standard, as Felix came to see and to treasure it, was established in that struggle.

His father was passionately attached to the antislavery cause. Deeply moved by the personality of Lincoln, he could also be described later by his son as having been "an ardent black Republican." For the rest of his life Felix never forgot the morning after Lincoln's assassination. "I was then fourteen years of age. I came down to the breakfast table and found my father weeping. I had never seen tears in his eyes before." The waves of these events and the moral feelings associated with the person and leadership of Lincoln (Father Abraham) never lost their motion in Felix's soul. During his early adolescent years the war drew forth a tumult of emotions in him. A depressing sense of suffering and tragedy pervaded the *Weltschmerz* which Felix recalled as having afflicted him in 1864 during a summer stay at Lake Placid. But at times before that, the romance of running off to be a drummer boy in the Union Army had also been one of his fancies.

In the family Felix was regarded as having a rather dreamy nature that would need directing and steadying. Samuel Adler's self-discipline had grown strong in the difficult course of his own development. His memoir and letters are markedly objective and unemotional. Whether his upbringing of his sons was in any points particularly repressive (in standards regarding sex, perhaps) is not clear. But the calm strength and equanimity of his father was without doubt a vital and lasting influence in forming Felix Adler's character and his own subsequently demanding ideals. His warmer and more imaginative nature, however, made the achievement a gradual and arduous one. "Both father and mother," he relates, "were anything but sentimental in regard to the big decisions of life. Implied suffering and self-denial did not count, but the daily details of our life and happiness were constantly on their minds."

In 1864 Isaac Adler enrolled at Columbia College. Two years later Felix followed in his brother's footsteps. Columbia College then occupied three brownstone buildings at 49th Street and Madison Avenue, which was considered far uptown. A row of old trees stood on a beautiful lawn sloping southward. But the college in the 1860s was not part of a great university, as it became several decades later. In fact, the following picture, hardly flattering, had been drawn of it.

When Barnard arrived as President in 1864 Columbia College had only 150 students. . . . The President knew every student by name and gave some personal attention to each. If any student was late to class, he went to the President with his excuse.

All instruction was by rote. The entire student body of the college attended Chapel at nine forty-five, where it found the whole faculty of seven or eight professors. At ten the boys went to their first recitation. At eleven they proceeded to the second. At twelve they recited so much Latin or Economics to a third professor; and at one everybody went home for the day.

The library was open for an hour or two after lunch. . . . Inside, the fifteen thousand books were kept in locked glass cases. Indeed, the librarian felt a thrill of pride in returning to the treasury each year a large part of the thousand dollars he was allowed for purchases.

Before the day of many electives a standard course was offered to all at Columbia College. Felix Adler found the intellectual fare rather skimpy, even moldy, and did not take fire from it. The offerings in philosophy, to which he inclined, seemed particularly arid and limited. Logic and ethics were taught by a professor who gave instruction also in English literature, history, and political economy. President Barnard himself gave the customary courses on Christian Evidences, but a broader presentation of religion in its history and in relation to expanding horizons of the times was wanting.

On the matter of religion there was correspondence between Samuel Adler and President Barnard of Columbia, asking that Felix be excused from compulsory attendance at chapel. Samuel was apparently unwilling to view this requirement simply as a college community symbol. A different estimate of his religious bias no doubt arose from Samuel's long efforts for equity for Jews in the German schools, and may also have been influenced by his expectation that Felix would follow him into the rabbinate.

Before finishing college Felix taught some Sabbath school classes at the Temple Emanu-El; toward the end of 1869 he also delivered a number of sermons at the Hebrew Orphan Asylum, of which his father had been one of the founders. Two of these sermons—his "first attempts at preaching," Felix says—have been preserved, and it is interesting that one of them centers on a description of the martyrdom of Castro-Fortas in the Spanish Inquisition.

It appears that the annals of martyrdom held a certain fascination for young Felix as heroic testimonies to "the spirit in triumph over fiercest pain." The sermons at the Hebrew Orphan Asylum show both a firm grasp of Jewish piety and a forensic eloquence, an intellectual coherence and linguistic force, with a special gift for imaginatively projecting vivid and dramatic pictures. Felix himself noted this gift as a personal discovery, and it remained a permanent asset.

At college Felix probably enjoyed his literary studies most and made progress in writing. In his third year he was class poet, and also became secretary of a literary society. On the playful side are some satiric verses entitled "1968," which offer a dream vision of New York City a century hence. At that time he sees the mud still "three feet high" along Broadway and "the courthouse" is still "incomplete and old." In the court sit a female judge and jury— fashionably dressed and sipping tea while they, first, exonerate a corrupt congressman in "a whiskey case," next, send to prison a blue-law violator, then follow "in succeeding course one hundred cases of divorce, disposed without a single speech, at only just one dollar each," and lastly, fine a poor man trying to collect damages for injury on a railway for "libeling the company." The closing lines bid all unite to drive these diseases away from "the Great Republic of the West."

Hardly an exact forecast of New York in 1968, the verses may yet in an odd, jocose way be a bit prophetic of Felix Adler's later involvement with the city's moral sense and issues of social justice. His firsthand, early awareness of poverty through his charitable visits as a boy in the company of his mother, were growing now in his college years to maturer reflections and to moral indignation over class relations.

If in Felix's disposition while at college there was a mirthful streak, there was also an attitude more sustainedly watchful and perhaps even a bit wary. A significant testimony to his watchfulness comes from the *Reminiscences* of Professor John W. Burgess, who met Adler in the summer of 1876. At the time Burgess was planning to leave Amherst to come to Columbia, where he subsequently played a major role in building important graduate departments in political and social science. Burgess recalled that after working at Amherst that summer he went for recuperation to the White Mountains, where

Dr. Adler and I sojourned in the same hotel for several weeks. He was an alumnus of Columbia College . . . and was then forming his plan for the Society for Ethical Culture, which now for nearly half a century has been such a power for good in the city of New York and elsewhere in our country.

We spent many profitable hours together talking over our projects, and while he received little value from my suggestions in regard to his work, I have always felt under obligation to him for the help he rendered me when I most needed it. I was especially indebted to him for giving me a very clever student's idea of Columbia, as obtained from his four years of recent work there.

He estimated very correctly the faults of the curriculum and methods of teaching there, and his character sketches of the members of the faculty made me well acquainted with my colleagues at Columbia before I had met them personally.

Felix's objections to the curriculum and teaching seem to have been strong enough to keep him away from a great many classes in his last year at Columbia. The College responded by denying him a speaking part in the commencement exercises. An entry in the records of the Board of Columbia College dated June 14, 1870, reads:

With respect to Felix Adler of the Senior class the following resolution was, on motion, adopted:
"Resolved that considering the great inattention of attendance during the past year, it does not appear to this Board that he can be justly allowed to take part in the literary exercises of the Commencement."

Adler was, however, recommended to the Board of Trustees for the degree of B.A.

A Columbia College class a century ago was small in numbers and could be relatively intimate, engendering some of the fraternal feeling and relations characteristic of a gentlemen's club. The thirty seniors who graduated with Adler included men who were quite distant from him in experience or viewpoint but also a number—including Seth Low and Edmond Kelly—who in later years fought along with him in support of various civic and cultural causes.

On June 29, 1870 the members of the class of 1870 received their diplomas from Columbia College at its 116th commencement, which was held in the Academy of Music. Seth Low gave the salutatory, and George Livingston Peabody the valedictory address. Two other members of the class also spoke: Edmond Kelly on "Women's Rights," and Robert N. Shepard on "Truth." Felix Adler, not quite nineteen then, stood eighth in the scholastic ratings of his class, but it would appear that Felix Adler did not attend. His brother Isaac, who had left for the Continent after his graduation from Columbia, had written Felix more than once extolling his experiences abroad and urging his sibling to hurry over. And so Felix did.

There is a tender letter to the two brothers signed by their parents and sister dated June 27, 1870, recapitulating and reflecting on Felix's departure earlier that day. The letter suggests the nature and warmth of the ties that bound the members of the Adler family to one another and seems a fitting close to this review of Felix's upbringing.

June 27, 1870
My dear Isaac and Felix:
    This is the first letter that I am writing to both of you at the same time. Naturally the greater part of it is for Felix who is burning with a desire to know if New York is still standing or at least whether our household is going on as usual, now that he has turned his back on us. Don't feel hurt if I tell you that we are all still living and working as serenely as ever. The events of the week from Saturday until today are as follows.
    After the St. Laurent was out of sight, we all climbed into the carriage and drove to the Fifth Avenue Hotel, where we refreshed ourselves with soda water. From there home for a little rest. Then we went up to 66th Street for a glorious bath. Yesterday was the hottest day of the summer. We drove for an hour in Central Park. At home wash-day is in order, the sewing machine is whirring and Mamma would have no time if she wanted to grieve for her young son. Truth to tell she has been braver than I thought would be possible. Her only cause for grief is that she could not journey with you. Sarah, so unhappy at losing you, has resigned herself to the new order of things and is glad to have a beautiful room all to herself. As for me, your departure has this advantage. I have one person less to remind about letter writing.

Don't have any anxiety about me. You can imagine, dear Felix, how anxiously we are waiting for your first letter. I ask no questions and I hope that unasked you will answer them all.

Your Pa
S.A.

My dear Children:

You have already heard from dear Pa how brave I was. It is truly due to the goodness of God that I was able to go through the parting and face the gap at home with so much resignation.

When you left, Isaac, it took me three whole days before I was myself again and now that Felix has gone I have kept serene through it all. The next few months, Felix dear, while you are in Germany without any special work to do you can use for rest and recuperation. You would have been away from home even if you had been in America. Then when the time for your studies comes every day will bring you nearer to your goal, and hence to your return to us. With these hopes and trusting in God I am cheerfully anticipating your letters.

I believe, Felix dear, your anxiety about us made the parting very hard, but I hope the wonderful voyage and lively company soon put sad thoughts out of your mind.

Let us know soon, Isaac dear, how you found your brother. What do you say to his nice little moustache? I hear that there are no signs of any such prospect for you as yet. Tell me, don't you think he is a splendid fellow?

Your Mama

[3]

STUDENT YEARS IN EUROPE:
1870–1873

FELIX ADLER ARRIVED in Paris on July 6, 1870, on the eve of momentous events. On July 19, the Franco-Prussian War broke out, and in the following twelve months France and Germany were caught in the turmoil of conflict and its aftermath. In France, defeat led in rapid succession to the overthrow of the Second Empire, the establishment of the Third Republic, and the bloody confrontation of the Paris Commune. For the visitors there followed the establishment of the German Reich under Emperor Wilhelm I and the chancellorship of Bismarck.

Felix Adler witnessed the crowning moment of German glory in Berlin in January 1871:

I saw the triumphal entry of the German troops, with the old Emperor at the head, the Crown Prince, Moltke and Bismarck at his side. They rode through the Brandenburg Gate. Through the favor of our Ambassador, the historian Bancroft, I had a privileged card, and stood close to the municipal councillors who received the Emperor. The chief mayor delivered an address of welcome. Bismarck on his horse with his silver helmet and white uniform, was within two feet of me. I could see his eyes shoot lightning flashes of anger at the poor Burgermeister, whose address was far too long.

The victory scene in Berlin, ushering in the modern German Empire, made an impression which lasted as an event to recall and ponder, not only for its political but for its general moral significance. Bismarck and his policies symbolized ever after for Felix Adler a crucial moral problem: the tangle of might and right in the exercise of power and in the conditions of its human validity.

Adler had come to Europe with a plan to pursue studies in Berlin, both at the university and in an adjacent new Academy for Jewish Learning (the *Hochschule für Wissenschaft des Judentums*) which was on the way to becoming an intellectual headquarters of Reformed Judaism. Yet one suspects that from the start his attention became divided between this aim and a compelling interest in the more general social and cultural scene.

Felix's brother, Isaac, had earlier decided not to continue in the rabbinical calling of his father and grandfather. Attracted by advancing knowledge and having a scientific turn of mind, he had chosen to pursue medical training when he arrived in Germany. By the summer of 1870 he had acquired enough knowledge of medicine to be caring for wounded soldiers at a military hospital in Heidelberg. In August he wrote to Felix, who was still in Paris:

I have sixty-eight patients in my charge, in fact the entire hospital, all wounded soldiers, many of them very seriously and dangerously so. I got to bed last night at three and was up at five, but it's a glorious feeling to be of use to one's suffering fellow-men.

He did not mention the fact that a Red Cross nurse added romance to the excitement of a war hospital.

Felix's vocational aims were by no means as clearly defined as his brother's, and his *Lehrjahre* were not without their problems. On the personal side, he never felt at home with the bohemianism of European student life, particularly in matters of sex, and he suffered considerably from a sense of loneliness and isolation during his Berlin years. Nor was intense concentration on study through the long dark winters there particularly conducive to health and happiness.

Yet his existence in Berlin was made more than tolerable, indeed proved memorable and formative, by the new range of intellectual power that he acquired there. The German universities were at a stage of highly developed discipline and productivity. And a major revolution in thought was breaking upon the world, transforming man's knowledge of his past and his conception of himself. The languages, literatures and monuments of ancient civilizations were being recovered for critical study as never before. Together with a new science of primitive cultures and ethnology, this advance of historical knowledge was freeing thought from traditional and provincial views of the human past. And evolutionary biology introduced a stupendous change of perspective regarding man's origins, nature, and development. In contrast to the limited offerings of his college studies, Felix now experienced this opening up of new horizons as a liberation which it was always thrilling for him to recall.

Attraction to a wide range of historical, psychological, and philosophical studies strongly worked upon him. Henceforth it seemed impossible adequately to understand or to deal with human affairs by mastering simply one historic tradition. Adler also recalled that, even in Berlin, he still met with "Protestant and Jewish theologies of the most repellent kind."

In Berlin there were also some accidental circumstances that conspired to move Felix's focus beyond his Jewish studies. He was able to study with some top Jewish scholars who taught there independently of the university, including Moritz Steinschneider, whose knowledge of Jewish and Arabic literature was quite exceptional. But the program of the *Hochschule für Wissenschaft des Judentums* and its relations with Berlin University were slow in developing. Abraham Geiger, leader in the ranks of Jewish reform, came to a Berlin rabbinical post in 1870, at the age of sixty-one, but he could not begin directing and teaching at the *Hochschule* until two years later. It was his dream to see similar standards and status accorded to the study of Jewish theology at Berlin University as were assigned to the study of Christian theology. But there was resistance to such a course, and instead forms of collaboration between the university and the *Hochschule* were gradually developed. Felix, who had met Geiger, was able to study with him and to pursue work in Semitics with other distinguished scholars outside the university.

Within the university his studies tended to be in philosophy. He heard Eduard Zeller on Greek literature and thought; also the outstanding Aristotelean scholar Hermann Bonitz, of whom he recalled:

I ought perhaps to include among those who strongly attracted me— Bonitz, professor at the University of Berlin during my student days, and who opened to me the vision of the Hellenic world. That was a call to penetrate beyond my limited range.

Greek thought was hence added to his lasting and cherished life-resources. On modern philosophy he heard Eugen Dühring, who emphasized the critical influence of science. The importance to him of Heymann Steinthal's introduction to psychology and to philological methods will be explained presently. Also notable were lectures by F. A. Trendelenburg on the history and theory of pedagogy.

There was correspondence from the family about the trend of Felix's studies. Letters from his father express both definite expectations and some misgivings. Toward the end of 1871 his father wrote:

To know the history of philosophy, its chief systems and their development is useful. More than that is effort without a goal and leads to just one conclusion—namely, that the deepest and most profound in the universe is not to be plumbed.

I am anxious to hear whether you have any studies in Arabic for this semester. I consider Arabic an important adjunct to Jewish theology, and it must be earnestly studied in order to be thoroughly known and easily used. I am also anxious to hear about your work in Biblical Criticism, and am looking forward to your report about this study.

Felix did at least begin the study of Arabic, but he could not confine his interest in philosophy within the limits suggested by his father.

By the beginning of 1872 he seems to have realized that he was getting rather far from home base, and his father commented: "you mention a complete change of thought, but without saying in what the change consists." Samuel Adler, recalling his own spiritual struggles, then advised his son: "Don't wear yourself out worrying over the future. Time will bring counsel."

Cousin Isidore Walz, a young chemist who at the time lived with the Adler family in New York, wrote Felix several strong letters that same year, aiming to reinforce the paternal counsel and also to persuade by argument.

April '72: Make up your mind to this, our age is a pushing, energetic, material one, especially so in our country; if you want people to occupy themselves with philosophical or religious questions, you will have to take them by the collar and force them to do so.

May '72: Your last letter leaves me in deeper darkness than before with regard to your metaphysics. I wish you would look into Herbert Spencer if you find time.

November 22, '72: I would like to be able to say that you have convinced me. . . . You have at best confirmed previous suspicions of your natural tendency to cultivate the faculties of imagination and fancy, and to allow reason to follow in their wake. . . . You live in a poetical and ideal world.

There are thousands of points on which cultivators of *positive*—not "empirical" as you call it science agree, *without exception*. I challenge you to adduce a single one on which philosophers agree without exception. You say, Kant is the rock of modern philosophy; I am aware that it is the rock on which his immediate followers split.

Thousands of giant intellects have grappled with the problem and failed sadly; but Felix Adler, student phil., in the blessed year of 1872, entertains a hope of finding the philosopher's stone. Do you really believe that ends of practical morality will be better attained when your theory of ethics is discovered?

As your cousin and friend I protest emphatically against your continuance in this line of studies, which are not studies, but guesswork, fancies, nothing! I am resolved, however, to write no more on this subject for I am convinced . . . you *will* go on; and I fear that even if I add the remark that your father shares my views in this regard, it will cause you but a moment's hesitation. Yet I have no doubt that in a few years more, when the friction of actual life has taken effect, you will perceive the folly of such pursuits, and hope that you will not then regret too much the loss of valuable time which they have cost you.

Yours affectionately,
Isidore

The counselors at home all wanted Felix to achieve a "positive" scholarly competence in Judaic studies. They feared he was inclined instead to philosophical *Schwärmerei*. For Felix there was no immediate way to argue down this tough-minded advice. He had either to give in, or to trust his own tender-minded idealism. As his cousin had predicted he chose the latter course. He had to leave it to the later "friction of actual life" to prove the consequences. Many years later he recalled how narrowly he had escaped from being "squeezed" into the familiar rabbinical cloak.

The particulars of Felix's Berlin studies need not be described in detail at this point. But they led him into what were to become three areas of permanent interest. An introduction to pedagogical theory—then a regular part of the philosophical curriculum in Germany—presented him with many of the ideas of modern educational reform, especially those of Friedrich Froebel. In later years, concern with child development would loom large among Adler's interests.

More to the fore at the time was the stimulus he got from the work of Heymann Steinthal, who together with Moritz Lazarus had launched the interesting *Zeitschrift für Völkerpsychologie und Sprachwissenschaft* (*Journal of Social Psychology and Linguistics*). This was devoted to studies of ethos and social mentality, to problems that Wilhelm Wundt was then also exploring in Leipzig. Steinthal's method sought ways to turn philological and exegetical study toward understanding the psychic patterns and thought forms of different peoples, Semitic, Aryan, Chinese, and so on. This approach introduced Adler to the ethical systems and religions of mankind and brought with it the possibility of making comparisons among them. His Judaic studies could now be placed within a larger context, and for Adler the consequences were to be far-reaching. In the winter of 1872, Felix wrote his father about the possibility of studying in Leipzig with Wundt. The reply was:

If you wish to take up scientific studies in Leipzig, I have no objections to your spending the summer semester there, but only if you return to Berlin in the fall. Remember that from next autumn you have only at most another year in Germany. Therefore you can not waste your time in scientific studies, but must limit yourself to the study of Talmud, which is the kernel of your future career.

Felix did not go to Leipzig, but he did continue to pursue his philosophical interests.

Forms of neo-Kantianism were having a heyday in German philosophy at that time, and Felix Adler was significantly influenced by one of their important exponents, Hermann Cohen, then a *Privat-Dozent* in Berlin. Cohen was not yet reigning as professor of the Marburg School of neo-Kantianism, but he had just published the first two of his interpretive books: *Kant's Theory of Experience* and *Kant's Foundation of Ethics*. Eventually Adler came to consider Hermann Cohen's construing of Kant as too intellectualistic. Yet he was probably led by Cohen to relate Kant's views on "causal necessity" to the equations for energy transformations in our mathematical physics. Whatever might be moot in such an interpretation, by adopting it Adler could later think that his view of natural science, in this respect, was in line with the progress that moved through thermo-dynamics, electro-dynamics, and radiation phenomena, to a kind of climax in the formula, $E = mc^2$.

Felix was also influenced by his reading of Friedrich Albert Lange, professor of philosophy at Marburg, whose interpretation of the history of materialism from a neo-Kantian point of view well represented a current mode of thought. Both Lange and Cohen belonged at the time among the academic Socialists (Katheder-Sozialisten) who went beyond Kant's individualism in their ethics. While Adler was not persuaded when Hermann Cohen said that "for us there can be no religion except socialism," he recalled reading F. A. Lange's work on the labor question (Die Arbeiterfrage, 1865) "with burning cheeks," and later claimed that it had a "revolutionizing effect" upon him. He also took note of Lange's book on John Stuart Mill (1866) in which Lange followed Mill in attacking economic individualism.

It is not evident that Felix made a minute study of Kant in these Berlin years. That came later. In 1871–72 he had much else to study. But the grand intent in the outline of Kantianism won his allegiance in suggesting the right intellectual and spiritual directives. He could see in Kant a three-fold charter of freedom—freedom for experimental science, for progressive morality, and for nondogmatic religious faith. Kant's theory of knowledge stood for a progress of experimental science toward precision in publicly demonstrable understanding of phenomena. His theory of ethics attributed an even higher rationality to moral precepts when accordant with an absolutely imperative Moral Law transcendent over phenomena. And finally, the source and authority of this Moral Law, i.e., to treat every person as an end and not as a means, only could be interpreted either humanistically or, in a liberal sense, theistically. For as being rational, the law had to be freely acknowledged by human reason, but as universal it did not need to be regarded as given to the universe by man alone.

In 1873, Felix transferred to the University of Heidelberg—such moves then being common for students in Germany—and became a candidate for a Ph.D. in Semitics. In his orals, Felix was examined by Gustav Weil in Hebrew and Arabic, by Carl Alexander Freiherr von Reichlin-Meldeg in philosophy, and Professor Stark in Latin.

Though preparation in these subjects must have taken up most of Adler's time, the faculty included several notable men in other fields that much interested Adler, notably the Swiss liberal, J. S. Bluntschli, whose field was political thought and to whom Adler still referred years later, and Kuno Fischer, who lectured on Kant.

Heidelberg offered more than just work, however. In the springtime, Felix found himself emotionally refreshed by excursions up the Neckarthal and along the Bergstrasse which gave him "intense joy." Here he also enjoyed the company of friends of his brother Isaac. He had a copy of the German student songbook, the *Kommersbuch,* and joined in the pleasures of student life.

His *Lehrjahre* ended successfully for Felix when he could finally report to his family that his doctorate had been awarded April 26, 1873, summa cum laude. His father answered: "I was overcome with surprise and delight and gave thanks to the Almighty." Abraham Geiger also wrote in commendation, and made Felix Adler a present of a handsome, vellum-bound copy of the *New Testament in Syriac* (1667).

Looking back on his student years abroad some forty-five years later, Adler saw certain of his experiences then as having had a profound effect on the development of his ethical principles and, hence, on the conduct of his life. In the first chapter of *An Ethical Philosophy of Life,* entitled "Prelude," he described his reaction to the bohemian life of his fellow students and of the strengthening effect on his character of his refusal to depart from his own position:

One of the leading principles to which I early gave assent, and to which I have ever since adhered as a correct fundamental insight, is expressed in the statement that every human being is an end *per se,* worthwhile on his own account.

Every human personality is to be safe against infringement and is, in this sense, sacred. There is a certain precinct which may not be invaded. The experience which served me especially as the matrix of this idea was the adolescent experience of sex-life—the necessity of inhibiting, out of reverence for the personality of women, the powerful instincts then awakened.

The fact that I had lived abroad for three years in frequent contact with young men, especially students, who derided my scruples, and in the impure atmosphere of three capital cities of Europe—Berlin, Paris and Vienna—where the "primrose path" is easy, tended to make the retention of my point of view more difficult, and at the same time to give it greater fixity, also to drive me into a kind of inner solitude. I felt myself in opposition to my surroundings, and acquired a confidence, perhaps exaggerated, to persevere along my own lines against prevailing tendencies.

Continuing further, Adler outlined "the decay of theism which took place in my mind in consequence of philosophic reading," noting his "reaction against the narrow theology of the lectures on Christian Evidences" as taught at Columbia, and the influence of the men he heard in Germany: Zeller, Dühring, Steinthal, and Bonitz. "Above all I came into contact with Hermann Cohen . . . and undertook to grapple in grim earnest with the philosophy of Immanuel Kant. The net outcome was not atheism in the moral sense—I have never been what is called an atheist—but the definite and permanent disappearance of the individualistic conception of Deity."

The third seminal experience Adler recalled was his reading of Friedrich Albert Lange's *Die Arbeiterfrage,* which though he judged it as "not a great book" was one which "opened for me a wide and tragic prospect, an outlook of which I had been until then in great measure oblivious, an outlook on all the moral as well as economic issues involved in what is called the Labor Question." While he did not accept Hermann Cohen's claims that "if there is to be anything like religion in the world hereafter, Socialism must be the expression of it," Adler believed that there was a "measure of truth in what he said, and that I must square myself with the issues that Socialism raises. Lange helped me to do this."

As he prepared to return to America, Adler was already dedicating himself to certain ends:

I would go out as the minister of a new religious evangel. Instead of preaching the individual God, I was to stir men up to enact the Moral Law; and to enact the Moral Law meant at that time primarily to influence the young men with whom I came into contact to reverence womanhood. . . . And . . . I was to go out to help arouse the conscience of the wealthy, the advantaged, the educated classes, to a sense of their guilt in violating the human personality of the laborer.

[4]

NEW WORLD'S MISSION:
1873–1876

A RECKONING AS TO Felix Adler's future career came soon after his return to New York, when the trustees of Temple Emanu-El invited him to deliver a sermon to his father's congregation. The sermon, delivered on October 11, 1873, was entitled "The Judaism of the Future." Adler began by reflecting on the changes Judaism had survived in the past and then went on to consider the challenges it must confront in the future.

Praising the work of the followers of Moses Mendelssohn, leader of the German Jewish Enlightenment, Adler spoke of their achievement in using "the hammer of argument and the pickaxe of criticism."

Ceremony after ceremony was abolished, custom after custom declared obsolete. No feelings of misplaced reverence for the relics of a hoary past could deter them, for they knew that there was danger to the living in such false love of the dead. . . . None but those familiar with the vast debris which had gathered in the course of time can appreciate the magnitude of their labor by the self denial involved in its execution.

But their work had been only the first step, for while those reformers had torn down the old, the new "has not been reared in its place," Adler continued.

Looking to Europe, where the movement of Reform took its origin, what a spectacle meets the eye! Stagnation everywhere; hopes that were once so high changed into hopeless indifference. The best spirits of the age are turning their backs upon religion . . . the ministers of religion have lost the confidence of the people. . . . On all sides, we hear the end of Religion predicted, and no wonder, considering the sorry condition in which it finds itself. The question for us to answer now is not this form or that form, this reform or that reform. The question is—life or death— is Religion about to perish?

36

Having summoned this dark possibility, Adler proceeded on a more hopeful note, pointing out that "If, from the history of religion, there is one lesson to be learned, if from its woeful past there is one bright hope to be drawn it is this . . . religions may pass away, religion shall endure." And how did this apply to Judaism in America? Addressing himself now specifically to the situation of the congregation before him, Adler pointed to the proud Jewish heritage of three thousand years "decked with what noble deeds, bright with what high names—legislators, scholars, statesmen, prophets, martyrs." But, he asked,

Does not the same blood flow in your veins as in theirs, and do not the creative powers live in you as in them? . . . A few decades have passed since you came to the shores of this new land, homeless, friendless, shelterless. And now—what a commanding position have ye built up for yourselves in the world of commerce. And what an augury for the future! Not in the market-place alone, but in the field of letters, in the high places of the political and social world, above all, in the great arena of religion, shall you be the leaders, and lead to great and noble ends. They know you little who believe you wrapt up in the sordid pursuit of gain. The ideal powers are slumbering within you, they need only be aroused to the resuscitating power of Judaism. Draw in your breath and listen to the clear, metallic notes that ring from the pulpits of the Free Religionists here and elsewhere. Do you not hear the great humanitarian doctrines of Judaism re-echo in their words? Are not they, too, the children of the prophets—our brothers?

Asking his congregation to fulfill the demands of the time and prepare the way for a union of life and religion, he exhorted:

It is history which shows us the origin and practical working of ideas. . . . Let us then strive by its aid to educate the masses, to create among them an enlightened judgment which shall teach them to discriminate between the passing form and the immortal idea. . . . Let us teach the history of Judaism, the history of religion. Let us show in its changing phases the unchanging principle. The forms which it must assume in our own practical and busy world will then arise naturally and of themselves and gain many and ardent adherents.

He concluded by asserting:

Judaism ever claimed to be a religion—not of the creed but of the deed—and its destiny is to embrace in one great moral state the whole family of man.

It was not a sermon calculated to inspire the trustees of Temple Emanu-El with confidence that Felix Adler would be an appropriate successor to his father as rabbi. There were too many negative assumptions about the state even of Reform Judaism as encumbered still by decaying traditions; and it was too broad, perhaps, in its emphasis on the brotherhood of man. It was too vague about particulars intended for the Jews and too silently evasive about God. A yeasting idealism, still rather unmolded, could hardly suffice the trustees or the congregation as a reliable investment. Would anyone have expected it could?

One should remember that in America at that time Reform Judaism was still without a common platform. The new country spurred reaching out beyond old world customs, and the outer boundaries of Reform had not yet been defined. So it is just possible that Felix meant to see if the Reform movement in the United States could take up his challenge. But the fact remains that once the gap between his thinking and that of the temple leaders had been exposed, Felix Adler ceased to seek a rabbinical post. This speaks rather strongly for the view that, in delivering his sermon, he did not expect or want to qualify for the customary rabbinical role.

For the Adler household the situation was clearly distressing, as it meant that Samuel Adler would close his eminent career with a defeat. He would not see a son succeed him in the temple. But in this great disappointment his fortitude and breadth of character were extraordinary. Though he retired from active service at the temple in 1874, at age sixty-five, he never wavered in an understanding and a trust of his son's honest idealism.

And the latter's sermon did in fact arouse some effective support. Ten days after he had spoken, Felix received a letter with forty-seven signatures. It is noteworthy that twenty of the signers would subscribe three years later to the lectures that led to founding of the Society for Ethical Culture. The letter began as follows:

Dear Felix Adler, Dear Sir:
Impressed with the merits of your late address, and believing that we represent the wishes of many of your audience on that occasion, we cordially invite you to give a course of lectures during the coming winter.

In response to this invitation Adler gave six popular lectures at Lyric Hall in New York on historic episodes in the world's religions. The leading lecture, decisive in his position toward Judaism, was called "The Fall of Jerusalem." Though he spoke of it as "the closing event in the national life of Israel," he said it should not be bewailed, because it marked "a beneficial change . . . an epoch in the progress of mankind . . . the rise and spread of a democratic movement in religion and politics." It is especially through the great social prophets and the democratic Pharisees, he avowed, that Judaic ideals are linked with American, so that one can say "the republican idea of our Declaration of Independence is the legitimate consequence of a doctrine proclaimed thousands of years ago in the valley of Samaria and on the hills of Judah."

In the other Lyric Hall lectures, Adler launched forth into the wide field of "comparative religion" with a discussion of Islam, of universalism in Indian and Buddhist religion, of "martyrs and martyrdom" (emphasizing Giordano Bruno and intellectual freedom in religion) and a final lecture on "Spiritualism," which was then enjoying a popular vogue. These lectures were never published: they are youthful performances with pictorial eloquence and perhaps a touch of martyr fantasy.

But what was now to be the young man's career? A turn to scholarship and teaching seemed indicated by his university studies and his Ph.D. Early in 1874 Mr. Joseph Seligman wrote Dr. Andrew D. White, president of Cornell University, a letter on behalf of Dr. Felix Adler. Seligman and his brothers were prominent Jewish bankers of German background; and though a leading trustee of Temple Emanu-El, Joseph Seligman found young Adler's ideas appealing. He was also a friend of Rabbi Samuel Adler and surely acted in part to help him establish his son. Cornell University had been established in 1865 with a charter proscribing religious discrimination in the appointment of faculty. The letter to Dr. White asked: Would Cornell wish to offer instruction in Hebrew and oriental literature in the context of world literature? Replying to Joseph Seligman, in a letter of March 10, 1874, Dr. White wrote that funds were not then available for instruction in Hebrew and oriental literature, but that special endowment of a "non-resident professorship" in that field would be welcome, and probably well-suited both to Cornell's and to Dr. Adler's interests. He went on to explain that:

We have here about five hundred active-minded, energetic, scholarly young men from every state of the Union, ready to absorb any good idea and to make it bear fruit in the part of the country to which they go. . . . Besides, ours is one of the very first institutions ever established in this country on the basis of complete equality between men of every shade of religious ideas and of complete liberty in the formation and expression of thought. Dr. Adler, if I mistake not, is a man calculated by his lectures as well as by his influence in other ways to promote those studies calculated to break down all unfortunate barriers of creed which have so long afflicted mankind. And this it was that led me at the outset to take a real interest in the case.

These statements of President White's were very much in harmony with Felix's direction of mind. They also seem to imply that White was informed about this young man's "lectures and influence in other ways."

Adler's teaching at Cornell began in the spring term of 1874; one-third of a full year's time (or six weeks) was expected of "non-resident" professors. On June 29, during commencement week, he delivered a formal inaugural address, which the *Ithaca Journal* carried in full. Only a slight impression of its oratorical style can be imparted in this quotation:

He was entering upon his professorship, the speaker said, "conscious that beneath the chafing, uproarious tide of political action, a silent current of *education* is steadily working out changes in our national life." The study of Oriental Literature, he admitted, might seem remote from this current. But philosophy and literature contain the keys to an understanding of the "national psychology" of different peoples and thereby of their unique contributions to the development of mankind. (Adler referred to his teacher, Steinthal, in saying this.) In the language, myth, and poetry of the Aryan peoples is revealed a genius for "objectivity," while Semitic studies, especially those of Hebrew literature, acquaint us with another and more "subjective" type of genius. The prophetic moral cast of the latter summons us to be not only "the bearers but the promoters also of the traditions of the Human on earth," preparing a way "for the grander man."

America, Adler concluded, has been given a birthright of freedom prepared of the ripest fruit of the past. Here where "individuals from all quarters of the earth are received into the community of the people, the true essential idea of this people rises above the national, is the idea of humanity itself . . . wherein may be consummated the union of the Aryan objective and the Semitic subjective . . . the union of the Real and Ideal of which the true manhood and womanhood will be born."

It was a vision of an American destiny that he had already proclaimed in his sermon at the temple, and again in the lectures given soon after in New York's Lyric Hall. Perhaps to some cool-headed listeners, whether in New York or amid the hills of Ithaca, it seemed impossibly idealistic, but for Adler it expressed an inspiration and goal which with important variations he would continue to pursue to the end of his life.

Adler's readiness to give popular lectures in the town as well as to his classes must have heightened a sense of his confrontation with orthodoxy and fundamentalism. Moreover, critics could not fail to note that whenever Adler discussed Judaism, it was his own view of it, rather than more familiar ideas, that received prominence. "The old is dead, the new has not yet been born," he said. Reform has taken new ground in biblical and historical study, yes, but has "lacked the constructive genius needed for the creation of new institutions." It has not extended "the symbolism of association," so central in Hebrew history, with new effect for the glaring issues of contemporary industrial society.

Adler discovered he was not alone in his ideal aspirations. He found encouragement and pleasure in meeting with a group of Emersonians at Ithaca. He mentions a Dr. Winslow and Miss Stebbins as being among them. They took walks in the neighborhood and held "Sunday meetings in the woods." Adler's nonresident status allowed him much time to spend elsewhere, and this came to include visits to Boston as well as New York.

On one such visit to New England, in 1875, Adler met Emerson at his home in Concord. While the visit was chiefly taken up with Emerson asking Adler about his studies abroad, the eminent man's influence on Adler was, for a time at least, considerable. In *An Ethical Philosophy of Life*, Adler later recalled that:

I came in touch with the Emerson circle and read and re-read the *Essays*. The value of Emerson's teaching to me at that time consisted in the exalted view he takes of the self. Divinity as an object of extraneous worship for me had vanished. Emerson taught that immediate experience of the divine power in self may take the place of worship. His doctrine of self-reliance also was bracing to a youth just setting out to challenge prevailing opinions and to urge plans of transformation upon the community in which he worked.

The positive effect of Adler's teaching at Cornell for some of his students can be glimpsed in a letter he received from one who had attended his course in its first year.

Rochester, April 1, 1875

Dear Sir:

While at Cornell I attended all your lectures from the very first. The impartial manner in which you treated your subject made a deep impression upon my mind and the ideas you advanced opened up a new field of thought into which I had never dreamed of entering. The idea of studying the history of the Jews as you would study the history of any other nation, of reading their works as you would Homer, Virgil, Goethe, or Shakespeare, had never occurred to me. But after hearing you the scales fell from my eyes, and now I am able to see somewhat. I have begun to lay aside those prejudices to which unreasoning orthodoxy gives rise and to look upon those grand old records of the Jews with some degree of independence. . . .

s/ F. P. Smith

Appreciative comment of this kind represented, however, but one side of the response to Adler's work at Cornell. The university was frequently attacked in the church press by denominational bodies for its toleration of what seemed to them tantamount to godlessness. The breadth of Adler's interest, as for instance in "the Hindu trinity," also gave offense. Though President White was unwilling to make concessions to this illiberal spirit, the issue did not subside.

During the summer of 1875, Adler visited Europe once again. While there he got in touch with Trübner, the publisher, and with J. Estlin Carpenter in London about the possibility of getting scholars to cooperate in an international *Journal of the Science of Religion*. Carpenter drew up an English list, to which Adler added the names of some Continental scholars, including Abraham Kuenen and C. P. Tiele. A prospectus was circulated by way of inquiry. In November Trübner forwarded to New York the replies received from T. K. Cheyne, James Martineau, T. W. Rhys Davids, A. H. Sayce, and E. B. Tylor. They evinced interest, but also a clear awareness of many difficulties intellectual, financial, and editorial. In view of these Adler found himself unable to forward his plan for the journal.

While abroad, Adler also took the opportunity to visit Pastor Gustav Werner in Reutlingen in southern Germany. A pioneer in developing social Christianity, Werner had been supporting homes for needy and wayward children by means of a set of very successful cooperative farms and industries for more than a quarter-century. "Was nicht zur Tat wird, hat keinen Wert" (What does not become deed has no value), he told Adler. It was a message with considerable appeal for Adler, since a religion of deed pertinent to the times was what he too was working toward.

Adler's preoccupations during the summer of 1875—the attempt to organize an international scientific journal concerned with religion and his visit to Pastor Werner—reflected his growing need to take action. On the one hand he was moved to seek greater truth in religion through increased knowledge; on the other, he felt the urge to deal with the pressing social and human needs of industrial society. His academic role at Cornell satisfied neither of these urges sufficiently.

From the outset of his time in Cornell, Adler had longed for companionship in his idealism. Among his Cornell papers were two handwritten sheets dated July 2, 1874, signed by Adler and eight other men, "members of Cornell University and others" forming themselves into a "Union of Religion." They pledge themselves to thoughtfulness in religion, to honest working out of their inner freedom, to purity toward women, and to a modest simplicity in their mode of life, in view of the wide divergence between the fortunes of different classes of society, an unsound state of affairs that calls for correction.

The signers empower Adler, "as their guide," to admit others to their union, and to reconvene them "if he sees good, at the end of three years." Nothing suggests that this particular group so reconvened. But the pattern remained a permanent one of drawing around himself a close band, a fellowship of high resolve. With variations this continued through Adler's whole life.

In a letter to his teenage sister, Sarah, with whom he corresponded often, Adler expressed his sense of the distance between his own religious consciousness and that of his fellow townsmen in Ithaca. Dated Easter 1876, the letter reflects:

What a wonderful transformation the spring brings. . . . It is Easter morning. I have the lively impression of another Easter morning, which I celebrated four years ago with my brother Isaac in Vienna. How profoundly was I then moved by the Passion-music, which all week long filled the churches with such tones of fear, distress, struggle, and pain. And how profoundly was I seized on that Sunday morning by the deep and eternal significance of the idea of resurrection! For is it not the inmost history of Everyman which is here present to the multitude in the guise of a fable?

And it is not (as in Goethe's *Faust*) only a low estate that comes from its cramped existence and poor uncultured circumstances (*"aus niedrigen Häuser dumpfen Gemächern, aus Hand-werks u. Gewerbes-Banden"*).

No, out of spiritual bogs and desolation humanity ever strives to rise to its true life. And where the supreme realm of the Ideal opens up to him, man will enter in, clarified, and will recognize that there is his true, abiding home.

To be sure, the sceptical world of today seems to have little appreciation left for what reaches beyond the moment. Those infinite world-goals, which bestow meaning and character upon life's cramps and poverty, the mighty messianic promises of future perfection, which once radiated their blessing into human existence, have faded and no longer avail to penetrate the dust of markets and the smoke of factories.

Yet, could not some new strong breath of spirit, nevertheless, still clear the prospect? The future must answer.

Now people are coming out of the churches here in Ithaca. Their faces are stolid and unrelieved by imagination. My Vienna devotees were after all more congenial in this respect. These here believe in their fables with all the crude prose that is natural to them. The genuine deeper meaning is mostly lost upon them.

Early in 1876 Adler entered into a correspondence with Julius Rosenbaum in New York about the possibility of his giving regular Sunday lectures in the city while retaining his nonresident professorship at Cornell. In a letter dated April 11, Rosenbaum noted:

You are undoubtedly anxiously awaiting a detailed report concerning the progress or results of our initiatory movement, but the time devoted to its development has been so short that I can scarcely furnish anything more definite than the gratifying assurance of certain success. The number of subscribers has already reached 35 & if our other friends shall succeed as well, we can surely count upon the support of 100 from the start. As anticipated we meet with various difficulties . . . although there are many who hail our proposed Sunday lectures with delight & offer their support cheerfully, there are others who hesitate to join us urging their objections in various forms, without however absolutely declining. Some do not approve of the day chosen . . . and would prefer any evening of the week, others express a fear that it may injure the future standing of the Temple Emanu-El to which they belong & others again desire to find out first what it would cost them before attaching their signature. I am however determined to prosecute the work in hand, being convinced that no success was ever attained in any undertaking without an Earnest Effort & hope only that your courage & faith may not fail you in spite of any disappointments or obstacles that may present themselves & meet us on the way.

Rosenbaum persisted in his Earnest Effort and Adler did not lose faith or courage. On May 5, 1876, Rosenbaum reported on a meeting held the previous evening at the Standard Club attended by "Messrs. Lauterbach, Goldman, Wolf, Sol Moses, Geo. Einstein & myself" at which "After an informal exchange of views which consisted largely of the various objections raised against Sunday lectures, we finally concluded not to deviate from the course already adopted & issue a general invitation for a public meeting to be held on Monday Evening the 15th inst., at Standard Hall at 42nd St. & B'dway, there and then to proclaim frankly the substance of our future plans."

The invitation was issued on May 12. The meeting three days later was to set the course that would shortly lead to the founding of the Society for Ethical Culture. For the time being, however, Adler's commitment was to give a series of lectures in New York during the fall of 1876. In the eyes of his supporters in the city, and in the terms of his duties at Ithaca, the two undertakings seemed compatible. Mr. Joseph Seligman informed Cornell University that he and other contributors to the fund for Adler's professorship were ready to renew the grant supporting Adler's appointment which was due to come to an end in December 1876.

After some friendly and candid correspondence with Vice-President William J. Russell of Cornell, they were told

The Executive Committee of the Cornell Trustees object to having professors nominated to them from the outside. . . . They, therefore, will not again accept any propositions for endowment where the choice of the incumbent is not left without restriction to the Trustees.

There can be little or no doubt that this was a generally sound principle of university administration for Cornell to adopt.

In their historical study, *The Development of Academic Freedom in the United States,* Professors Richard Hofstadter and Walter Metzger devote a page to the experience of Felix Adler at Cornell. Perhaps the university gave something less than a fighting round of support and defense of Adler in the face of his critics. But I have very deliberately drawn attention to his own interest in activity beyond ordinary academic usage. And one should add that without malice some critics had reason to think that Adler's emphasis on his own viewpoints was hardly a representative offering of Jewish and Oriental literature.

Clearly the life of an academic at Cornell had not been totally satisfying to Adler: throughout the three years he had kept closely in touch with his group of friends in New York and had been willing to go down from Ithaca on Saturdays to give his Sunday lectures, returning Sunday evenings to Cornell. He remained preoccupied with the ideas that had first taken root during his student days abroad and he was fired with the possibility of a religion based not on revealed dogma and fixed church tenets but on practical morality.

[5]

ETHICAL CULTURE—
A NEW CALLING: 1876–1877

I N HIS CORRESPONDENCE with Adler about the possibility of giving "regular Sunday lectures" in New York City, Julius Rosenbaum mentioned "various difficulties and objections" that had been raised in opposition to the idea. He explained that some felt it might be prejudicial to Judaism and the temple to hold meetings on Sunday morning, "it being the Christian Sabbath." Others thought the plan to include music "might give the exercises a too religious tendency." Confronted by such crosscurrents Rosenbaum advised Dr. Adler to take his own ground boldly.

"We shall effect our object with more certainty and greater satisfaction," he wrote, "if we promulgate our ideas frankly and fearlessly. We shall either succeed on their strength alone or fail altogether." Adler, in reply, was definite in approving the choice of Sunday and in wanting to have music supplement his lectures. With regard to the "object," events show that he hoped to establish a permanent effort in the city, not only for moral enlightenment but for a free approach to the whole elevation of life. This pointed to religious innovation, which was suspect both to those who wished to preserve the customary religion and to others who wanted to reject it. It was necessary, therefore, to proceed discreetly if also "fearlessly."

Eventually the following invitation was sent out:

New York May 12th, 1876

Dear Sir:

Your attendance and that of the ladies of your family is earnestly requested at a meeting to be held on Monday Evening the 15th at 8 o'clock at Standard Hall Cor. of 42 Str & B'dway, where measures will be considered to inaugurate Sunday lectures during the approaching Autumn.

47

Prof. Felix Adler will be present and State his views concerning the movement.

Respectfully

The Committee

May 15, 1876, has come to be regarded as Ethical Culture's birthday, although the words "ethical culture" do not occur— either as a name or in any other way—in the text that has come down of what Adler said that evening.* This is clear from the bare statement, signed during the next months by 264 subscribers, which read simply as follows.

We, the undersigned, agree to cooperate in a movement about to be initiated for the purpose of enabling Professor Adler to deliver lectures on Sunday mornings during and after October next. The same to be accompanied by suitable music.

Whatever the large range of his interest Adler had a marked gift for directing himself on occasions to specific targets. On the occasion of May 15 this can be seen, for example, in the strong plea he made for the inclusion of music in his Sunday lecture plan. Music, he said, "speaks in its own wordless language of an ideal beauty and harmony far transcending the prosy aspirations to which we confess."

Another immediate and crucial target was to secure financial support for the project. It is clear that Adler was on that occasion talking and appealing to a distinctly middle-class group, including some people of affluence. And he sought to identify with his audience by approaching American conditions with sympathy for the trials and the better hopes of men in the business community.

---

*In describing the purpose of the proposed lectures Adler explained: "The exercises of our meetings are to be simple and devoid of all ceremony and formalism. They are to consist of a *lecture* mainly, and, as a pleasing and grateful auxiliary, of music to elevate the heart and give rest to the feelings. The object of the lectures shall be twofold: First, to illustrate the history of human aspirations, its monitions and its examples; to trace the origin of many of those errors of the past whose poisonous tendrils still cling to the life of the present, but also to exhibit its pure and bright examples and so *to enrich the little sphere of our earthly existence by showing the grander connections in which it everywhere stands with the large life of the race.*" Felix Adler, "Address of May 15, 1876," *Ethical Addresses*, series 3, no. 5 (Philadelphia: S. Burns Weston, 1896). Editor's insert. F.W.

He spoke of them as people one-sided in their mercantile prowess yet justly substantial and proud of it. The effects of the depression which followed the Panic of 1873 were still prevalent, and Adler felt for those whose happiness was undermined by business failure when "a great crisis sweeps over the land." He dwelt on the human toll exacted by fierce competition for enrichment. He deplored a nervous and artificial quality in American "pleasure." He excoriated the private and public corruption that was so rife in the Grant administration and under the Tweed Ring's control in New York.

At this May 15 meeting Adler did not play up criticism of religion nor did he elaborate his own religious views. It was not until the fall and winter lectures that these issues received much attention. On the earlier occasion he must have assumed that his general position was sufficiently familiar to his special audience. Yet he did say explicitly that two fundamental features of customary religious practice would be rejected in his proposed Sunday meetings. In respect to moral care of the young, he denied the value of teaching them "to repeat some scattered verses of the Bible, and of doctrine which at their time of life they can but half comprehend at best." Second, he said: "in our Sunday meetings *we propose to entirely exclude prayer and every form of ritual.*"

Immediately he added that this exclusion did not so much aim at utter rejection as toward the positive "purpose of reconciliation." It aimed, that is, to take a stand on "common ground" where "believers and unbelievers" could meet and deal directly with moral and practical issues of contemporary society. He identified this "common ground" with a stress upon deed as he had been doing for the three years since his temple sermon. He proclaimed, *"Diversity in the creed, unanimity in the deed!* This is that common ground where we may clasp hands as brothers, united in mankind's common cause."

The spiritual note which Adler struck in this May meeting, largely devoted to projecting a plan, was linked strongly with a desire to do well for one's children.

There must be wider vistas . . . and sublime emotions which do not fail to exalt and consecrate existence. . . . You struggle and toil to leave them a store of earthly goods. Far better to feel the assurance that they will be true men and noble women. . . . strong even in adversity, because they believe in the destiny of mankind and in the dignity of man.

There is a great and crying evil in modern society. . . . It is want of purpose. It is that narrowness of vision which shuts out the wider vistas of the soul. It is the absence of those sublime emotions which, wherever they arise, do not fail to exalt and consecrate existence.

Five months later, on October 15, 1876, in the first of his series of "Sunday lectures," Adler returned to develop this same theme more fully.* And now that he was addressing a more general public, and not a special audience of close supporters, he stressed the goal of a greater and more equitable community as an essential ethical ideal. In short, he included his concern with "the social or labor question," which had perhaps been taken for granted but not explicitly developed in his May 15 address. Thus, in his opening October lecture he said:

Amid all changes the essential principle of ethics alone is changeless. The attempt to express its meanings in all the relations of life, to admit new and ever larger classes of society into the old bond of inalienable right and fellowship, this is what has constituted the supreme contest in the moral conquest of humanity. Today it manifests itself in the great social problems that agitate our age, demanding a higher justice, if they shall be solved, threatening anarchy and disruption, if they are met with in a spirit of selfish greed, promising a finer future than the world has ever seen, if dealt with in a spirit of wisdom and forbearance.

The keynote struck in the Opening Lecture on October 15 was this: *a new dedication,* a fresh applying of moral principle was needed to lift people out of the morass into which they had sunk. Traditional religion, by its orientation and its waning credibility, was impotent to supply a sufficient directing impulse. An ampler freedom in religious thought and relevant action toward a greater human community had to take hold.

It is revealing to see how Adler pitched his program of Sunday lectures that first year. He devoted the Sundays of the first four months mainly to criticism of fundamentals in the traditional religious heritage, Jewish and Christian. Not until the end of Janu-

Ethical Problems. Inaugural Discourse, Specially Reported by Miss Jennie Turner (New York: Charles P. Somerby, 1896).

ary 1877 did he proceed more positively with an address on "The New Ideal."

At the start, five consecutive lectures, those from October 22 through November 19, were devoted to discussions of "immortality," from diverse angles of modern inquiry. The positive aim in this was to associate life-dedication with a relevant this-worldly ethic. And the tenor of argument was that mankind's ideas about the afterlife were historically so various, so uncertain, and so vague as not to furnish effective direction for present action on "common ground." Dr. Adler also rather savored the tale of a clergyman who, when asked whether he believed in "eternal bliss," replied: "Yes, but why bring up such an unpleasant subject?"*

Probably the majority of his audience was already attuned to such arguments for a this-worldly ethics. It was crucial, however, to stress that to become effective such an ethic would require "enlightenment of the masses." On November 26 the Sunday lecture, entitled "The Enlightenment of the Masses," was devoted to underscoring this as "the problem on which the future of society depends." Liberal religious institutions, Adler added, must become centers of public enlightenment not just on Sundays but on the other six days of the week as well.

In December, a month replete with traditional religious holidays, his lectures examined prevailing attitudes toward the Bible, toward Jewish Reform, and toward Jesus, much as had his articles published in several journals during the preceding summer and fall months. Speaking for a developmental, historical view of the Bible, he said it is not to be held as divine teaching once and for all given to Moses, but as offering witness in changing eras to an evolving moral and religious consciousness. In this Adler was but following a trend toward critical history common among Jewish reformers. Yet he failed to see the needed development of that principle in the new temple modernism of the Jewish reformers.

* Beside these main conclusions, much of these five lectures gave current information on life-after-death discussions from literature in anthropology, comparative religion, ethics, psychology, and philosophy. The series was widely informative as well as argumentative. Works of Tylor, Lubbock, Bastin, Tindall, and Dubois-Reymond were cited.

On Sunday, December 31, 1876, the subject was Jesus. Looking for what had made possible a great outreach in religion, Adler said:

We shall not touch the true secret of his power until we recall his sympathy with the neglected classes of society. . . . The novelty of righteousness is not in itself, but in its novel application to the particular unrighteousness of a particular age. It was thus that Jesus applied to the sins and mock sanctities of his day, the ancient truths known to the prophets and to others long before him.

In later years Adler had much more to say than this in vital tribute to Jesus, not as a God of course, but as a fresh and essential contributor to ethical insight, a point about which many scholars disagreed.

Following this, in January 1877, three other "great religious emancipators" Buddha, Luther, and Spinoza were presented.* The aim in each case, as with Jesus, was to uphold elements of expanding religious truth which needed to be preserved despite the rejections of critical modern thought. Buddha's compassion transcending caste, Luther's sense of a possible priesthood of all believers, the serenity and power that Spinoza divined in an understanding of Nature's Order were underscored. Appealing as these lectures remain for their lucid manly speech and honest reverence, it should be added again that Adler later reached fuller views of these and other figures from the past.

Not until the religious heritage of the past had received this much critique (from October to January), did Adler attempt to explain how he viewed the next steps of change. In the flood of his ideas there came two crests, one on January 28, 1877, when he spoke on "The New Ideal," and again on Easter Sunday, April 1, when "The Form of the New Ideal" was the topic.† By "The Form" Adler meant the necessary ways of truly expressing and implementing the Ideal. In the intervening lectures much relevant matter was discussed.

---

*The addresses of January 7, 14, and 21, 1877, are in typescript, but that on Spinoza is printed as ch. 8, *Creed and Deed* (New York: Putnam, 1877). The lecture on Jesus follows as ch. 9. And on pp. 130–31 of the same volume is a passage on Buddha.

†Chs. 3 and 5 of *Creed and Deed*.

Although in the address on "The New Ideal" Kant is not explicitly mentioned, there can be little doubt that Adler chose the term "the Ideal" in some continuity with Kantian and neo-Kantian (cf. F. A. Lange's) usage. "The Ideal" could refer not only to something man-made but could be also a symbol pointing to a transcendent, part hidden, divine unifying ground of the universe. Probably there was some deliberate ambivalence in his choice of this term, although in his lecture of January 28 Adler referred to "The New Ideal" with a markedly humanistic emphasis, saying that it pointed to the "new conceptions of the purpose which we are here to accomplish and of the means of help we can command in the attempt to realize our destiny." Still, when facing critics in the near future, Adler avowed that "he had never been an atheist." His meaning in saying this must be presently considered, and also why he distinctly preferred to uphold a "religion of The Ideal" rather than a "religion of Humanity" then advocated by Comteans and others.

There is also a dual position, though not a flat contradiction, in what Adler said on January 28, 1877, about the relation of the old and the new. On the one hand, he predicted that "The new ideal of spiritual emancipation" would not destroy, but would fulfill what remains true in the old religions, especially concerning the law of righteousness. At the same time he said:

We stand at the portals of a new age. The old religions and science are at war. . . . The religious conceptions of the past are poetry, often of the sublimest kind. But to us the mystery is still mystery. . . . The riddle is unread. . . . Our business is to know a world with which we are but half acquainted more thoroughly.

We can no longer rely on prayer to affect the universe. We have really lost that sense of special protection, which bids us give to a personal deity a trust like that of a child to its father.

Less dogmatism, greater humility about knowledge of the universe, but greater responsibility in directing human affairs was the crucial plea in these statements.

In the Easter address, "The Form of the New Ideal," certain essentials of this greater responsibility were spelled out. Adler had already said it could not be satisfied by ritual worship. Now he declared that only "a new order of life and society" would avail.

"Liberalism," he said pointedly, "must pass the stage of individualism, must become the soul of great combinations." It must *organize* to produce institutions as well as personalities, and "institutions grounded in needs of the present." Basic human relations are themselves spiritual ends as well as means for developing individuals.

The "New Ideal" was linked in all this with a definite call for measures of social reconstruction. Instead of the corruptions and extravagances of that gilded age, the new order would again aim to produce a "true simplicity in living and a sincere purity in manners and morals." In the education of the masses, of women, and of the young, all was still sadly impoverished and constrained. For many years Adler continued to identify the labor problem, the role of women, and a new view of childhood as the deepest moral issues of the times.

How strongly the great spring holidays moved Felix Adler has already been seen in the letter he wrote his sister from Ithaca a year earlier, on Easter in 1876. Now, in 1877, he closed his Easter Sunday address by remarking on the church bells pealing "the resurrection," and said:

What we cannot credit of an individual is true of the nations. After long periods of seeming torpor and death, humanity ever rises anew from the dust, shakes off its slumbers, and clothes itself with fresher vigor and diviner powers. Let such a hope animate us.

By February 1877 the response to Adler's appeal proved sufficient to activate measures for permanent organization. A certificate to incorporate the Society for Ethical Culture in New York was filed on February 21. It explained:

The object of said Society will be mutual improvement in religious knowledge and the furtherance of religious opinion, which shall be in part accomplished by a system of weekly lectures, in which the principles of ethics shall be developed, propagated and advanced among adults, and in part by the establishment of a school or schools wherein a course of moral instruction shall be supplied for the young.

The preamble to the bylaws of the Society, adopted that same month, further stressed the need for:

a permanent and effective organization to support the cause of enlightenment. . . .
to further the moral elevation of the masses in particular. . . .
to train the young in enjoyment of the inestimable benefits of
liberty. . . .
and to recognize the great truths of man's moral nature as the essential
safeguard of life.

In a series of four addresses delivered in February 1877, Adler
sought to explain and justify the religious nature of the proposed
Society by discussing the nature of religion and its main types.
The basic, generic nature of religion, he held, is not creed, nor
sacrifice, nor even prayer. It "has its roots in the feeling of the
sublime, which the presence of the Infinite in the thoughts of man
awakens within him." Religion takes different directions according to whether the feeling of the sublime is evoked predominantly
by the mysterious, as in fetichism; by exhibitions of superhuman
power, as in paganism; by vastness, as in Hinduism; or by the
morally infinite, as in Judaism and Christianity.

The contrast which Adler felt most concerned to drive home
was that between "the gods of force," such as are celebrated in the
nature rites and myths of paganism, and divinity conceived as essentially having a moral infinitude. This ethical type of religion
was the only kind, Adler stressed, that could still legitimately make
an absolute claim upon man's conscience. But even the claim
made by this type could not be confined within any single credo
or theology. "It were sad indeed," he concluded, "if morality de-
pended upon the certainty of dogma. On the contrary it is true
that all that is best and grandest in dogma is due to the inspiration
of the moral law in man. . . . Dogma we will keep in abeyance—
this is our point of departure, and the deed superior to the
creed."*

Joseph Seligman was chosen as the Society's first president and
served in this office until his death in 1880. His prominence, his
wealth and business standing, and the continuous interest he had
taken in Adler's ideas during the three years since the temple sermon of 1873 were vital assets in launching the new Society.

*Compare these views with ch. 2 of *Creed and Deed*.

Fifteen trustees were provided for who could elect to membership in the Society by a three-fourths vote.* "No subscription to any formula of faith, belief, or creed was to be required of members"; the identity of the Society was lodged in purpose not in creed. It was further stipulated that "as long as ten members shall desire to perpetuate the organization of the Society the same shall not be dissolved."

At the start the powers of professional leadership in the new Society presented at least a verbal problem, and in the run of later years a number of more genuine ones. Felix Adler always felt the need to involve a group of professionals, of individuals specially prepared for and continuously employed in leadership. The bylaws accordingly stated that the Society was to elect "a Lecturer or Lecturers" who would have ex-officio membership on the Board of Trustees. But rather surprising is the further statement in the bylaws that these lecturers would be in general charged with "the intellectual concerns and powers of ministers in religious societies." At the May 15, 1876 meeting, though pleading for "specialists" in moral teaching, Adler had avoided the word "priest," saying in fact: "Do not fear friends that a priestly office after a new fashion will thus be introduced." Yet now, in a Sunday lecture of March 1877 he used the title "The Priesthood of the Ideal," though he did repeat that "with good reason the very name of the priesthood has become odious to the modern mind."† Still he went on to explain the need of "a new priesthood of the Ideal" in these words:

The time will come, when single men shall no more be needed to do this ministry, when in the brotherhood and sisterhood of mankind all shall be priests and priestesses one to another. . . . Yet until then, the power of the new priest is in this, that he speaks what all feel. . . . and brings us face to face with the inner life. . . . Not only to instruct, but to be an interpreter on those special occasions, when the ideal bearings of life come home to us with peculiar force, do we require the priest.

---

*The fifteen trustees elected for the first year were: Joseph Seligman, president of the Society; Albert A. Levi: Henry Friedman; Edward Lauterbach; William Byfield; Joseph Seidenberg; Max Abenheim; Max Landman; Emil Salinger; Meyer Jonasson; Jacob Stettheimer, Jr.; Samuel A. Solomons; Julius Rosenbaum; Marcus Goldman; Samuel V. Speyer.

†Ch. 4. of *Creed and Deed.*

In particular, he said, "at the grave is the office of the priest," and at marriage, which he called "the supreme festival of humanity." It is very clear that he wanted much to exercise personally these "priestly" functions of which he here spoke. And one must add that he proved to be unusually gifted for it. Many of his services for the departed and his words on commemorative occasions, public and private, stand up enduringly as among his finest expressions.

On the last Sunday of the season, May 13, 1877, Adler initiated a custom of giving an "Anniversary Discourse," reviewing the first year's course of thought and its forward intent. It was announced that 234 had joined the Society, "exclusive of the original subscribers," which, allowing for withdrawals, would suggest a roster of around 400.

A contemporary account of the impression Adler made on his audiences is to be found in the March 29, 1877, issue of *The Index: A Weekly Journal Devoted to Free Religion*. The article, reprinted from the *Christian Register*, February 24, describes one of Adler's Sunday lectures in some detail. It begins with the general comment:

The new exponent of radical ideas, Prof. Felix Adler, is attracting a good deal of attention, especially among the more liberal Jews. He lectures on Sunday at Standard Hall. . . . It is a snug little place, that will hold three hundred people, and on Sunday morning last was crowded with as many as it could comfortably seat. . . . There was also a considerable sprinkling of Gentiles. . . .

Describing the nature of these lectures, the reporter indicated:

The service is purely secular without a prayer or hymn, text or benediction. A choir up in a little gallery sings a few selections from Mendelssohn and Rossini to an organ accompaniment, and then Prof. Adler takes his place at the reading desk.

After commenting on Adler's background, the writer went on to describe his appearance: "slightly built and scholarly-looking, with a well-formed head and massive brain. . . . The slight pallor of the student is contrasted with the black hair and eyes, and a close-cut beard of the same hue."

Finally the writer addressed himself to Adler's lectures, their style and content.

He speaks entirely without notes, and from the first sentences it is apparent that his intellect is of a keen, relentless, and incisive order, and his scholarship ripe and rare. Absolute fearlessness seems to be one of his leading characteristics, and some of the things he said on Sunday must have been peculiarly startling to his Jewish auditors, but he said them as if he deserved thanks for his almost pitiless sincerity.

Commenting on Adler's method, the reporter noted:

A profound interest is developed in the audience as soon as the speaker begins his lecture. He is now delivering a course on the "History of Religion". . . . Though his manner is quiet, at moments, through the warmth of a fervid nature, it rises to an intense but ungesticulatory kind of eloquence.

Coming to the essential message of Adler's lecture, the reporter wrote:

He partially refuted the common opinion that religion had its origin in fear. It sprang equally from the instinctive reverence for power. The old gods were men deified, vast human images cast upon the screen of the unknown. God made man in his image, man has made God in his own likeness.

The reporter ended his account in a prophetic vein:

He announced that the founding of his society would take place this week, and judging from the lively interest of the something more than handful he has already drawn, it is safe to predict that Prof. Adler will soon have a not inconsiderable following.*

Later in 1877 G. P. Putnam's Sons published Adler's first book, a small volume called *Creed and Deed,* which in somewhat abridged and revised form contained the substance of his first year's addresses in launching the Society for Ethical Culture. The book received rather widespread press notice in towns as well as cities, showing the attention then given to religious and moral controversy. Estimates of the book varied extremely, from those which found it "dreary," "unwholesome," "pharisaical unbelief," to one reviewer who proclaimed "this logical, beautiful and valuable work . . . is the fruit of a courageous, earnest, cultured, thoroughly masculine and yet sympathetic and poetic mind." One critic, however, complained of weakness in "the author's ethical system, as well as in his philosophy of religion and revelation.

*Editor's insert. F.W.

What he calls his moral sense is more an ideal sentiment than an imperative law . . . or dynamic principle."

Within a few years Adler himself felt the need to give his ideas sharper definition and stronger application. His chapters in *Creed and Deed* are not works of commanding direction nor of matured experience. But they have the open and tender air of a young idealist's romance through the springtime of his hopes for a larger morality and freer religion. As such his lectures of 1876–77 did take hold and did impart a lasting practical impetus.

Felix Adler was a complex enough person to satisfy a variety of interests among his followers. The scope of his thought and superior delivery made his lectures culturally eventful and beyond ephemeral commentary. His ideas on social progress drew helpers who chiefly shared the ardor for such effort. But above all he was a dedicated man engaging intensely the vision and power he now possessed. This dedication and its range of purpose qualified him for many as their religious leader.

A wide impact on the life of the city could not yet be claimed. But a band of intelligent and constructively minded people had responded to Adler with excitement and with serious purpose. After hearing his addresses they went home to engage in discussions that were often intense and purposeful. And they felt liberated from ties and practices that they perceived as too narrow and outworn.

But what could be done with the challenge? Whether the call of the first year would be of lasting consequence was still in the power of ensuing events to determine.

[6]

A SPEARHEAD OF SOCIAL ETHICS:
1877–1880

THE SUMMER OF 1877 saw unprecedented and widespread industrial violence throughout much of the United States. The long business depression which followed the Panic of 1873 had not yet ended. In railroading, especially, financial distress showed in a sharp stock decline and a rise in receiverships. Early in 1877 some of the country's railroad barons conferred and decided "to earn more" by boosting freight rates and "to spend less" by introducing a 10 percent cut in wages. Rail workers, then weak in organized support, knew that ordinary strikes could be soon overcome by strikebreakers. In July their unrest seethed into violent strike actions that spread rapidly from Baltimore and Pittsburgh through the Midwest, with minor disorders that reached as far as the West Coast. In one place after another car yards were set afire. Though chiefly on the railways, many concurrent strikes took place, and unruly discontented crowds swelled the disturbances. Both state militia and federal troops went into action, especially in Maryland, Pennsylvania, West Virginia and Illinois, as well as in other states. Bloodshed among rioters occurred in many cities.

The unrest came near to bursting into a nationwide upheaval, and it spurred important developments in our industrial system. It gave a new impetus to wider organization of American labor. As Samuel Gompers recorded in his autobiography, *Seventy Years of Life and Labor*, "The railroad strike of 1877 was the tocsin that sounded a ringing message of hope to us all." But the different remedies proposed and initiated formed a wide spectrum. New repressive measures such as the formation of the "Coal and Iron Police" were undertaken by private companies to deal with labor unrest. Appeal to the courts and other government offices to intervene in critical industrial disputes became more common. At the same time there appeared a Marxist revolutionary party, the Workingmen's Party of the United States (reorganized in 1878 as the Socialist Labor Party), which demanded the nationalization of the railroads and an eight-hour working day.

Less radical suggestions included various proposals for industrial arbitration. Little welcomed, these hardly seemed promising in a period when immigration furnished such a steady flow of unorganized labor. Nevertheless, a disposition to reconcile led Felix Adler to wonder about the possibilities of arbitration. So in the midst of that flaming summer he wrote a letter to the editor of the *Railroad Gazette* in England asking for information about the system of arbitration in British industry. The long reply dated August 23, 1877, from Mr. Thomas Hughes gave details on unions and industrial negotiation and arbitration, but prefaced all with the general remark:

I do not however see how my experience or that of any English arbitrator can help you, for it seems to me you are quite in error in supposing that the condition of things disclosed by your recent railroad war is analogous to that which has long existed here, or is likely to exist.

The anarchic conditions in American industry, with its ruthless, driving ferocity, now precipitated a significant release of moral concern for a more responsible and humane industrial order. If for some twenty years or more Felix Adler named "the social or labor question" as "the chief moral question of the day," he clearly was not referring to wages and working conditions alone. It was the growing edge of a new stage of society that he saw in the general state and future prospects of industrial workers. It was a concern for the entire education and development of the workers, for their homes and families, their life structure and outlook. And it was concern, as well, that they have a voice in the making of economic decisions. These economic, intellectual, and moral dimensions led Adler to view "the liberation of labor" as of crucial ethical moment to all society.

Though he built on his own distinctive principles, he was not a lone voice in now urging that "Religion must step in between the contending classes. . . . and preach the sermon of justice as it has never been heard before." To be sure, during the 1877 railroad war, the Reverend Henry Ward Beecher had told his comfortable Brooklyn congregation, in a sermon that became notorious:

It is true that a dollar a day is not enough to support a man and five children, if the man insists on smoking and drinking beer. Is not a dollar a day enough to buy bread? Water costs nothing. . . . A family may live on good bread and water in the morning, water and bread at midday, and good water and bread at night. . . . The great laws of political economy can not be set at defiance.

But the reactions to Beecher's "bread and water" sermon, even in the business press, were not all so favorable as he might have expected. And some American ministers and teachers had by this time begun to criticize the prevailing economics of laissez-faire. They were seeking a social ethics and gospel more suited to the developing industrial situation.* W. J. Tucker at Andover Seminary and Francis Peabody at the Harvard Divinity School were also beginning about 1881 to introduce new courses in social ethics.

In New York City during these years the spectrum of religious and moral teaching included more heterodox doctrines as well, such as the Comtean Positivism preached by William Frey and Edward King as the Religion of Humanity. The flow of such preaching during the seventies and eighties in New York may be glimpsed in part through accounts of men who worked to unionize the garment trades. Thus, J. M. Budish and George Soule tell us:

Every year small and transient trade unions sprang up. . . . rather debating societies than real trade organizations. The members were often more interested in the theoretical battles between the different philosophical schools fighting for supremacy on the East Side than in their trade activities.

These men suddenly found themselves under the influence of three main schools. The teachers who dominated the three schools were idolized by their followers. One of them was William Frey who taught Positivism and the "religion of humanity;" another was Felix Adler who

---

*Among voices thus raised were: Washington Gladden in *Workingmen and Their Employers*, 1876; R. Heber Newton in *The Morals of Trade*, 1876; Dudley Rhodes in *Creed and Greed*, 1879; Henry George in *Progress and Poverty*, 1879; Edward Everett Hale in *The Life in Common*, 1880; J. H. W. Stuckenberg, in *Christian Sociology*, 1880; and J. H. Rylance in *Lectures on Social Questions*, 1880.

preached Ethical Culture; and a third was Johann Most who taught Anarchism. Eager audiences flocked to all three. But, at the beginning, the teachings of the three were confused in the minds of the youth into an Ethical-Anarchistic-Positivistic hash.*

Felix Adler was sensitive and averse to having his ideas hashed up; indeed, he remained strongly so throughout life. Intellectual distinctness was for him part of ethical integrity. Thus, on a November Sunday in 1877, he sought to distinguish his views from the Positivism of William Frey and Edward King in his address, "The Religion of Humanity." He wanted to explain that he had wrongly been called a follower of Auguste Comte's Positivist Religion of Humanity. Adler, however, praised Comte "as one of the few moderns who perceived the inherent relations that ought to subsist between religious and social progress." He expressed a strong sympathy with three of Comte's particular views: his emphasis on labor, and on a larger role for woman, and his critique of the Golden Rule as an ethical principle. But then he proceeded to criticize, in graphic and rather devastating detail, features which Positivism had cultivated as "a religious sect." The historical, so-called "positive religions," Adler said, made the mistake of taking their ideals for facts of existence in supernatural heavens and hells. Now this new Positivist Religion of Humanity was making the opposite mistake of idealizing certain contemporary facts of science, society, and femininity. To avoid ending up in "positive confusion," Adler concluded, it will always be necessary to keep clear a distinction between facts as facts and ideals as ideals.

To idolize man as he is, is the weakness to which a Religion of Humanity is prone. To avoid it Adler spoke for a Religion of the Ideal. "The Ideal" transcends "the all too human." It stirs an aspiration to re-envision humanity's essential part in a universe of infinite grandeur. In wanting to preserve such a reach of religious feeling Adler adhered to a transcendent idealism. But no less did he want to grapple with facts as facts, as a realist in the immediate human scene. He did not mean to direct his course into a life of ideal contemplation.

For some years Adler had been calling for urgently needed

*J. M. Budish and George Soule, *The New Unionism in the Clothing Industry* (New York: Harcourt Brace and Howe, 1920), pp. 208–9.

deeds. And now in an address soon after his criticism of the Comteans, he explained that in engaging itself in deeds Ethical Culture should not aim to be a new sect. Its aim should not be to display a creed, but to forward "a universal task" by attending to the "great practical problems of the age," by spreading "truthfulness among the people" and "education for moral welfare." It is inspired by feeling that the "peaceable revolution" taking place through science demands "a new emotional life," in which heart and head may be reconciled.

The Ethical Culture Society began its deeds with two modest yet well-directed practical projects. A first proposal, before the end of 1877, was to send nurses to visit the homebound sick in poor districts. A beginning was made with a single nurse, Miss Effie Benedict, a college graduate with training from Bellevue Hospital. She was based at the DeMilt Dispensary, where at that time some of the best medical men gave their services free. A careful routine was worked out and the nurse reported on her visits to a doctor. He in turn instructed her and when necessary, visited the sick with her. This practice, at first called "district" and then "visiting nursing," caught on readily and became eventually a vital adjunct in city health systems. The Ethical Culture Society was interested in its being a nonsectarian service, and it soon became permanently organized as such, largely through the work of Lillian D. Wald and the Henry Street Settlement.

The second project was to launch a free kindergarten. The educational outgrowths of this venture are detailed in later chapters. But its initial motivation for Adler was broadly related to "the social question"; its aim was to take children of workingmen's families off the streets and to give them some of the care needed in the early years. Toward the end of 1877 Felix and a close friend, Alfred Wolff (an engineering graduate of the Stevens Institute), promoted the project themselves, by giving out handbills in the Gas House district on the West Side, inviting neighborhood people to send their children to the Free Kindergarten. Most had never heard of such a thing, and some, it seems, even suspected a kidnapping scheme! But on January 2, 1878, eight "small persons," six boys and two girls, ventured to appear. And presently the group began to be eagerly sought out.

Since both these measures had appeal beyond the membership of the Society for Ethical Culture, an auxiliary arm called the United Relief Works was established promptly, through which support could be given to specific projects by people who were not moved to join the Society. Yet each January in 1878, 1879, and 1880 Adler began the new year with prominent attention and explanation in his Sunday addresses of his developing efforts in social ethics.

The pitch of his argument and his program for industrial reform drew wide public notice and sharp controversy in these years. On January 13, 1878, he took as his topic for a Sunday address, "The Ethics of the Social Question." Social justice is its alpha and omega, he declared. The idea that the present system rewards labor according to merit overlooks the great inequalities of opportunity caused by glutting of the labor market, insecure employment, and poverty of education. There must be a threefold liberation—economic, moral, and intellectual—within the condition of labor. For the laboring man justice will no longer be satisfied by indulging the dream wherein "the laborer of today expects to become the employer of tomorrow." Lincoln had so described an expectation typical of earlier America. But the real problem now, Adler concluded, is "to raise them in their capacity as laborers," and this must mean "a just remuneration, constant employment, and social dignity." Adler's statement at the start of this address that "I am the speaker of my society, and hope, in some respects, their mouthpiece" probably disclosed his wish rather than the complete fact. It is not likely that the Society's members, nearly all middle-class people, were of one mind with him on labor questions.

On April 4, 1878, there appeared in the *New York Times* an account of the Society for Ethical Culture "by a visitor," who explained, among other points:

Though the reverse of alarmist, Adler sees danger in the present condition of things in the concentration and glut of laborers in the cities, the hostile feelings between labor and capital, the lack of intelligence on the one hand, the want of sympathy on the other; the absence of recognition of the humanity and manhood of the toiling millions. . . . The laboring classes, to be truly and permanently benefited, must feel and see that the more fortunate and prosperous have their interest at heart, and are willing to help them to help themselves. They have the right to live, meaning the right to work, the right to cleanliness, and the right to be private and virtuous, which in the crowded and poisonous tenement houses of the city, they can never enjoy.

The whole account in the *Times* gave a very attractive, positive picture of the Ethical Culture Society and its leader. And it must have been especially welcome at this time because Adler had been subjected to a bitter, maligning attack only a few weeks before.

The occasion of this was an invitation that in March 1878 he might address the Sinai Literary Association of Chicago (an organization connected there with the Reform Temple) on his way to a lecture engagement in Milwaukee. News of Felix Adler's doings in New York was spreading and evidently evoking interest. Yet his standpoint was highly controversial and objectionable to many who viewed him as now grazing on flatlands of social work and simple philanthropy after unwisely leaving the Jewish religious fold. Did he conceive his social ethics as substitute for true religion? So it was hardly surprising that Dr. Kaufmann Kohler, eminent as an intellectual leader among the Reformed rabbis in America, saw fit to deliver a sharp rebuke to his colleagues on the subject of the Chicago invitation to Adler. Dr. Kohler wrote:

To my great surprise, I hear that in the Sinai Literary Association a motion is on foot to invite Professor Felix Adler, of New York, to deliver a lecture before the members, he being expected to come here next week. Of what benefit to a society of Jewish young people the lecture of a man can be who has deserted the Jewish flag, and openly professes his disbelief in God and immortality, I really fail to see, unless the eradication of the Jewish faith is the object contemplated. But, I suppose, very few of your members, if any, know anything about the young professor, who merely by his fine oratory, combined with great arrogance, created for a while some sensation in New York. At any rate, I shall not allow my temple to be disgraced by a lecture to be delivered within its walls by one who blasphemes God and Judaism.

The abusiveness of this blast gave offense in turn. A response in an open letter from Julius Rosenthal, indicated that there was no intention to desecrate Rabbi Kohler's temple, which moreover was not really "his" temple. The immediate outcome was that Adler did give a lecture in Chicago, but at the Standard Hall there.

The occasion led Dr. Kohler to further invective wherein other persons were mentioned. He wanted it understood that "his friends and colleagues, Drs. Felsenthal and L. Adler" of Chicago, did not approve, that indeed no Jewish minister could approve "the teachings of Felix Adler," whose derivative and mistaken ideas "would hardly have created such a sensation in Jewish circles, were he not the son of the venerable Dr. S. Adler, and the pupil of the late Dr. A. Geiger, misleading thereby, and by fine oratory, many an advocate of Jewish reform."

Felix Adler did not himself respond to these harsh ad hominem charges. But it meant much to Felix to have the warm support of his father expressed in an exchange of letters between Samuel Adler and Rabbi Felsenthal in Chicago.

Dear Dr. Felsenthal,
 Your lines of March 1st reached me and added to the joy and solemnity of the Sabbath. I want to express to you my gratitude for your words of esteem and friendship as well as your appreciation of my son.
 And yet it is difficult for me to answer your letter fully for I do not feel strong enough to discuss the subject. In fact I try not to feel harshly against those who have joined in branding a pure and idealistic soul as godless and immoral because it does not agree with their own ideas. It is quite natural that they should attempt to make me too a target for their arrows. I am to be forced to exert my fatherly authority in order to silence my son. Honest fanaticism is blind, but hypocritical fanaticism aims to obstruct and confuse people's vision. They do not understand nor wish to recognize that in the face of a deep and honest conviction and a passionate search for truth a father's authority is at an end. Even if I had such authority I should consider it a sin to exercise it.
 I am convinced that the aim and purpose of my son's work is a deeply sacred and religious one, that the attribution of Atheism and Materialism and other impure motives are purely malicious slanders. If his convictions in some respects are not the same as mine, they are nevertheless his honest convictions and are entitled to as much consideration as my own. For this reason I allow all these mean and contemptible criticisms to pass over me and endeavor to support them with as much patience and resignation as my sense of duty and devotion to God allow me to do.
 In love and friendship,
 Yours,
 Samuel Adler

In New York, Felix Adler told his Ethical Culture followers at a Sunday meeting that, of course, he never wished to substitute social reform for religion. "Religion must bring us nigh to the Infinite," he said.

Shall we think it a recompense for the lost kingdom of the universal, of the Infinite, that we can cultivate a little better this small plot of land whereon we stand? Shall our hearts beat never more to the sublimest emotions induced by the aspect of the All? Religion dwells upon what this whole universe means for me.

People want a confession of faith, I am told. Hear then mine—a simple one. I believe in the supreme excellence of righteousness; I believe that the law of righteousness will triumph in the universe over all evil; I believe that in the law of righteousness is the sanctification of human life; and I believe that in furthering and fulfilling that law I also am hallowed in the service of the unknown God.

Those words "the unknown God" signalize the reserve with which Felix Adler in those early years turned away from explicit formulas of theology.

Kohler's emphasis on historic faith and God-belief surely raised a genuine issue. For what Felix Adler was saying and doing in his new movement obviously raised crucial questions for Jewish community and identity. There was as yet no common convention as to the boundaries of Reformed Judaism in America; in 1885 a platform, drafted largely by Kohler, was adopted at a rabbinical conference in Pittsburgh. Ethical Culture was clearly outside its guidelines, as indeed it was by its own definition. It was one of the "universalizing" movements widely present in liberal religion of the day.

Furthermore, while Adler advised against mixed marriages between Jewish and Christian adherents loyal to their distinct religions, he welcomed them between persons who, having departed from these backgrounds, had reached a common ethical faith. In this respect he was definitely an assimilationist. And in the long prospect he ventured to predict, in an address on December 16, 1878, that "eventually the Jewish race (like others) must die."

Its prophets had themselves with rapture predicted the time when their people should be relieved of their separate mission; as Greece is dead and still lives in its poetry, philosophy and art, so the genius of the Hebrew people will live on in the immortal heritage of moral truth which they left to mankind.

Such a prediction must have cut the more sharply because sensitivity on matters of Jewish identity and solidarity was rising in this country after the Civil War. New trends of social discrimination against Jews were spreading, and liberal belief and deed conferred no immunity. This was dramatically illustrated in a cause célèbre close to Adler's circle when Joseph Seligman in the summer of 1877 was refused accommodations at the Grand Union Hotel in Saratoga, where he had been a long-time patron.

Adler's universalist turn in religion is prominent in his relations to the Free Religious Association. Though he served as president of this association for four years (1878–82) he found its members unresponsive to the main initiatives he proposed. Still, as will become evident, his contacts with the Free Religious Association brought the first applicants to join him in professional leadership of the Ethical Culture movement. They came, not out of Reform Judaism but from universalizing tendencies having Unitarian and liberal Christian backgrounds. This fact worked no doubt both to qualify and to curb the effect of Ethical Culture as a schismatic influence upon Judaism.

Adler did not permit the religious issues and crosscurrents of these years to deter his activities in the name of social ethics. But not all his efforts in this line were successful. During a strike, in 1878, in the printing trades in New York, he sought help to establish a cooperative printing shop. Some capital stocks were issued in the name of the New York Cooperative Printers' Association. Yet presently, when the strike was settled, most of the cooperative printers abandoned their shop and reverted to their familiar competitive employment, expecting it to be individually more profitable. Adler had been warned by a well-wisher that the men accepted taking advantage of one another as the way of the world in their business. This experience nourished his convictions that working people would have to be taught to cooperate through an education that improved both their economic and social outlook.

So Adler, assisted again by Alfred Wolff, Heber Newton, and others, now channeled considerable effort into several projects aimed at providing relevant education for industrial society. One of the first, launched on March 23, 1878, was a "Workingmen's

Lyceum for the spread of correct economic knowledge." It was observed that "such institutions exist in many of the large cities of England and Scotland and elsewhere," and it was hoped that it might eventually "be housed in a Mechanics' Institute which would contain a free Library, Reading Rooms, a Hall for Meetings and the like. Not any one class," the promoters said, "but the whole community, mankind at large, are interested in this vital issue of the elevation of the working classes." Adler, it seems, drafted a constitution of sorts, indicating that

It shall not be a political organization, nor a trade organization; it will assume an educational mission only. . . . But all classes of the community will have a right to speech on this platform. We do not believe it to be dangerous to hear communistic arguments.

During 1878 and 1879 the Lyceum conducted a notably active forum, with lectures at Cooper Union and a number of other halls. The variety of topics treated is suggested by Parke Godwin's series, "The Social Problem," Heber Newton's address, "The Wrong of the Wages System," and E. C. Seguin's lecture, "Diet." In a lecture on May 1, 1878, Felix Adler declared that "to make men fit for cooperating is the work of the Lyceum." And in the following year, on November 1, 1879, at Cooper Union, the progress of the cooperative movement in England was reported by an English exponent, George J. Holyoake.

Also in January 1879, and again in 1880, Dr. Adler brought his own specific thoughts on a program for the reform of industrial society onto the Sunday platform of the Ethical Culture Society. In 1879 he did this with a series of three lectures on "Social Ethics," and in January and February of 1880 with another series of five lectures on "Just Measures of Social Reform." In the opening address on "Social Ethics" he focused on the problem of moral aim and motive. The ethical doctrine of enlightened self-interest was much used to condone raw competition and a devil-take-the-hindmost attitude. But the effort to correct this in Christian and in other religious teachings by a purely altruistic system of ethics, Adler said, is an over-compensatory reaction. It encourages "remedial charity," doing good to the poor who are "always with us." A preventive, not just remedial, charity requires an ethics of "jointness" or mutuality which is both other-regarding and self-interested. In reply to new charges of heresy, he called it "arch-heresy" to deny the possibility of progress in removing license, slavery, and poverty. He asked for no sudden change, no world-wide panacea, but only a diligent and tireless and immediate pursuit of the needed liberation of labor.

His second "Social Ethics" lecture tackled "the ethics of property." Here he sought to answer, with some irony, the charge that his views were tainted by "communism." Since there are ideal values in communism that have appealed to many noble spirits, it is crude and unworthy to use the term as one of abuse. But from the long-term historical viewpoint, Adler declared, it could be seen that it was the advocates of private property who had been the real revolutionaries. And, since it is "arch-heresy to deny the possibility of progress," he concluded that he must rank himself on the side of private property as a condition favorable to personal freedom.

This lecture also criticized the labor theory of property that each is entitled to the fruits of his own labor. "What fruit does anyone produce apart from the heritage of the race? . . . My ethical right to private property lies, not in what I make by my labor, but in what I need to do my proper work well." In this case, only the great transition now bringing more cooperative industrial organization can avail. And government must aid with appropriate measures of taxation and of education. On this matter Adler referred to John Stuart Mill's advocacy of income and inheritance taxes.

The last of these three "Social Ethics" lectures ventured into the question of the management and control of factories. A distinction was drawn among "three forms of government possible for factories: monarchical, constitutional, and republican."

In the monarchical form there is one master and all others are dependent upon him. The constitutional government of a factory is found where there is still one master and others are dependent, but the working men have a share in the profits and a voice in the management, as was the case in one of the largest industrial establishments of this city for many years. The republican form of government is to be found where the employer and the employed are identical, the laborer being the capitalist and the capitalist being the laborer. . . . The working classes are not ripe for it, they have not yet learned that self-restraint which is necessary for this form of industrial government. . . . But the working classes should not relax their efforts until they have gained this goal, for by this means they will wed democracy and industry.

So, in light of his experience with the attempted cooperative printing shop, Adler concluded that under current conditions the change to work for is one from a "monarchical" to a "constitutional" government of industries. But beyond this he envisaged the "republican form of factory government," a more thorough industrial democracy, as a desirable eventual goal.

In 1880 a still longer series of five lectures was given, titled "Just Measures of Social Reform," in the cause of implementing these ideals. The first measure submitted was *a new and better education of the working classes*. The aim in this, Adler said, should be not merely to increase the workingman's skill for breadwinning but to develop him as a human being and citizen for a greater cooperative freedom. A second measure of reform must be *a reeducation of the possessing classes*, which would involve "reformation of the churches." People need to be guided beyond familiar conceptions of "remedial charity" toward measures of "larger preventive charity" by "a science of ethics." The churches would continue to have a vital role, because the imagination must be appealed to by art, and the intellect by science, in order to foster a "right love." Third, in democratic states legitimate measures of preventive charity would include *a graduated system of income taxes*, instituted by government to support the proposed development of public education and in other ways to aid the transition from competition to cooperation in industry. Last, *graduated inheritance taxes* would prove sound in the interest of the children of the rich as well as of the community at large. "The rights of children" do include a right of inheritance, Adler said, but not one to unlimited wealth. In advancing these thoughts on taxation, he again cited and expanded upon the ideas of John Stuart Mill.

Reporting on these lectures, the *Evening Post* of February 9, 1880, commented that "The Society for Ethical Culture, we understand, is nothing if not practical, and it is doing very praiseworthy practical work of an educational and charitable kind; yet so impracticable is its leader that he has proposed a plan of taxation under which the treasury would be speedily and permanently empty because it would soon leave nothing to be taxed." Hardly a far-seeing remark! Adler was not moved in the course of later years to abandon any of these early proposals. These lectures of 1879 and 1880 were a first gathering of views on social reform, but they already contained a structure that would inform Adler's later, more developed position based on his mature experience and thought.

After the passage of many years Rabbi Kaufmann Kohler would come to admit that Felix Adler was a more religious man than the rabbi had recognized at first. And for his part, in retrospect, Adler could say that the social question, the liberation of labor is not *the* raison d'être of Ethical Culture. But espousal of this cause had in the early days "given the movement life."

[7]

EARLY ASSOCIATIONS
AND MARRIAGE: 1878–1882

FROM 1876 TO 1880 Felix Adler lived on the top floor of a house at the corner of 59th Street and Lexington Avenue, where his older, married brother, the physician Dr. Isaac Adler, had his residence and office on the floors below. Already in these years Felix's active initiative in numerous projects brought many people to his top-floor study for conference and counsel. It is said that one of Isaac's young sons remarked: "You, uncle, have a great many patients coming to see you, lots more than father has."

Dr. Isaac remained skeptical of his brother's philosophizing and its possible religious sense, apparently even to the point of doubting whether he had "a real message." Years later he could still caustically refer to one of Felix's associates as "the assistant Messiah." Nevertheless, as a physician he did give precious service, not alone in personal needs, but in helping the Ethical Society's school promote superior medical care for its members.

Isaac's mind remained strictly committed to scientific standards and his repute as a doctor was connected with this. For his part, Felix, although he rejected "scientism" as too limited a philosophy of life, did seek to admit the crucial and progressive bearing of advancing science upon ethical enlightenment. He repeatedly stressed this as an essential feature and policy in describing the Ethical Culture movement.

I want the advantage and the strength . . . the essential ethical strength, that comes from touching hands with those honest people who are ethically-minded, but who do not take the same religious view of things that I myself do. . . . The religious teacher has some indispensable elements; the world, the scientists, the practical men, the artists have others.

Though his relation to Isaac was not one of reciprocal and equal enthusiasm, he sought to keep it a steady and fruitful one. Doubtless it was one intimate source of his deep conviction that human

74

interdependence must embrace productive differences rather than seek only for accords.

The associates who helped Felix Adler in his work during the 1870s were volunteers, except for the nurse employed in the district nursing and the directress of the Free Kindergarten. Adler himself was the only Ethical Culture lecturer, and his notes for the lectures were written in his own hand, not typed by a secretary. But the Ethical Culture movement received help from whole families, whose members became absorbed in the problems and aspirations that Adler presented to them. Among these were the Alfred Wolff and Julius Rosenbaum families. This was also the case with the Seligmans; not only Joseph Seligman himself but his son Edwin and his daughter Frances (Mrs. Theodore Hellman) were prominent and active in the Society for Ethical Culture. Edwin became a president of the Society, and Mrs. Hellman was a warm friend and supporter of Felix Adler's plans and activities.

The people who came to assist Felix Adler in developing the Ethical Culture movement were not all found in New York, however. Some entered through Adler's connections in New England, which proved especially important in bringing him several of the first applicants for Ethical Culture leadership as a professional career. His relations to The Free Religious Association played a significant part in this.

In 1878, at its December meeting in Boston, Felix Adler had been elected president of the Free Religious Association (F.R.A.). Octavius B. Frothingham was retiring from the presidency for reasons of declining health, and it was believed that Adler's youthful energy and constructive aims might bring fresh life to the Association, which was then entering its twelfth year. In May 1877, at the close of Ethical Culture's first year, Francis E. Abbot (editor of the F.R.A. journal, *The Index*) had written Felix Adler to ask if he was correct in thinking that

you have taken a position respecting Judaism very analogous to that I took respecting Christianity in 1868—that is, a frank advance from the limitations of all *special historical religions* to the freedom of *universal spiritual religion*.

We do not have Adler's reply but we know that through Ethical Culture he was aiming toward a stronger *ethical* commitment in practical affairs as well as toward religious advance from "special historical" forms to freer universal validity.

Yet Francis Abbot was right that both the Free Religious Association and the Society for Ethical Culture had established "free platforms," open to the expression of religious thought not bound to historic creeds. When he became president of the F.R.A. in December 1878, Adler proposed development of a center of higher learning for "the training of leaders of free religion," that would combine the intellectual freedom of Continental universities with the New World's zeal for building a freer social order. "The great complaint," he observed, "is that with few exceptions our liberal leaders are not profound enough." In May 1879 he pressed this thought again at the Ethical Culture Society by noting the need for an advanced "school for the science of religion."

This was indeed a challenging educational proposition in the context of that day. It was prophetic of directions eventually taken, or at least half-taken, in some of our foremost university-connected seminaries. But the Free Religious Association was not able to respond to it effectively. The same idea, in various guises, continued to bob up from time to time in Ethical Culture planning but without reaching large consequence there either.

The F.R.A.'s dominant bent remained that of a forum for the interchange of independent religious thought, chiefly among some liberal spirits, Brahmins, and scholars of New England, England, and India. Having become greatly occupied with new projects of social and educational reform in New York, Felix Adler decided to withdraw from the F.R.A. by the time of its 1882 meeting, despite pleas tendered through W. J. Potter that he should remain. Reviewing his experience as president of the Association, he wrote Potter the following explanation:

When Mr. Frothingham resigned from the Presidency I understood from him that the Association had of late years declined in vital form, that he himself felt the need of giving a new direction to the society's efforts and that he believed that I might be the means of accomplishing this desirable result. I accepted after some hesitation in the belief that I was to do or attempt to do a definite work . . . .

The impression has deepened on my mind that the purpose indicated by Frothingham and held in view by me from the moment I entered the Association *cannot* be fulfilled, at least by me. The temper of the Association is surely not friendly to a new departure. The Free Platform idea is still the predominant one. That idea is thoroughly good. Fourteen years ago it was new. The Association grew on the juice of that idea. But it has exhausted that juice, and so far as I can judge it is not willing to draw upon a new idea.

These are the reasons that have determined my action. . . . I do not wish my action to appear as a shifting of base or desertion of the cause, when in reality I retire from the Association because I find it slow, even unto deadness in our cause, and because I do not believe that energies should be spent on resuscitation which are all required for the joyous work of new construction.

People who presently read in the papers that Felix Adler had left "the Free Religious ranks" did not need to fear, as did Miss Agnes Watson, who wrote him a long letter from Binghamton, N.Y., to implore him (in the name of George Eliot, Mill, Darwin, Huxley, Tyndall, Spencer, Parker, Channing, and Emerson) not to return to "conservative religion!" Adler had merely given up trying to convert the "Free Religious ranks" to his own more active strain of ethical religion and social reform.

But if he was thus disappointed in his efforts to renovate and redirect the F.R.A., his contacts with New England free thought brought him in touch with individuals who themselves were attracted by Ethical Culture's activism. The Free Religious movement was of importance for S. Burns Weston's awareness of Felix Adler, and it had at least a tangential bearing on W. M. Salter's coming to Ethical Culture.

And as it happened, liberal Unitarianism also played a role in bringing Adler his closest lifelong companion, his wife.

Helen Goldmark was the eldest daughter of Joseph Goldmark and Regina Wehle. Her parents had migrated to this country from Vienna and Prague, respectively, a year after the failure of the 1848 revolution. Joseph was a half-brother of the composer Karl Goldmark. As a young physician at the University of Vienna he had joined with the students in fighting for the revolution and was accused of implication in the lamppost hanging of War Minister Latour. He fled to Switzerland and from there came to the United States. In 1868 he returned briefly to Vienna and was successful in clearing himself of the criminal charges against him.

After settling in Brooklyn, Joseph Goldmark became a manufacturing chemist and inventor. His invention of amorphous phosphorus enabled him to make percussion cartridge caps of superior utility for the Union armies in the American Civil War. The Brooklyn home of the Goldmarks was a large one with a pleasant garden containing fruit trees. Here the Goldmarks brought up seven daughters and three sons. The business prospered sufficiently to support good educations and other cultural advantages for all of them.

Both of Helen (Nellie) Goldmark's parents, in their religious convictions, had become independent of synagogue traditions; indeed, the family had acquired something of an anticlerical bias. Joseph Goldmark had rationalist "scientific" views.

Nellie and a sister, Christine, were in the habit of attending Dr. John M. Chadwick's liberal Unitarian church in Brooklyn. It is possible that they first met Felix Adler there, and they heard him speak there in 1879. Adler being the new president of the Free Religious Association now had special entree to liberal Unitarian circles. It is possible that these two families—the Adlers and the Goldmarks—each distancing itself in its own way and measure from Jewish custom might never have become connected save for the Unitarian mediation! When the Felix Adler and Nellie Goldmark betrothal became known, Dr. Chadwick wrote Adler a congratulatory note. Dated February 1, 1880, it read:

My dear Mr. Adler,
    I write to congratulate you that you have made good the prophesy of your name (Felix), for I am sure that you are very happy. And I am sure that you have good reason to be, for though my acquaintance with Miss Goldmark is of the slightest, intelligence and goodness shine so in her face, she is so unspoiled by what is called "society," has so evidently kept her maiden artlessness, that I feel as if no further acquaintance with her could make me feel more sure of your good fortune. You will do your great work better than ever with a great love for your continual rest and aspiration.

Felix was indeed marrying a rare person and also becoming associated with what proved to be a remarkable family group. Nellie's older brother, Henry Goldmark, became a distinguished engineer and later designed locks for the Panama Canal and other important constructions connected with waterways. A sister, Alice, in 1891 became the wife of Louis Brandeis, living in Boston until his appointment to the United States Supreme Court. Her two youngest sisters, Pauline and Josephine Goldmark, went to Bryn Mawr in the nineties and retained a lifelong active interest in the college. Josephine wrote several social and historical studies, the best known being that on *Fatigue and Efficiency*, which served Brandeis with data for his Oregon brief defending the regulation of working hours for women. Her book *Pilgrims of '48* is an account of the family forbears in Europe, and of their new homes in America.

Nellie Goldmark and Felix Adler were married on May 24, 1880. The *New York Times*, May 25, reported the event as follows:

A very simple ceremony was performed yesterday in Mayor Howell's private office in the City Hall, Brooklyn. The contracting parties were Professor Adler, formerly of Cornell University, and Miss Nellie Goldmark, daughter of Dr. Joseph Goldmark, a well-known resident of Brooklyn. The bridal party arrived at City Hall some minutes before eleven o'clock and were ushered into the Mayor's private office. The bride leaned on the arm of her father. She was dressed in black silk and wore a straw hat with a yellow feather. She is a petite brunette graceful and willowy of figure, and of high accomplishments.

Later in the day a second ceremony took place, conducted by Felix's father, Samuel Adler, in the home of the bride at Second Place, Brooklyn, where a garden party followed in the evening.

Nellie Goldmark was a spirited little person, yet also shy. She had attended the Brooklyn Heights Seminary and also passed entrance examinations for Harvard (which her brother Henry attended), but there was then no "annex" providing for the admission of women. Her feelings could be strongly partisan, both for and against. Her native spontaneity took the direction of loving attachments and much self-effacing devotion. After her marriage she eagerly identified herself with Felix's humanitarian ardor and ethical outlook, disciplining herself to share his work as well as his household. But within her shyness and her careful breeding, there lurked a delightful gypsy touch. Eventually, in late years especially, the charm and freedom of her being found an outlet in flower sketches and in pottery and textile designs that were beautifully living and never tight or thin. There was a genuine artistic impulse, but no perfectionist demand, in Nellie Adler.

The young couple's first residence was in the Sherwood Studios at 57th Street and Sixth Avenue in New York. Here they enjoyed the close company of artist friends, particularly the Douglas Volk and George de Forest Brush families. The building was constructed to provide for elements of cooperative living by a group of families. Besides spacious living rooms and studios, there was a large common kitchen from which meals could be furnished without duplicating family labors. Felix found esthetic satisfaction in these arrangements, which also seemed to fit in with views he then held on "cooperation" in labor and economy. Alas, living in the Sherwood Studios turned out to be rather expensive, and early in 1882 the Adlers moved to an apartment at 63d and Park Avenue, which then was not the high-cost area it later became. Here their first child, Waldo (named in homage to Emerson), was born on January 9, 1882.

[8]

APPRENTICING WITH ADLER—
FOUR PROFESSIONAL COLLEAGUES:
1880s

D URING THE 1880s Adler's views found a widening audience. His addresses on social reform and ethical culture were not confined to New York City. In the spring of 1882 he gave six lectures in Chicago. Their purpose was to encourage the formation of an Ethical Culture Society in that city and on October 9, 1882, the Chicago Ethical Society was formally initiated.

In the course of these years local action also led to the establishment of Ethical Societies in Philadelphia (1885) and St. Louis (1886). Each of the locations presented distinct problems, but the strong influence of New York and its leader directed all the societies into a pattern of Ethical Culture existence that was largely the same. Moreover, Adler had been working in New York with applicants who presented themselves for a possible career of professionally leading Ethical Culture Societies and these men went on to serve the newly formed societies in other cities.

Adler welcomed a variety of backgrounds and experience in these applicants but demanded two things of them. First he wanted to have the opportunity to know them personally through working together with them. Second he demanded that they undertake advanced studies free of enshrined dogmas. Those who proved broadly qualified to become his first colleagues as leaders of societies were William Mackintire Salter (1853–1931), S. Burns Weston (1855–1936), Walter L. Sheldon (1858–1907), and Stanton Coit (1857–1944). All were of Adler's own generation, and each of them sought him out rather more than they were sought out by him. All these contacts occurred during or close to the time of his presidency of the Free Religious Association. Two of them,

81

Salter and Weston, were divinity school graduates and had preached in churches before meeting Adler; Sheldon and Coit had done neither of these things. But all four, in one way or other, thought to find moral freedom and intellectual integrity in a career such as Adler's, which they had not found in the pursuit of previous theological or academic studies and customs.

It is significant that Adler wished all four to have further post-graduate study abroad. He did not, it should be stressed, insist on uniform paths of study, except that religious history and philosophy were to be included. But not having prevailed in his early proposal for a "seminary to deepen the education of liberals," he usually recommended Berlin University, where he had himself profitably studied, and sometimes also Leipzig, where he had wanted to study with Wundt and others.

Another feature common to all four apprenticeships was working in close association with Adler for several years in New York. With this there was sometimes combined part-time study at Columbia University, especially in the new graduate departments of political and economic science that Professor John W. Burgess was inaugurating. But the principal point for these men was to acquire personal knowledge of Adler and to evolve their response to his then-prevailing interests. The roles these men developed in Ethical Culture lasted over many years; here only their initial relations and their apprenticing with Adler are discussed.

William Mackintire Salter was only two years younger than Adler himself; and his whole life was marked by strong intellectual conscience and self-direction. Much of his way toward Ethical Culture was made through an independent progression before he knew of Adler. Indeed, Salter seems to have been freer and more independent and at times appears to have enjoyed a more equal companionship with Adler than the latter's other colleagues.

From a devout Congregational home in Iowa, Salter first went to Knox College in Illinois. Here one of his most admired teachers was John W. Burgess, whom he later met again when the latter was playing a prominent role in Columbia University's graduate faculty. In 1871 Salter enrolled in the conservative Yale Divinity School to study for the ministry. He was encouraged in his choice of career by reading Channing and Emerson but at cost to his Christian orthodoxy, and in 1873 he moved from Yale to the Harvard Divinity School with its Unitarian connections. During 1874–75 he also served a Unitarian pulpit in Wayland, Massachusetts, while pursuing his studies at Harvard.

Following graduation from the Harvard Divinity School in 1876, Salter proceeded to Göttingen. He remained there from Michaelmas 1876 to Easter 1877 hearing lectures by Lotze as well as by some Comtean positivists. The strain he placed upon himself in all these studies affected his health, and he decided upon a needed respite in Colorado. In a radical change of activity he worked for two years as a sheep herder.

It was upon his return to Boston from this sojourn that Salter first met Felix Adler, probably late in 1879. During the next two years he resumed his Unitarian ministry in Wayland, but also gave one or more talks under New York Ethical Culture auspices. During this same period Salter developed a friendship with S. Burns Weston, who was also having difficulties with Christian Unitarianism in his post in Leicester, Massachusetts, and was himself seeking career advice from Dr. Adler.

William James remarked some years later that a talk of Salter's on "the practical meaning of religion" (1881–82) impressed him as just "rather dreary conscientiousness." A long letter to Felix Adler dated June 5, 1880, however, lays out many points Salter was then trying to be conscientious about. It was written after hearing an address in which Adler presented many innovative suggestions to his Free Religious audience in Boston: the possibility of a community of families living together; more cooperative industry to be forwarded with State aid; income taxes; church taxation and church schools; and the relations of Ethical Culture to Christianity and to Free Religion.

Assuring Adler that he agrees "in the general policy that society needs a moral awakening and renewal," Salter adds "we must go into details and agree on some practical definite platform." He then proceeds with questions and reservations about each of Adler's proposals, asking the following questions:

[On family life, he says]: Has not all Jewish and Christian morality been very closely connected with the idea of the family . . . . and tho many families might well live in community and have some common interests, this should not be inconsistent with the privacy and soundness of the old-fashioned family life.

As to the State, I am shy of all theories of government intervention. . . . Cooperation by men's voluntary association I believe in, tho I realize we have got to have a generation or two of education for the working-classes, before they can get the wisdom and self-control and forbearance sufficient to enable them to be successful. . . . But governmental socialism is quite another matter.

A graduated income tax I believe on general principles to be just, though . . . if 50 or 100% were taxed, there would be few if any who would try to have incomes of large wealth. Would you say such are not desirable?

(On population control): As I have been reading Mill, I have felt strongly that the moral law ought to be uttered in its relation to self-control in the begetting of children and the increase of the population. . . . Excessive population is half the cause of poverty and misery.

Religions in the sense of dogmatic instruction should be kept out of the schools; . . . but moral instruction there should be, or shall we leave it to the Sunday Schools and the Ethical Schools we propose to have?

If the churches really exist for moral ends and to some extent fulfill them, I think they should no more be taxed than educational or charitable institutions. . . . But I wish the wealthy clubs that go by the name of churches in our large cities, might be taxed up to their full value; but this cannot be said of the Catholic churches that are supported by the poor and are used by them—that make in fact almost the only quiet retiring place for any man, Protestant or what not.

I cannot agree with you in your desire to have people give up the Christian name on the grounds of disbelief in many Christian doctrines. . . . I regretted the time you gave to the name discussion. I shall never take an attitude of hostility to Christianity, the new faith will be in advance of Christianity, but it will not be in contradiction to it. I don't mean by this that I should take the Christian name, if I went out to work; I would not anymore be Unitarian. I should call my Society an Ethical one. . . . No more should I identify myself with Free Religion. . . . I am thankful that you have been brought to the attention of Boston in this way . . . but I have an interest in your movement just because it is not a negative thing, as Free Religion for the most part is, but means a positive moral advance. . . . You may turn Free Religion into Ethical Religion, I hope you will. . . . none the less in idea they do seem to me to be distinct.

Salter's letter is quoted rather fully here to illustrate his careful deliberation and independent questioning without regard to source of authority. At the time of this letter, in 1880, he was in his twenty-eighth year and felt himself ready to apply for Ethical Culture leadership. He explained that he was willing "to go where there is most need, most work to be done," yet suggested that "there are places nearer you than Minneapolis, which should be first attacked. I want to know you more and understand you better." Adler agreed to keep him near New York for a while, but by April 1882 took him along to Chicago, to see if a group interested in forming a Society there would accept him as a leader. It did, and Salter departed for that city.

S. Burns Weston, four years younger than Adler, had, like Salter, graduated from the Harvard Divinity School, where the aura of Emerson affected him strongly. Born the son of a Maine farmer and reared amid "the mildest type of New England Puritanism," he was sent to the Preparatory School of Antioch College in Ohio, from which he received his A.B. in 1876. After entering Harvard Divinity School he discovered the thought of the Free Religion movement and also learned from journals of Felix Adler's work in New York.

In 1879 Weston took a Unitarian pulpit in Leicester, Massachusetts, but without formal ordination, for the particular church was endowed by a will to preach "Unitarian Christianity," while Weston, in the manner of free religion, considered his Unitarianism to be more broadly religious than specifically Christian. Despite this latitude, his congregation voted on June 10, 1881, "not to accept the resignation I have offered." But the Council of the National Unitarian Conference decided that the terms of the will required its acceptance.

Coming to New York, Weston next sought out Felix Adler, who advised him, first, to undertake further study in a German university. He went to Berlin and to Leipzig (as Adler himself had wished to do), but his philosophic and social studies were without commitment to Judaic learning. Weston did not take a doctorate, either abroad or at Columbia University, but back in New York by 1883 he continued some part-time study in the Columbia Graduate Faculty of Political Science under Professor John W. Burgess. At the same time he served an apprenticeship with Adler for two years in Ethical Culture activities.

Weston's bent was one of practical usefulness to his fellow men, coupled with an open quest in matters of religious feeling and ideas. He did not have Salter's turn for theory, and he became probably the least doctrinaire of Ethical Culture's founding leaders. In ensuing years Adler relied much upon Weston for steady practical judgment and managerial energy in many matters including publication.

In 1885 Weston was given charge of the Philadelphia Ethical Culture Society and five years later he assumed the editorship of the *International Journal of Ethics* as well. As Adler would write him many years later: "You, more than anyone else, have been in touch with every phase of the Society's growth."*

Walter L. Sheldon was discovered by Weston in 1881 as a fellow American student in the University of Berlin. He proved to be an interested listener to what he heard about Ethical Culture. Born in Brooklyn, Sheldon had been raised by his mother in Vermont after his father died in a drowning accident during the boy's seventh year. Reared in a devout Congregational faith, he went first to Middlebury College and then to Princeton, from which he graduated in 1880. But "by the time of my graduation being far outside the pale of its theology," instead of continuing to the seminary he embarked on a period of travel in the Middle East, visiting both Egypt and Palestine.

It was from there that Sheldon decided to proceed to Berlin for study, with a possible academic career in view. The acquaintance with Weston developed into a close and lasting friendship (Sheldon later became his brother-in-law), and Weston wrote to Felix Adler that he had discovered another potential candidate for Ethical Culture leadership.

Meanwhile Sheldon spent another year, 1882–83, in Leipzig, studying psychology and philosophy with Wilhelm Wundt and others. Adler was at this time interested in finding a man whom he could entrust to lead an Ethical Culture group that was forming in St. Louis. In July of that year he wrote Weston, urging him

---

*From a letter dated October 7, 1910, asking Weston to "take an important part" in the dedication of the New York Society's meeting house at 2 West 64th Street, by pronouncing "the word of fellowship and felicitation on behalf of what may be called the historic past of the Ethical Movement."

to return to New York *now*, and about Sheldon he added "it all depends upon the man."

Both Weston and Sheldon came, and during the next two years they worked under Adler's direction in New York, at the same time pursuing some studies at Columbia in philosophy and in political science. But Sheldon suffered much intellectual agony over theoretical questions of mind–body relations; the problem of free will had been troubling him from college years on. He had to trace a long path, step by step, to reach (c.1884–85) a view of the self as a directing moral agent.

Sheldon believed that the physical aspect of man's constitution was insufficiently emphasized by Adler and at one point he looked toward medicine rather than a career of ethical teaching. In the winter term of 1885 he even returned to Berlin University to enter the Faculty of Medicine, and heard lectures by Helmholtz and others. Adler was then inclined to give him up. In a long letter to Weston, dated September 3, 1885, he commented on Sheldon's situation and went on to make what was, in effect, a policy statement:

I too see Sheldon depart with regret. I cannot conceive that medicine should be his proper sphere.

Sheldon despairs of an assured intellectual basis for his moral convictions. I on the other hand should despair of the movement without such a basis! You tell me that Sheldon "believes and would teach the freedom of the will, but when it comes to a philosophical explanation of it he finds contradictions which he cannot reconcile." With what confidence then can a belief be promulgated of which the teacher is aware that he cannot state it without self-contradiction?

I must work until I can get a satisfactory *reason* for the faith that is in me. But Sheldon refuses to do this, and what is more asks that his state of intellectual indecision be erected into a precedent and a rule in our movement. To this demand I can only return an inflexible negative. I need not repeat that in requiring reasons for his faith it is not implied that he should give *our reasons*, only strong reasons, reasons that will make him feel that he has a *right* to teach what he does teach, and that will guarantee the permanence of his moral convictions.

A mere common purpose, such as the aim of elevating humanity is not enough as a bond of mind between Ethical Teachers. The history of the present century is full of warning examples to show us what the mere enthusiasm of humanity may lead to. Enfantin & his fellows in France, the early leaders of the "Young Germany," the author of "Conventional Lies" among our contemporaries, are sufficient instances. Many of these men were filled with the most genuine desire to "elevate humanity." Progress & Humanity were their very Religion. But in the name of progress & Humanity, the abolition of marriage and the like were their practical proposals. Without the firm leadings of Principles our Movement which began on the mountain top will be likely to end in the mire!

The view stated in this letter remained Adler's permanent belief: ethical light requires intellectual integrity, but a variety of intellectual conclusions can be, not only compatible with, but even favorable to ethical forwarding of purpose.

By the spring of 1886 Sheldon returned to New York and to serve in the Ethical movement. Indeed, in May of that year Adler introduced him to a group forming in St. Louis as a possible choice for leadership there. And later that month he sat on the platform with colleagues celebrating the tenth anniversary of Ethical Culture at the New York Society. Yet still in 1890 Adler had occasion to write Salter, "Sheldon is a walking volcano and must be permitted from time to time to emit fire and smoke."

Stanton Coit, who was born in Ohio into an Episcopalian family, already "counted himself a disciple of Emerson" at the age of fifteen. While at Amherst College in 1881 he was telling a friend of his enthusiasm for Emerson's idea of "a cultus of pure ethics," when the friend said: "You ought to hear Felix Adler, the radical! *He* is *doing* the very thing of which *you* are *dreaming!* Soon after, Coit went to New York to hear Adler, and then "all uninvited" called on the latter to say that he had decided "to be an Ethical Lecturer."

Coit explained it was ethics and its concrete applications that attracted him. "Preaching is not our chief means of furthering the spread of goodness; . . . rather to help change the physical and social environment of men, so that it shall be more favorable to a truly human life." Adler advised this impetuous student to do further academic work first, and in the next two years Coit did so. He continued giving some instruction in English for a while at Amherst. Then, he too went off to Berlin in 1883.

From the lectures he heard there a lasting and independent

interest in philosophy developed, and in 1885 he earned a Ph.D. with a dissertation on "the inner sanction of moral judgment." One of the points he argued was that "Kant's assertion that ethics requires a transcendent ground is unjustified."

Leaving Berlin in 1886, Coit spent three months in London. There he was vitally impressed by what he saw of social work in a city environment at Toynbee Hall, a university settlement founded in 1885 in memory of economic historian and social reformer Arnold Toynbee. When Coit returned to New York to work with Adler he founded the Neighborhood Guild (later renamed the University Settlement), the first American center of its kind.

In 1887, however, Coit returned to England to officiate at London's South Place Chapel, which had been long served by another American, Moncure Conway. Coit insisted that the chapel, which had its own strong liberal traditions, be renamed the South Place Ethical Society, a condition accepted only by a narrow vote. Five years later, in 1892, Coit took a unique course and left South Place to establish a West End Ethical Society which he named "The Ethical Church."

Here at last, as will eventually appear, he developed his own version of a "cultus of pure ethics," drawing heavily upon Anglican forms and national feeling sans theology! The Episcopalian and Emersonian passions of his youth made a peculiar match here, little congenial to Adler or to most of his colleagues. Yet as a strongly self-motivating man in many ways Coit fully earned his unique place among the founding leaders of Ethical Culture. Whether from Adler or from Toynbee Hall or from both, he developed his own genuine social idealism. And in his personal style he did so with a generous worldly grace. Following his example and tutelage a number of young Englishmen became themselves leaders in the Ethical movement, and some of them were invited by Adler to serve American Societies.

The advice given to Weston, Sheldon, and Coit about their studies throws strong light upon the high intellectual standards that Adler attached to Ethical Culture leadership. He wanted his colleagues well-disciplined in philosophy and well-grounded in the development of sociopolitical institutions. He did not demand

Ph.D. degrees, but he required work under first-rate teachers in philosophy and social science faculties. Not having available that ideal center of learning of which he dreamed "for the training of leaders," he generally steered his candidates to Berlin University for philosophy and for American social studies to the new Graduate Faculty of Political Science at Columbia University in New York. Though the lack of a specific independent seminary made for uneven levels of preparation, it favored a desirable variety in the education of Ethical Culture's leaders.

But intellectual strength in itself was not the top aim of preparation for working with Felix Adler. The prime aim was spiritual self-development and active concern for moral progress in socially organized as well as personal life. This Adler hoped to further by having his candidates participate with him in various efforts of education and social reform, and at the same time in an intimate circle devoted to self-culture. The motives of religious and of social progress were for him inseparably fused in this program.

When Adler had accepted young Coit as a candidate, Salter wondered whether "religious" motivation and elements of ministerial training (such as he and Weston had) were not to be required in preparing for Ethical Cultural leadership. Adler appeared to accept Coit without such insistence. In the end it turned out, whether predictably or not, that both Sheldon and Coit—the two men accepted without seminary training—were the ones who eventually gave the more churchlike patterns to the Ethical Societies they led. Under Coit The Ethical Church in London developed an entirely unique ceremonial style of "worship," and under Sheldon the St. Louis Society achieved a strong congregational identity still unmatched in the Ethical Culture movement. Salter and Weston, and indeed Adler himself, having each prepared for specific ministerial careers from which they withdrew, pursued their Ethical Culture leadership through more flexible, multirole activity.

An address at the close of Ethical Culture's seventh season, on May 13, 1883, throws some light on Adler's position during this time of expanding activity.

If religious progress is impossible without dropping the thought of social progress, then I for one am content rather to drop the idea of religious emancipation, for there is neither religion to me, nor emancipation, in the cold teachings of a prudent egotism. The gospel of the religion of the future well understood must be a gospel for the poor. . . . must be a sunrise over the hills, shedding light into the dark places and penetrating into the deepest valleys of human society.

Yet after making this strong pledge to social progress, he went on to devote this same address to such familiar religious questions as: What can bring us peace amid bereavement? And how are the tortures of conscience over personal wrongdoing to be dealt with?

The charge that a purely ethical faith in "the Ideal" is fairweather religion, and lacks power to restore "the sinner," went deep and pressed Adler to profess the following reach of faith.

It has been said that the sermon of the moral ideal may be apt and sufficient for those who are morally sound . . . but what hope can it offer to the morally unsound? We must face the facts as they are; . . . we must probe into our inward being, we must penetrate into the depths of our soul, and though we may at first shrink back, when we see so much gross and base metal, still deeper and deeper we must delve, and we shall come at last upon the gold at the bottom of the mine.

Down underneath, in the very depths of our humanity, flows the crystal fountain, ever clear; for this is the great truth by which we abide and upon which we will build—that at the core human nature is sound, that in the most sinful of sinners at the bottom of his soul there is gold, in the veriest depths there flows the spring of purity.

The image of a "crystal fountain flowing in the very depths of our humanity" is beautifully refreshing, but at the same time highly metaphorical. In 1883 Adler was not yet ready to give his faith in "the sound core of human nature" the kind of definite and distinctive expression to which he eventually came. It took years more—mostly from the 1890s on—for him to arrive at it. In the 1880s, and for some time after, his avowals of religious faith remained general and were often expressed in wording much derived from the current "genteel tradition" of idealistic philosophy. We have a "cosmic anchorage" for our efforts, he told his hearers, with an intention to assure them that "all is well in the great universe" (1882). Yet he himself discerned a weakness in such expressions and felt that he must press on to describe the meaning of his faith more compellingly and distinctly. At the tenth anniversary of Ethical Culture, in 1886, he openly declared, "I have never delivered my message, never yet been able to speak fully."

It was in intimate meetings with small groups of his associates that Adler was likely to contribute most to the self-development of his fellow-workers, as of himself. In the early 1880s he still used the name "Union for the Higher Life" for such a circle, and repeated the pledge of its members to sex purity, to intellectual development, and to putting aside funds in aid of working people. Under various names ("Circle," "Fellowship," "Seminar") the pattern of meeting regularly with small, selected groups continued throughout Adler's life as a chosen method of close communication. The initial pledges remained as tacit implications rather than being continued as explicit declarations.

During his last year with Adler in New York, 1881, William Salter acted as secretary for the Union for the Higher Life. Rather sketchy notes of his exist on meetings between December 26, 1881, and February 27, 1883. They show concentration on various aspects of "the social question," with use of F. A. Lange's book *Die Arbeiterfrage* and Henry George's *Progress and Poverty* as background reading. In the absence of government income taxes, the merits of self-taxation were proposed. And the members did tax themselves to provide a fund for maintaining a home, called the Schaefer Home, for a small group of orphaned children. Some meetings were concerned with this venture, others with problems of family life and of cooperative living by families, still others with the menace to family welfare in the tenements, of vice and prostitution, and other corruptions in a great city.

In April 1882, the question of women members was raised and discussions lasted the better part of a year before it was decided to continue the group "in its present form for two more years." The absence of women members may well have lasted longer. In 1903, however, Mrs. Anna Garlin Spencer was appointed as an associate leader in Ethical Culture. Adler himself, it appears, had to battle for this step.

In his autobiography, *All in a Lifetime,* Henry Morgenthau admits that among his Ethical Culture connections he "treasured above all the fond remembrance of having been a member of the Union for the Higher Life—an organization of a few of Adler's devotees." It was the growing and deepening reach of his mind and spirit that counted most in the influence Adler could impart in these close circles of associates.

For Adler and for most (if not all) people receptive to him there was relief and moral increase in their shedding observances and doctrines which they judged to be no longer part of the realities they had to face. But this was not followed by a sight of utopia around the corner. On the contrary, expectations were soon invaded by a new realism; experience brought a fresh sense of obdurate human weaknesses and limits that had to be dealt with, it was to be hoped, in ways more effective than formal hand-wringings. Instead of withdrawing from his reforming efforts, Adler increased them manifold in the 1880s, but at the same time his more idyllic youthful perspectives were giving way to a maturer and more comprehending sense of duties and severe tasks.

[9]

CONSCIENCE IN THE CITY:
1880s AND 1890s

THE 1880s HAVE BEEN called "the ardent eighties," and not without reason. Especially in the expanding cities, growth and activity were at a high pitch. It was a decade of the largest immigration into New York City, and that alone was enough to cause a stirring. As people became aware of the grave problems of the cities, they were moved into dealing with them from many angles. There was the housing problem with tenement residence growing greater (due to newcomers) during the very stages of manifold attack upon it. By 1890 New York's 35,000 tenements contained more than two-thirds of the city's total population of approximately 2.5 million.

Extreme poverty drove many children into work instead of school. Moreover, the public schools themselves were now attacked from many angles. Universities found them giving poor preparation for scholarship, and churches were little satisfied with what they did for work and religion. But Felix Adler's criticism was different and broader. He complained of their deficiency for the common advance of humanity in the growing industrial society. They were not educating the working people for an understanding of their problems and the making of constructive changes. In New York the success of Tammany Hall's political candidates generally prevailed. The reformers proved to be minorities in origin and in voting. This and many social ills were condoned by the exploitative and one-sided government.

Felix Adler was in his thirties in this decade and although his views on social reform had not yet reached their full development he threw himself into the thick of various reform efforts to bring about needed changes in city life.

It is impossible in this limited space to follow all the manifesta-

94

tions of his activity in the 1880s. But this chapter will in turn deal with three aspects of Adler's main efforts in respect to schooling, to housing, and to city government. These are so vital and formative in his whole career as to demand attention here.

The Workingman's School

In 1878 Adler and his friend, Alfred Wolff, capably organized a tuition-free kindergarten, the first of its kind in the eastern United States. They personally distributed handbills in the Gas House district to gather children. Neither of them was minded to be an educator, but they wanted to get the children of workers off the streets, and to have them taste some of the thoughtful care a young child needs. Adler had already shown his interest in a lyceum for workers. Moreover, his failure to keep a cooperative printing shop together had made him feel all the more keenly the need to educate workers for cooperation.

But what followed beyond the kindergarten in 1880–90— namely a new eight-grade, tuition-free elementary school—was not limited to any social class, but aimed to build an elementary education suited to everybody in our growing industrial culture. Even though it was called the Workingman's School, what Adler built had a universal intention. Neither public schools nor the prevailing private schools had this kind of comprehensive, timely aim. The public schools kept their programs in abstract clerical subjects, while the private schools catered to various special elites. Adler's Workingman's School built instead a model elementary schooling of lifelike character for all members in the developing industrial society. It did this by having the school program deal in germ with the nature of the child's actual experience. The contrast in roots, old and new, was of course not absolute, but it was very profound.*

On October 24, 1880, in an address to the Ethical Culture Society on the Workingman's School, Adler discussed the reason for founding such a school and the course it must pursue. Beginning with the assumption that only education could extirpate poverty at the root and alleviate the misery of the poor, he went on to

*Editor's insert for following four paragraphs. F.W.

quote the conclusions of various experts on the inadequacy of the existing school system. Among these was the characterization of such schools as a "combination of the cotton mill and the railroad with the model State's prison. . . . From one point of view children are regarded as automatons; from another as india-rubber bags; from a third as so much raw material."

What was to be done? "Agitation alone will not bring about the desired result, because a system of teaching so widely ramified, and upon which the employment of thousands of persons depends, cannot be assailed without exciting violent hostility; nor can it be changed in a month or a year."

The solution was for a number of persons "because the improvement of their fellow-men by education has their whole interest" to guarantee the means "necessary for the building up of a *Model School*, in which the right methods shall be demonstrated, and if they will have a care that only the most competent teachers are employed in connection with it."

A salient feature of the program of instruction which Adler advocated was the inclusion of industrial education, which would give students an understanding of what they were doing rather than simply teach them manual skills. The point would be that unlike other such programs, this would be introduced in the lower grades and "would be combined organically with the whole scheme of education . . . to support and coalesce with all the other studies." In this context industrial education

becomes a means of teaching mathematics, for instance, more thoroughly, causing the pupils to work out mathematical truths with their hands. . . . It becomes the means of making the hand a wise and cunning hand by putting more brain into it. But . . . it also makes the brain a clear and vigorous and enlightened brain, by giving it the salutary corrective of the demonstrations of the hand.

Adler's program meant departures in other aspects of education too. It meant attention for the physical side of life, for health through examinations and through activity indoors and out. It meant recreation together. It meant a diversified program of arts and crafts—"the gate of labor" (learning by doing) as well as "the gate of study"—bringing plants, animals, and art objects into the classrooms, workshops, and art rooms. It favored more student organization and relation to community needs. It included the germs of "science"—through care for observation and for the rational connection of thoughts. In literature it meant reading originals instead of excerpts from standard readers. Classics continued to be studied but with teachers having zest of personality as well as technical mastery of their subjects. There was also the beginning of a second modern language (at first German in the third grade, later French) in this elementary schooling. Music, moreover, thrived in a wealth of fine school singing. And festivals gave dramatic collective expression of the school's thousand interests.

These features did not appear all at once. They evolved piece by piece in the course of ten years. In fact, the Workingman's School grew, as it were, two years at a time, as the kindergarten graduates moved up. Thus at the start in 1880 there were, in addition to the kindergarten, 51 pupils for the first two grades; in 1883 there were 144 for the first four grades; and 217 for the six grades the next year.

Adler himself took special care to find teachers who understood his viewpoint and had innovating capacity. In respect to science the first principal, Gabriel Bamberger, a German, "was strong in mathematics, and the exercises which he planned had a slant toward demonstrating mathematical concepts and relations. W. H. Bristol, from the Stevens Institute of Technology, introduced a further mechanical emphasis in the exercises devised in drawing, word instruction, and elementary physics."

But when Henry A. Kelly came in 1889 to head work in natural science a further correlating of physical and biological studies became notable. During long years of service Dr. Kelly was a leading teacher in forwarding the school's excellence. In his work, ability in science was joined with regard for its vital human bearings.

As was necessarily the case in the kindergarten, so serious contact with parents continued in the Workingman's School. Regular parent meetings became a feature about 1883, as the principal then reported:

On the first Wednesday in each month the fathers and mothers of our pupils, often bringing their children with them, come in the evening to the school hall as to a festival. Sometimes the children sing; sometimes our method in a certain line of hand or mind instruction is illustrated, and the results exhibited in the children's work. These meetings have an appreciably good effect on school discipline. They afford opportunity for the closer study of pupils, for hints as to diet, clothing and cleanliness, and for the presentation in familiar language of rational educational methods.

Adler was advised by a council of interested people who aided him in supplementing the teaching staff. Such men as Douglas Volk, George de Forest Brush, Walter Shirlaw, and Walter and Frank Damrosch gave help in arts; and in medicine Dr. R. C. Wiener and Adler's own brother Isaac, who was on the school executive committee in the early years, gave their time. An excellent description of the Workingman's School can be found in print as an "Educational Exhibit of the State of New York, Hand-book 17" (1894). It may have been prepared for the World's Fair at Chicago in the preceding year, where Adler gave an address on American Education.

At the end of the 1880s the repute of the school was such that President Hunt of the New York City Board of Education said "If I could have my way, every public school in this city would be conducted in accordance with the system of instruction adopted in this School." There was also popular acclaim, as in the *Herald Tribune* of December 27, 1891:

Eureka! I have found it at last! A school where children actually like to go. A school which goes on excursions to park and dell, to those wonderlands of childhood, the big factories, the steamboats and locomotives, in order that the little ones may learn about the big wheels which make this big world move. A school which deals with living things.

The school instead of drilling in certain needed skills gave its pupils a rather full experience of youthful life in a growing modern city. In subsequent years, this approach became so widespread as to become almost a universal practice. Indeed one can regard the new model of elementary education in the Workingman's School as the greatest single institutional success of Adler's life. In content and practice it became an epitome of actual child life and not an artificially imposed scheme.

Yet success can also raise problems. In this case by 1890 the school was threatened by its costs, which in ten years had reached a point of crisis. At this time, those people who could afford to pay tuition proposed having their children admitted to the hitherto tuition-free school. They wanted both to benefit from its excellence and to keep it going. Much controversy ensued, and some members of the governing board, such as Alfred Wolff, were among opponents of the change. But in 1890, after long debates, it was voted to admit twenty tuition payers, provided that in future at least half of the places in the school would remain tuition-free. Though it proved impossible to maintain this ratio, scholarship funds continued to cover near twenty percent of the student charges for tuition in Ethical Culture schools.

Besides bowing to financial need in this decision, Adler justified the admission of tuition-payers on the ground that in democracies elementary schools should be representative of the whole society and not draw their pupils from a single economic level. He mentioned George H. Curtiss as calling attention to the fact that philanthropy for the children of working people might produce an undemocratic, class school. Whatever the force of such argument it is a widely held and a forceful view that in the course of time the admission of the tuition-payers radically changed much of the character of the Ethical Culture School.

But it was not only this decision of 1890 that brought change. A second decision, taken in 1895, added a high school and at the same time the name Workingman's School was replaced by the name Ethical Culture Schools. In the selection of students and in the development of curricula, the goals of high school and college thereafter played a more determining role. Had the school remained only an experimental, elementary school it might well have been easier to keep in it the comprehensive scope of cultural diversity for which Adler had argued originally.

In his address of October 24, 1880, Adler had explained the choice of name for the Workingman's School as follows:

And here it becomes apparent why our School is not an industrial school in the sense which commonly attaches to that name. . . . We do not propose to give our pupils an aptitude for any particular trade; we do not propose to make them tailors, or shoemakers, or printers. We would consider that a retrograde step rather than a step in advance, if we were to prevent these young lads and little girls from spending even a few years in gaining knowledge, without any reference to the pitiable necessities of their after-lives; we do not propose to yoke their young souls before they have had time to expand at all into the harness of trade, merely for the sake of getting their bread better afterward. We propose to give them that which will secure them bread thereafter, and many of the higher treasures of human existence, we hope, besides; we propose to give them a broad and generous education, such as the children of the richest might be glad in some respect to share with them which will prepare them for their future station in life, but also make them capable of living in a truly human way.*

This statement had proved prophetic in numerous ways.

City Housing—the Tenement House Commission

Concern with city housing in New York during the latter decades of the nineteenth century came to be widely directed toward tenement house reform. Nevertheless the number of tenements and their residents continued to grow during the 1880s, due in large part to massive immigration. Many continued living in over-crowded quarters because they could not afford better housing.

The New York State legislature led the way in passing the first tenement house law in this country in 1867. It concerned "the use of cellar rooms as dwellings." During the next ten years, and coming to a head in 1878–79, there were further important measures projected in New York, although strength in design and in enforcement often failed. Nevertheless, a tenement house law of 1879 gave the Board of Health absolute control over all the plumbing and draining in tenement houses. In 1881 such control was extended to all buildings.

The magnitude and variety of tenement house problems was tremendous. Virtually all agencies of reform now found in them targets for persisting criticism and increasing attack. The city government appears to have been significantly two-faced in its attitude toward the tenements; and many people preferred living in familiar though squalid conditions rather than to be turned loose into uncertain new conditions.

Felix Adler had first been touched by the conditions of tenement living as a child, when he accompanied his mother on char-

*Editor's insert.

itable visits to the poor. As a young adult, in February 1884, he fired off a blast of speeches attacking the tenements. While his aim was to do away with them, he was realistic enough to know that change would have to be piecemeal and gradual.

A scare over epidemics in 1883 had aroused public interest in the relationship between crowded tenement conditions and an increase in cases of contagious diseases such as scarlet fever, diphtheria, smallpox, meningitis, and pneumonia. Thus when Adler addressed himself to this question, the capacity of the hall was overtaxed by interested listeners.

Health was not Adler's only concern, however; he also attacked the exorbitant rentals widely demanded by landlords for tenement house dwellings. Although he did not believe in public provision of free housing, because that carried the danger of encouraging pauperization, he believed that there was another remedy.

"The evil that can be changed," he said, "is that the culture of greed should plunge its claws into the vitals of the poor and demand 10, 15 and 20 percent income on their investment. Let 3 percent be the reasonable income, and stigmatize everything above that as usury." Adler presently amended himself by recognizing that efficient management of dwellings might well result in "a six percent" gain. Yet he continued to urge that such additional percent should support improved aid for tenants rather than be taken as profits.

Gouging rentals and menaces to health headed the attacks in Adler's addresses on tenements. New York State responded to rising feeling by setting up the Tenement House Commission, of which Felix Adler was a member. But what was done under this commission, till near the end of the century, displayed a still hesitant and mild pace of change.

Adler's stature, however, as a leader in city affairs, rose as a result of his work for the commission. His speeches drew able workers to the cause, and he enjoyed an active, cooperative relation with some of them. Such was the case, for instance, with Jacob Riis, who became outstanding as a humanitarian pleader among tenement house reformers. His books, *How the Other Half Lives,* published in 1890, and *The Children of the Poor,* published in 1893, brought him to the fore in this cause. And at the same time,

Riis, observing the work of the Tenement House Commission, wrote about Adler:

One man the landlords . . . never caught off his guard. His clear incisive questions, that went through all subterfuges to the root of things, were sometimes like flashes of lightning on a dark night discovering the landscape far and near. He was Dr. Felix Adler, whom I met there for the first time.*

Riis shared Adler's view that in the main the characters and potentials of the depressed tenants were far better than the housing available to them.

Adler and his associates did not confine themselves to talking about housing. His moving lectures of 1884 promptly showed results. In 1885, the Tenement House Building Company was organized with Professor E. R. A. Seligman of Columbia College and of the New York Ethical Culture Society as a director. Its aim was to build "model tenements" requiring "rent of eight to fourteen dollars per month" and yielding "dividends not exceeding four percent." Moses Rischin notes that, "By 1887 the Tenement House Building Company had erected on Cherry Street six model buildings costing $155,000, and housing Russian Jews engaged in the making of shirts, ties, and cigars."†

Adler had at heart not only the physical facilities of "model tenements," but the forwarding in them of home life and its blessings. This inclusive aim, however, had its faults as well as its merits. It upheld a human ideal, but it was relatively expensive and at best it could reach only small groups instead of the masses. These faults were noted by many reformers who preferred another way of procuring tenement reform than by building "models."

Among such reformers was Lawrence Veiller, who by the turn of the century had become an outstanding leader of improvement. He took only minor interest in chances to build models. Instead he believed it far more useful to accumulate legislation restricting piece by piece the building of housing with plainly evident and harmful defects. He claimed that "until reformers could

---

* Jacob Riis, *The Battle with The Slum* (New York and London: Macmillan, 1902), pp. 246–47.

† Moses Rischin, *The Promised City* (Cambridge: Harvard University Press, 1962), p. 202.

incorporate the standards of the model tenement in [such] restrictive legislation, housing conditions would not improve for the majority of workers." And indeed statistics could be drawn which held that during forty years the financing of model tenements had benefited "some 18,000 people in 3,500 families, while housing legislation had debarred many serious defects from the dwellings of over a million people in some 253,000 families."

It seems that nearly every kind of social organization, volunteer and governmental, busied itself with city housing on various levels during this period. Active among these was the Charity Organization Society (COS), founded in 1882 by Robert W. DeForest and Josephine Shaw Lowell. Although it did not formally name its Tenement House Committee until 1898, this organization played a leading part in spreading a disposition for progressive change.

To widen reform, Adler recommended to the Gilder Committee (1894) that the city should purchase suburban land on which to build and thus relieve congestion in the urban tenements. This was not acted upon because of the great financial outreach that would have been required. In the stage of reform dating from the Tenement House Commission of 1900 and the new Law of 1901, Adler involved himself more with related special efforts for better home life than with greater building as such. In 1900 and 1901 he joined with the Committee of Fifteen to fight the prevalence of prostitution in tenements. His friend William H. Baldwin was chairman of the committee. A successfully accomplished object of this campaign was the election in 1902 of Seth Low as a reform mayor of New York.

Municipal Politics

City politics were tangled with school and housing reform efforts during the 1880s and 1890s. The abrasive issue was the simultaneous increase of great wealth and spreading poverty. It marked the period with ardent controversy and occasions of violent protest. In Chicago the Haymarket riot of 1886 struck with a wide blast of anger. "Anarchistic" extremes of rejection and destruction found expression in many parts of the world at this time.

In New York, Henry George's 1886 campaign for mayor was

uniquely "spectacular and fierce." Adler supported George in it, not because he agreed with George's solutions, but because George accorded political importance to labor and its problems. Adler was concerned with unifying the movement for political reform in New York. But the heavy influx of immigrants and crowded tenement conditions worked to the advantage of Tammany Hall. Instead of aiding in tenement house reform, Tammany preferred to carry the abundant votes of tenement dwellers. Only in a few signal campaigns did reform movements succeed in the election of non-Tammany mayors, such as William L. Strong (1895), Seth Low (1901), and John Purroy Mitchel (1914).

One can add that reform opposition also had effect in leading Tammany itself at times to provide abler and more honest candidates. Such was the case, in fact, in 1886, when the industrialist Abram Hewitt was nominated and elected to defeat Henry George and Theodore Roosevelt. The later mayoralties of George B. McClellan (1904) and of William J. Gaynor (1910) might also be counted as instances, though perhaps less radical ones.

Great ethnic differences impeded reform politics in New York, but efforts were made to organize "good government" and other "reform" clubs. Prominent in this endeavor was Edmond Kelly (1851–1906), a Columbia College classmate of Felix Adler's, and a founder, in 1886, of the City Club of New York, which remained outstanding among the many good government clubs that he promoted.

For the election in 1895 many citizens chose, independently of their usual party allegiances, to support William L. Strong, a mayoral candidate who was a strong Republican. His campaign was managed by W. Travers Jerome and he was elected. The frequent fraudulent voting was greatly cut because Jerome had "organized the first Honest Ballot Watchers" for this election. It has been said that Strong gave New York its first honest government in years.

Yet despite the election of Strong, and the praiseworthy conduct of his office, Edmond Kelly was frankly disappointed in the good government clubs. In his published reminiscences he makes the statement that their objective never rose higher than the defeat of Tammany. No positive view of the city's government and its many human problems emerged. This raises for us the question whether it did so in the mind of Felix Adler. Kelly at first was a Spencerian individualist, but like Adler he became a critic of this view and indeed eventually became an "avowed socialist."

In the main the good government club efforts were very welcome to Ethical Culture and its members. But this did not mean that they, more than others in the clubs, had a common idea of city government and what it should be. Some were Socialists though most were not. Dr. Adler himself was not a Socialist, either in general economics or politics, yet he did at times express himself as in favor of "municipal socialism." By this he meant city management—not necessarily ownership—of utilities, such as city transportation, public schools, and health care facilities.

The good government clubs had down-to-earth, concrete goals, but also ideal aims bespeaking their reformist views in municipal politics. Among concrete goals were clean and well-lighted streets, upright police, worthy schools and schoolhouses, more small parks, a better system of docks, and well-equipped public lavatories, laundries, and baths. Featured beyond these, the ideal aims stressed interest and civic pride instead of apathy in city government, honesty rather than fraud, guarding city business from predatory exploitations by national parties and their bosses, abler people in city officialdom, building justice for all rather than favoritism toward special groups, and seeing the laws faithfully executed.

Dr. Adler could not but approve of such goals. Yet he realized (and so did Edmond Kelly) that there was no panacea in purely political steps to raise the generally low level of city government. A better attitude of public mind and knowledge were needed. He kept his faith, as he said in 1886, in "the onward march, the triumph of larger democracy," instead of shifting his main reliance to experts. To that end his main emphasis was on suitable education; labor education to qualify workers for participation in management is "momentous," he declared.

But speaking on "The Problem of Poverty," he pointed also to the need for better pay for women, for workmen's insurance to cope with sickness, for drawing children from labor and into school. Besides attacking pauperism he battled against prostitu-

tion and crime. He did not conceive the Ethical Societies as political organs. Yet in matters of city politics he pointedly spoke his
views near election time in late October or early November in the
years 1884 to 1891 and again from 1893 to 1898.

In his comments he was apt to contrast New York's lack of municipal pride with the self-regard of Athens, Paris, Florence, and
other cities. The comparisons suggest that for a city to have this
kind of ideal "municipal pride" strongly, it perhaps needs either
to be a city-state or to typify the whole life of the state. Did New
York City have this dimension, or not? Was there an absence of
municipal patriotism of the higher kind? Was its character more
akin to that of an emporium than to that of a state? Its increase
of material wealth was, of course, not only outstanding but also
led to fabulous accumulation of cultural assets and opportunities.
The city's freedom of intake and choice of resources had no
measure, it seemed. But how did this identify those who lived
there? Surely many could and did love life in New York, but
could there also be love of the city for its mode of humanity?

Adler's view of how the mode of humanity might be served,
how the interests of society might be met, can be gleaned from an
address he delivered at Carnegie Hall on January 17, 1904. The
specific subject was "The Ethics of the Labor Struggle," but the
concluding paragraph had much wider application:

No one class may think of itself as the people to the ignoring or slighting
of the others, be they the rich or the poor, the highly educated or the
less educated. No one class may rank its interest above the total social
interest, but must conform to the latter, must harmonize its own interest
with the social interest. . . . The welfare of society, the progress of society as a whole, is the supreme law.

[10]

VISION AT NOON AND
ALLIES ABROAD: 1891-1896

THE YEAR 1891 in several evident ways marked a special moment in Felix Adler's life. He was at a midpoint in his span of years; he reached forty that August. But more significantly this midpoint was for him a high noon in his career and growth. The movement for Ethical Culture was now represented in four large American cities, where in each case its members were notably active in efforts to raise the standards of community life and enlightenment. In the preceding decade Adler had won prominence as a public leader, especially in New York City, where few movements for civic or social reform lacked his initiative and help.

Fifteen years of experience since the start of his public career in the city had brought manifest success, but with it an insistent need for critical inner assessment. If there was response to his liberal thinking and reforming zeal, what did it signify in terms of ethical growth in himself, in others, in society? This question loomed not for the first time, but in his fortieth year Adler felt a more pressing need to satisfy himself as to the validity of his purpose. He expressed his need and desire for a time of reflection in a letter to his wife, while visiting the St. Louis Ethical Society. Writing from the home of its president, Charles Nagel, Adler commented on the importance of a proposed trip to Europe, because it would give him time to stand back from his daily activities.

St. Louis March 13th /91

My dearest Wife

Such a delightfully quiet morning this has been! The whole house at my disposal and not a sound to break the silence except now and then the voice of little Hildegard (Nagel) singing to herself in the nursery. And not a caller! except Nagel's office boy who came in an hour ago with your letter of the 11th. . . .

I do feel the benefit of getting away from the accustomed routine of work . . . to stand on the bank surveying the course of the current of one's own life. This is an invaluable help. Only I feel the need of this help for a longer time. I do look forward very confidently and hopefully to our European trip. . . . I really must break away for a year. I think that a fresher and stronger intellectual life is quickening in me. I realize that, subject of course to incalculable interferences, the best part of my life is beginning—my real manhood. And I have a fund of thoughts and plans now accumulated which I can shape if I am given liberty to do so.

What the outcome of my development will be I cannot fully know myself, but I feel that I am certainly passing through a period of decisive growth. I must protect this growth by giving it room and time. . . .

Felix

What shall we make of the comment "the best part of my life is beginning, my real manhood," given that a remarkable unbroken continuity runs through the whole of Adler's career? As a later colleague, Horace Bridges, observed: "From his youth he walked through the world like a man who had received an authoritative command which he could not but obey." That command expressed itself in an unfaltering commitment to several aims: to uphold a high personal worth in everyone; to build a social as well as a personal ethic, including institutions needed to procure greater justice for the laboring groups of industrial society; to bring religious and social life into fuller and freer coherence; to develop the role of women; to give scope to "humanity in the child."

But if these aims appeared early in Adler's efforts, the way he pursued them, his assumptions and expectations, underwent important changes. At the start his assumptions regarding people were much too simplistic and his expectations of institutional reform far too utopian. As he himself acknowledged in retrospect:

At the outset of my career I began with a somewhat utopian enthusiasm for immediate reforms and their benefits; then, when difficulties appeared, I first fell back upon the simple dignity of the moral law. Finally, I found it necessary to seek a fresh and deeper understanding of what is in that law and its claims upon men.

In effect in his early years Adler was addressing a fervent summons to "the good," or to goodness in people, to unite in building better institutions, better schools, nurseries, homes, shops, and cities. But quite soon he realized that "the good" no less than "the bad" exhibited motley natures with various strong and weak characteristics. Adler, in fact, now came to be much impressed with the prevalence of "polarities" in character, with the idea that "people have the defects of their qualities," as a French saying puts it. He remarks to his wife that to understand this (dismissing the good and bad man opposition) must have revolutionary consequences for ethics.

And indeed, his conception of Ethical Culture matured and deepened profoundly in his later work. The simple and sanguine attitudes in the early Ethical Culture movement could invite some cynical doubts about "do-gooders." But the ethical charge was now being seen by Adler on the basis of different assumptions. Emphasis on "the good" uplifting "the bad" lessened, and gave way to a more diversified process of mutual maturing and developing. How to grow as human partners, to discover and reach for "more valid persons," whatever their strengths and weaknesses, favored freedom from complacency. The future path broadened steadily from this noontide vision of Ethical Culture and its "whole Promethean task."

In his famous lectures published as *The Varieties of Religious Experience* (1901), William James stressed a difference between "once-born" and "twice-born" religious types. In James's sense Felix Adler was not a twice-born man; that is, he did not experience a halt, a life-crisis in which he felt forsaken in spirit, or a void of meaning from which he had to be delivered to a new and changed life. What I call his noontide vision was definitely not a second birth or conversion experience. But with its expanding range and depth Adler became a decidedly and highly *developed* man. And his growing realism in regard to human failings and frustrations, together with the transcendence he extolled in the Ideal, gave his matured religious outlook its own share of the depth that James associates with "pessimistic" conversionist religions.

It is then the development of Felix Adler that we want to emphasize in pursuing the meaning of his feeling that the best part of his life, his real manhood, was beginning in the 1890s. Looking over the first half of his life, up to the age of forty, we can see a sequence of several spiritual responses. First, as a young student and teacher in his twenties, he had unburdened himself of that which he judged to be outworn and false in Judaic tradition; he had, to repeat the words in his temple sermon, "gone out from among the ruins." But accompanying this step of emancipation was a compelling imperative to renew enduring principles of ethical religion (found partly in Hebrew prophecy) and to remove the injustices and outrages of advancing industrial society. Then, in his ardent efforts at reform, Adler encountered the obstacles of human custom and prejudice and discovered the inadequacy of power to sustain efforts of substantial reform. And this experience by the early 1880s led to his stress on the importance of religious dedication to duty and moral principle beyond all expectation and satisfaction with specific reforms.

This is not to say that Adler in his thirties was turning from activism to an essentially contemplative attitude. Far from it. During the 1880s his activities were extended in more directions than perhaps in any other decade of his career. But he tended to justify his immersion in life's struggles not because of the immediate gains but as clearing the vision for the nature of truly valid human relationships.

The account to come—in chapters on the second half of Adler's life—shows the unfolding of this vision in word and action. One recalls that at the tenth anniversary of the Society for Ethical Culture, in May 1886, he had declared: "I have never delivered my message, not yet been able to speak fully." It remains to follow and reflect on what this message, this full speaking, came to be.

The following chapters then deal with what Adler tried to make the "best part" of his life, the distinctive message of his "real manhood." The noontide vision was not something completed in a moment, but was a connected development of views with their main reaches through the forty years still ahead of him. New and influential, however, was the much expanded context and range of his relations. His immediate family, his children, were growing up; his school was developing a high-school division; the Ethical Culture movement like the United States itself was gaining life in other nations; and Adler himself, after 1902, added to his philosophical contacts with part-time teaching as Professor of Political and Social Ethics at Columbia University.

In his philosophical outlook at large Felix Adler retained the Kantian view of Mind as a "reality producing," world-organizing power with transcendent eminence over natural cause and effect. Herein he remained a transcendentalist thinker and clashed with emerging dispositions of philosophic naturalism. But in his own critique of Kant's ethics he was sufficiently radical so that it would be a mistake to call his matured ethical teaching Kantian. Adler came to see the ethical ideal not as observance of universal Moral Law but as a complete relatedness of unique selves, realizing one another in the basic "stations" or stages of life. Moral stature lies less in exemplifying uniform rules than in one's partaking in relations such as family, vocation, and citizenship as a distinctive essential member. By its insufficient attention both to the social formation of personality and to the uniqueness of self, Kant's ethics is too individualistic and legalist.

Year Abroad: 1891–92

The year of leave which the trustees of the Ethical Society granted Adler was much needed. The preceding year of very demanding and continuous work had left him in a much fatigued condition. To this had been added the strain of his father's prolonged illness.

Reverend Samuel Adler died that June, in his eighty-second year. He had lived in quiet, scholarly retirement since 1874, when he became rabbi emeritus at Temple Emanu-El. He was not active in the developing American scene which so fully engaged his son, but he could look upon that engagement with much sympathy and pride. Until 1885, when his health failed, Samuel Adler quite frequently attended the lectures at the Society for Ethical Culture, for despite their distinct spheres and paths, Felix had the blessing of his father, who understood that a kindred ethical and liberal spirit animated them both in their life's work.

The Adler family left for Europe on the S.S. Nordland in September, reaching Antwerp on the fourteenth of that month. The family then included Waldo, eight years old, Eleanor, nearly seven, Lawrence, five, and Margaret, not quite two. The voyage took twelve days.

Once on the Continent, the Adlers took their ease in a leisurely progress toward Munich, which had been chosen for a winter residence. From Antwerp they went to Brussels for several days and thence to Aachen and to Cologne. They traveled on the Rhine from Koblentz, and for about two weeks lingered in the Rhine country, visiting Trier, Mainz, and several other places. Of course, they went to Worms and to Alzey, of which Mrs. Adler's diary relates that "on a beautiful sunny October day, the quiet little country hamlet was very dear to us, with tender love and reverence for the dear ones [Felix's parents and family] who lived a part of their lives here." After Worms and Frankfort they spent some days in Heidelberg which also had pleasant memories for Felix. With brief stops in Strassburg and Nuremberg, they finally arrived in Munich on November 2.

One must suppose that the change of scene gave the refreshment Adler was seeking. Yet considerable time had to be given to editing lectures he had recently given in America on the moral instruction of children; these were published in book form in 1892 by Appleton, as volume 21 in the International Education Series edited by W. T. Harris, then U.S. Commissioner of Education.

The art collections of Munich delighted the Adlers. And, of course, Felix came in touch with some scholars at the university. But here an impression of pedantry stemming from the intensive specialization of scholarship seems to have eclipsed more attractive memories. In the Adler family's table-talk this impression lingered long after, for example, in recalling a professor who had excused himself from general conversation on Goethe's poetry by saying: "Mein Fach ist Klopstock" (My field is Klopstock).

In March 1892 Dr. Adler went up to Berlin, briefly, "to meet a small committee chiefly of University Professors, and to report on the Ethical Societies in America." Here he did find a congenial reception. Attractive sponsors and a broad ground of concern were already present for developing a movement for "Ethische Kultur" in German cities. Adler was invited to return to Berlin later in the summer term to lend his voice to that effort.

But before that, during the spring, he took two other trips. The first was a short vacation tour to some cities of Italy, which he and

RABBI SAMUEL ADLER, FATHER OF FELIX ADLER.

HENRIETTA (FRANKFURTER) ADLER WITH HER CHILDREN
(L. TO R.) ISAAC, SARAH, AND FELIX, C.1861.

ISAAC AND FELIX ADLER IN THE MID-1860S.

FELIX ADLER AT CORNELL UNIVERSITY IN 1875.

FELIX AND ISAAC ADLER WITH THE LATTER'S FIANCEE,
FRIEDA, IN 1875.

FELIX ADLER IN THE 1890s.

HELEN (NELL) GOLDMARK ADLER.

FELIX ADLER WITH HIS DAUGHTER RUTH IN THE
ADIRONDACKS IN THE LATE 1890S. RUTH ADLER
MARRIED HORACE FRIESS IN 1923.

(L. TO R.) MARGARET AND ELEANOR ADLER AND FRIENDS WITH THEIR
FATHER FELIX ADLER (FAR RIGHT) ON AN ADIRONDACK MOUNTAIN TOP.

DERS OF ETHICAL CULTURE SOCIETIES AT GLENMORE IN THE ADIRONDACKS IN 1901.
TO R.) S. BURNS WESTON, WILLIAM M. SALTER, PERCIVAL CHUBB, FELIX ADLER, ANNA
RLIN SPENCER, ALFRED W. MARTIN, DAVID SAVILLE MUZZEY, UNIDENTIFIED, LESLIE
LIS SPRAGUE AND JOHN LOVEJOY ELLIOTT.

DR. AND MRS. FELIX ADLER ON THE ACROPOLIS IN ATHENS IN 1905.

ERS AND ASSOCIATES OF ETHICAL SOCIETIES AT THE HUDSON GUILD FARM IN THE 1920S. (FRONT L. TO R.) HENRY NEUMANN, MRS. DAVID SAVILLE MUZZEY, DR. AND FELIX ADLER. (BACK L. TO R.) ALGERNON D. BLACK, HAROLD K. ESTABROOK, JAMES MANN, ALFRED W. MARTIN, HENRY J. GOLDING, HORACE BRIDGES, JOHN LOVEJOY EL-T, DAVID SAVILLE MUZZEY, ERNEST JACQUES, STANTON COIT, AND S. BURNS WESTON.

LEADERS AND ASSOCIATES IN ETHICAL SOCIETIES AT THE HUDSON GUILD FARM, NETC
N.J., IN THE LATE 1920S. (L. TO R.) S. BURNS WESTON, GEORGE E. O'DELL, ROBERT F
ERT, MARK MCCLOSKEY, PERCIVAL CHUBB, HAROLD K. ESTABROOK, DR. AND MRS. F
ADLER, ERNEST JACQUES, DAVID SAVILLE MUZZEY, JOHN LOVEJOY ELLIOTT, HI
NEUMANN, JAMES GUTMANN, ALRED W. MARTIN, AND HENRY J. GOLDING.

DR. FELIX ADLER C. 1930.

HORACE L. FRIESS, AUTHOR OF THIS BOOK AND FELIX ADLER'S
SON-IN-LAW.

his wife greatly enjoyed together. Friends had been found to look after the children for them. The other was a longer visit to England, which Felix made alone during the latter part of May and June. For some of the time when he was gone, his wife and children moved out to a retreat in the country at Feldafing on the Stärnberger Sea. Adler's frequent (almost daily) letters to his wife are full of tender complaint about the separation. And his entreaties finally persuaded her to meet him at Dover toward the close of his English visit.

Allies Abroad

Well before Adler's visit in 1892 an Ethical movement had grown indigenously in England from various sources. And Felix himself had been in touch with English scholars both by correspondence and through Stanton Coit.

The English Ethical movement had no centralized system and showed no signs of wanting any. It represented a confluence of important currents in the national life, and it was marked by variety in philosophy and in group expressions. A strand of philosophic idealism came from the teaching of Thomas Hill Green at Oxford. But the various programs and pleas put forward by Utilitarians and Positivists such as John Stuart Mill, Frederic Harrison, and Leslie Stephen also continued to attract attention.

In his book *The Ethical Movement in Great Britain: A Documentary History* (1934), Gustav Spiller judges that by the turn of the century there were six relatively strong centers of the movement in Britain. Among these was a London Ethical Society, formed in 1886, and another established at Cambridge University in 1888. But in addition many small local groups, some fluid and some more stable, emerged. And with the strong moral concern among English intellectuals, even these small groups could often avail themselves of able visiting speakers. Indeed, a notable number of outstanding British thinkers spoke at least now and then to the English Ethical Societies. Among those who did so fairly regularly were Sir John Seeley, Edward Caird, J. H. Muirhead, B. Bosanquet, J. Bonar, Henry Sidgwick, Leslie Stephen, Frederic Harrison, and C. Deslisle Burns, as well as foreign guests.

On his visit to England in May–June 1892, Felix Adler lectured
for the London Ethical Society at Essex Hall on three successive
Sundays, beginning on May 15. The topics were: "The Ethical
Element in Religion"; "Ethical Standards Applied to Economics";
and "The Matter and Method of Moral Education." These themes
clearly represented Adler's leading concerns.

The first of these lectures was repeated on May 16 for the Ethical Society in Cambridge. Adler wrote his wife that the audience
there was stirred to lively questioning. He mentioned having a
long talk with Professor Sidgwick, his host, who introduced him
to Professor John Seeley and Mr. Keynes. On this, or on another
occasion, Sidgwick expressed some doubts as to the extent to
which the teaching of ethics might be expected to influence practical conduct.

The report to Mrs. Adler on a later meeting, on June 13, in
Oxford was not so warm. "It was found impossible," Felix wrote,
"to obtain for me a hearing in Balliol or Oriel," but I gave an
address this evening to about fifty people whom the Harcourts,
with the cooperation of Mr. Alexander, had invited." Reflecting
on the occasion, Adler added of Oxford:

The atmosphere is charged with conservatism. Even the scientific men
are more or less pledged to conventionalism, and are constrained to all
sorts of subtle compromises. . . . I felt that while my audience was far
too advanced to be shocked by anything I might say, the tone of my
remarks jarred against the system here in vogue.

The English are known for "doing ethics" and minding conduct
in their own way. And Felix Adler, unlike the Captain of the
H.M.S. Pinafore, was not an Englishman either by fate or choice.
The English regard for and protection of individual liberty at
home he always recognized as a moral achievement of outstanding magnitude. But the element of noblesse oblige in British culture aroused mixed and perplexing feelings in Adler. In theory
he rather consistently inveighed against it, especially as applied to
imperial rule of other peoples. Yet he was not unaware of the
advantages of upper class experience and training when it came
to importing Englishmen for leadership positions in the Ethical
movement in America.

On the whole, it seems to me that Adler gained more for his

knowledge of life from his many contacts with England than he was able to impart to that country out of his own style of Ethical Culture. Understanding of national character and institutions he always considered to be an important factor in ethical development. And his experience of English ways became for him a fruitful case of that interplay of differences, which he saw as the true pattern and symbol of a universal, as contrasted to an ethnically bounded, spiritual life.

His letters, of course, mentioned both old friends and the new people he was meeting. And he much relished travel to historic sites that he had read about. During this visit in 1892 he was a dinner guest of the Earl of Dysart at his country house in Petersham. The fine house, "a different world" Adler wrote his wife, "was built by James I for the Prince of Wales . . . and contains the so-called Cabal Room, in which the Cabal met." He added, "My host, Lord Dysart, is a radical Earl, a strange being . . . very 'keen' he says about his interest in the Ethical Society and wanting to help along."

Adler hoped to further Dysart's interest in the *International Journal of Ethics* and in the new West London Ethical Society, later called The Ethical Church, of which Stanton Coit was about to take charge. Meanwhile, he enjoyed this visit with its stimulus to historical imagination and a ride down the Thames in the Earl's launch to Kew Gardens, "where we had a pleasant walk. Lord Dysart thinks that hereditary aristocracy has not long to live. Coming from one who is the owner of twenty-eight thousand acres of English soil this forecast is interesting."

In still another letter to his wife Adler confessed that the lectures he had given for the London Ethical Society at Essex Hall did not bring him the assurance he sought, namely, that "he could speak to an English audience." What he meant was a general, uninitiated audience, for those who heard him at Essex Hall were already within the Ethical family, so to speak. But before he left England some of the desired confidence came, when he talked to a wide public at Prince's Hall, Piccadilly. Here, he reported, "we launched out boldly to throw ourselves on London. . . . There was a fine audience and a most encouraging reception." This lecture, on June 12, was in some respects the decisive lecture, he added. The same letter asked whether his wife was coming to join him: "Everyone asks me whether you are." After Mrs. Adler's arrival in England, the Adlers spent a few days in London, then Paris, before returning to Germany.

Back in Germany in July, Adler and his wife made their way to the planned meetings in Berlin. Before a large assembly in the hall of the Architectural Society he gave an address, in German, which made a deep impression and was most favorably received. Later, he and Mrs. Adler were guests at a dinner given by a committee of university professors and other professional people— lawyers, physicians, artists—presided over by Professor Wilhelm Foerster, rector of Berlin University and director of the Royal Observatory.

Dr. Adler was especially proud that the German Society, Deutsche Gesellschaft für Ethische Kultur, which was launched in October 1892, could obtain the active leadership of Professor Wilhelm Foerster as its first president. For this distinguished university man and astronomer was also a person of sterling character. Because he was there at the start, and because of German elements in his own style of thought, Adler in 1892 and in subsequent years could give some effective help in forming the German movement. Yet the latter's swift rise and spread can hardly be explained by that. The German Reich (First Reich) was still a relatively new political formation; in the Bismarckian regime, issues of socialism, clericalism, and militant nationalism had become critical. A response to these issues which was not dictated by government or by party had a timely appeal for many people. Only so can one understand that in two years (1892–1894) the German Society for Ethical Culture was able to form sections in eight German cities, Berlin, Breslau, Frankfurt-am-Main, Freiburg, Königsberg, Magdeburg, München (Munich), and Strassburg, with a total of more than 1,600 members. These sections, however, were centers of propaganda, spoken and printed, rather than membership organizations in the American or English mold.

Dr. Adler left Germany that summer with an encouraging sense that Ethical Culture had international application, that it was not nationally circumscribed. And in the next years (1893–1896) developments on the Continent gave the movement a further outreach. In 1893 a conference was held at Eisenach in Germany attended by representatives from Ethical societies in England and America as well as Germany. In addition to organizational planning the matters there discussed included ethical instruction, the relation of ethics to religion, the battle for social welfare (vis-à-vis class struggle politics), renewal of family life, art and the people, and natural science and ethics.

A major moral principle in regard to nationalism was also enunciated at Eisenach in 1893 in these terms:

Ethical Culture cannot and may not be circumscribed by national boundaries any more than by social class differences. It is a concern common to all mankind. . . . It must be international in principle, not because it deprecates the ethical worth of nationality, but because the highest flowering of national character seems to us possible only within a morally organized Community of Humanity (*Humanitätsgemeinschaft*).

The lasting weight of this position in Adler's own thinking will be seen in his subsequent attitude toward imperialism and in his interpretation of World War I.

In 1894 Professor Friedrich Jodl became leader of a Society begun in Vienna and eventually given the attractive name of Die Ethische Gemeinde (The Ethical Community). Jodl's philosophical orientation was positivistic rather than metaphysical, and this continued as a cast of thinking prominent in the Vienna group. In the twentieth century Wilhelm Boerner and Walter Eckstein became leaders there. In Lausanne and Zürich Jean Wagner, who had studied with Stanton Coit in London, organized the Ligue pour l'action morale.

Along with features common to all, in respect to freedom in religion, moral instruction, economic justice, the groups in these different countries each developed some distinctive local projects and emphases.

These several beginnings led in 1896 to the formation of the International Ethical Union (IEU) and to the convening of its first congress in Zurich that September, with delegates coming from England, Germany, Austria, Italy, Switzerland, and the United States. The French government also sent two official observers "to report on plans for moral education."

A stormy sign was the fact that the Social Democrats held a

convention in Zurich simultaneously with the 1896 meetings of the International Ethical Union. At that convention August Bebel and others warned against softening the class struggle with ethical reformist tendencies. It was part of the Socialist debate over "revisionism." Some discussion took place with delegates of the Ethical Congress, for though many of these held socialistic views themselves, they feared that emphasis on the class struggle would lead to a brutalizing of social conflict. This issue proved an augury of difficulties to come for the Ethical movement on the Continent.

Before the IEU Congress opened on September 6 there had been public lectures for some weeks, designed to arouse interest in the social and moral concerns of Ethical Culture. A galaxy of intellectual leaders gave these lectures including Ferdinand Tönnies, Werner Sombart, Wilhelm Foerster, Harald Höffding, and other prominent scholars. Felix Adler did not engage in these lectures, but when he arrived in Zurich he reported, in a letter, that "every one is in high glee over the success of the lecture course— some fifty lectures!—and the prospects are good for the coming week."

But Adler also had some unsettled feelings about his relation to the congress. He had been named its honorary president, and had a suspicion that this might be a polite way of stressing his "honor" while limiting his influence. He sensed "a little jealousy of American ideas, a little disposition to treat the American origin of the movement somewhat in the light of an historical accident." He still dwells upon this, in a letter written at the close of the congress to his American colleague, William Salter, but now adds a note of happy encouragement over the way things seem to have turned out.

Zurich, Sept. 12, 1896

My dear Salter:

I approached the Convention with some trepidation. I had a fear that antagonisms might be aroused and that irremediable differences between the ideas of our European friends and our own might disclose themselves. These fears were speedily and happily dispelled.

An externalizing tendency has predominated in the German movement, and no less so in the Austrian and Italian. In my opening address, I at once struck the chord that the Ethical Societies primarily exist for the moral improvement of their members, that participation in social reform must be valued not merely or chiefly because of its external effects, but as an indispensable means of personal development.

This position was to perhaps the greater part of my hearers new and at first startling. But it was wonderful with what joyful willingness the whole convention, after a moment's hesitation, advanced toward the position that had been pointed out. And now I feel for the first time as if this way of looking upon the Ethical Societies had received the assent of our friends on this side, and as if there were fundamental community of purpose between us.

Adler thus claimed a satisfying response, and the congress did ask him to draft its official declaration, or platform, which (he reports to Salter) was "adopted en bloc with the addition of two sentences proposed by Professor Tönnies and Dr. Reich of Vienna." Into this document Adler did introduce his emphasis on personal development, but it contained also "pronouncements on the Labor Question, on Marriage, on Education, on International Peace," as ethical issues of world-wide moment and concern.

Once more a familiar dream appeared, of starting in Zurich "a Pedagogical Seminary for the training of teachers in methods of moral instruction," as the germ of a larger Academy of Ethics which would develop in time.

The congress did establish "an international secretariat to be located in Zurich." And Dr. Friedrich Wilhelm Foerster, the son of Professor Foerster, was chosen to serve this office.

In the same year of these events at Zurich, 1896, the New York Society for Ethical Culture celebrated its twentieth anniversary with a meeting held in Carnegie Hall on Friday evening, May 15. The London Ethical Society was ten years old, and the German Society was just entering its fifth year. Other groups forming on the Continent (Vienna, Venice, Lausanne) were still in newer beginnings of only a year or two. These time spans and sites point to differences in experience and in problems which were bound to affect priorities. Whatever consensus and worldwide relevance Felix Adler felt glad to have sensed at Zurich, he was not in a position to direct the practical growth of an international Ethical movement. The pressure of situations would have greater effect upon this than any single person or doctrine. During World War I and its aftermath Adler could with good conscience, though with pain, disclaim responsibility for the failure of most Continental Ethical Societies to survive and to resist overwhelming, contrary political trends.

There was a significant turn inward to self-examination as Adler faced the widening relations of Ethical Culture in 1896. Both in New York on May 15 and in Zurich in September he appeared less preoccupied with reforms than with the traits of *reformers,* their moral development and relations to one another. This comes to the fore also in a letter to his wife from the Zurich Congress. There he comments on some of the notable people he met and their various pet causes. One was a clergyman "who became very excited and warlike on the peace question." Another was an alienist who "buttonholed me on the street about the temperance question," and who made me "wonder whether we are not all a bit crazy." He then added:

Most people treat their neighbors as a jumping board from which to give impetus to their own fancies, or as a convenient receptacle into which they empty their own overplus. There are so few people who have real consideration in conversation for the individuality of others. I speak feelingly on the subject as I am penitently conscious of innumerable sins of omission and commission of this kind.

The confession in this letter makes the rejection of a unilateral path of expression the more striking. Whether Dr. Adler in following years became more personally understanding and responsive himself, as well as directive, could be debated from several angles. In any case the idea of development together with joint regard for others and self became more explicit and sovereign in his mature thought. In the deepening of his vision at noon this was a central point.

[11]

ASPIRATIONS FOR SCHOOL
AND SOCIETY: 1900–1931

THE APPROACH OF A new century is apt to stir a flurry of hopes for progress ahead. Such was the case around 1900. And there were special and deep causes that gave strength to the hopes for education in America at that time. The population was growing, through heavy immigration as well as through natural increase. This in itself presented an expanded and urgent task for the schools. The new content and standards of thought contained in the sciences provided a widely compelling stimulus, as did the intensification of national consciousness brought about by the Spanish-American War and subsequent American involvement in the Pacific and the Far East.

It was a time when many looked to education to bring about a better social order. This chapter deals chiefly with the course of the Ethical Culture Schools after 1895 and under Felix Adler's continued leadership until the 1930s. What was done in the schools however must be seen in the context of the growing hope for democratic culture through a more effective and creative union of school and society. There were remarkable leaders in this movement and a special focus of idealism in this cause. These generated a spirit within which Adler's efforts in schooling flourished.

Outstanding among those concerned with the social mission of education were Felix Adler and John Dewey. Between 1894 and 1904, when he was head of the Department of Philosophy, Psychology and Pedagogy at the University of Chicago, Dewey expressed his views in influential writings about school and society. A leading book of his had, indeed, the title *School and Society* (1899), but he published other important works on this subject both in this period and throughout his life. He had also established a laboratory school in 1896 in Chicago, so that his ideas could be put into practice and thus be tested.

Dewey wanted schools to become model democracies engaged in inquiry and reflection about the real problems of their miniature community. As he put it in *School and Society:*

> . . . make each one of our schools an embryonic community life, active with types of occupations that reflect the life of the larger society, and permeated throughout with the spirit of art, history and science. When the school introduces and trains each child of society into membership within such a little community, saturating him with the spirit of service, and providing him with the instruments of effective self-direction, we shall have the deepest and best guarantee of a larger society which is worthy, lovely and harmonious.

Dewey firmly believed that this task for education was all the more important now that industrialism, urbanization, job specialization, and increasing mobility were rapidly eroding the personal role of the individual in the life of the community.

For some years before Dewey came to Columbia University and Teacher's College in 1904, he had been a summer resident at Glenmore, among the philosophers who gathered there around Thomas Davidson. From time to time that remarkable summer group included, besides William James, Dewey, and Adler, other notables such as (in 1893) W. T. Harris, Josiah Royce, James Seth, James Hyslop, F. N. Scott, and Charles Bakewell. Occasionally there were also foreign visitors. It was here that Adler would meet Davidson's English friend and former member of the London Ethical Society, Percival Chubb, and invite him to join the faculty of the Ethical Culture School.

By the turn of the century Adler too was emphasizing the role that his school must play in the reform of society. So, for example, he said in a key statement frequently discussed:

> The ideal of the School is not the adaptation of the individual to the existing social environment; it is to develop persons who will be competent to change their environment to greater conformity with moral ideals; that is, to put it boldly, to train reformers. But this must be rightly understood. . . . Children are to be developed into duly conservative men and women.
>
> The unbalanced reformer is most harmful. The lessons of history. . . . should give this balance. By "reformers" are meant persons who

believe that their salvation consists in reacting beneficently upon their environment. This ideal of beneficent activity, beneficent transformation of faulty environment, is the ideal of the Society and of the School.

He went on to declare that education should aim to unify mankind.

Such statements were addressed not only to the faculty of the Ethical Culture School but also to the trustees and leaders of the New York Society for Ethical Culture, which owned the school.

New colleagues in leadership of the Society—John Elliott, David Muzzey and, a bit later, Henry Neumann—were in those years taking direct part in teaching in the school. And Adler himself became more closely associated with other educators and philosophers when he accepted a part-time appointment as Professor of Social and Political Philosophy at Columbia University in 1902–1903. These new relationships had effects not only in the maturing of his thought but also in the extension of his knowledge of educational developments and personnel.

In 1895 Adler had moved to add a high school division to the Ethical Culture School. He had outlined a long-range plan for a series of secondary schools in his speech at the World's Columbian Exposition in Chicago two years earlier, explaining that: "The logical outcome of our plan is a series of secondary schools, growing like branches from our elementary school as their common trunk; a classical school, a scientific school, a technological school, a commercial school, and an evening school for the continued education of those pupils, who must earn their own living during the day."

His emphasis on occupations, "vocations" in his ideal, was doubtless influenced by German examples. Yet he strongly wanted to turn this to the advantage of America where he believed democracy was too "individualistic" and education too vague about how to deal with rising social problems. There must be a greater emphasis on cooperation and on excellence in one's work. "Learn to do your own work so that the work of the world is better done for it," he said.

But when the Society, in 1895, added a high school program it was of the kind that might be described as classical and scientific, by Adler's own definition, and did not include the technical, commercial, and evening classes mentioned in his Chicago speech. With the more universal ideal in mind, however, Adler continued to propose measures that would keep the school from becoming too narrowly tied to academic conventions. Moreover, he continued to do this until the end of his leadership of the Ethical Culture School.

A foremost care of his was to keep a watchful eye over the people he wanted as teachers and leaders in his school. He wanted people with high standards in their own fields who would bring this interest to bear on the development of the whole student. This had been a keynote from the first in founding the Free Kindergarten and the Workingman's School and it continued undiminished with the growth of specialties in the school's upper grades and high school division.

In accord with his desire to advance many distinct abilities, Adler viewed the study of history as offering a "central core" suited to correlate work in languages, literature, art, science, and ethics. Though he granted that historical studies should satisfy the intellect in a critical determination of facts and in a search "to trace causes and effects," he opposed the teaching of "laws of history" allegedly established by "social science." High school youth were not to be indoctrinated in uncertain explanations of social "phenomena as determined by inexorable laws." In his ethical emphasis Adler wanted instead to stress the role of human decision and will in the making of history.

History teaching should impart a sense of mankind's great struggles and efforts to progress in various ideal directions. It must appeal to the imagination, the feelings, and the will as well as to the intellect, "to awaken the sentiment of humanity, of understanding sympathy with human nature in its various guises." In Adler's own words:

History teaching should emphasize points of likeness to create sympathy and points of difference in order to overcome provincialism and widen the horizon. The student should learn about Egypt, Babylonia, Persia, etc. for the purpose of appreciating a different type of humanity from his own. The foreign type is often represented as too foreign and becomes unattractive; or the attempt is made to modernize excessively the foreign life, thus not only falsifying the facts, but depriving the student of the benefit of new mental adjustments. The whole civilization must be presented as in a picture, its leading traits standing out sharply, lights and shadows contrasted, and care taken that a unified impression shall remain on the mind. Such study will also lead in a natural way to the singling out of the permanent contributions made by successive types to human civilization.

In such pronouncements the strong ethical cast in Adler's attitude toward history teaching is highly evident.

Indeed, was not his ethicism so strong as to imply that the "Moral Law" or the "Ideal" ruled ultimately over the direction and much of the course of history? This is clearly a pivotal question and one upon which Adler's answer over the years shows both continuity and profound change. As a young man in the early years of his public career his answer to the above question might truly be regarded as an unqualified "yes." So, during his contention with Rabbi Kaufmann Kohler of Chicago in 1878, he declared as a "confession of faith": "I believe that the law of righteousness will triumph in the universe over all evil." In some measure this attitude continued during the next years in which Adler "preached the supremacy of the Moral Law," for this was regarded not only as a supremacy of authority but "as a power actually working in the world" to bring out the best in people.

But knowing "the best" became a new question as his reflections on history extended and deepened. Historical events and changes brought out the changing and unfinished contents and meaning of the Moral Law. They gave abundant, sure evidence of man's motley performance—full of devastations as well as nobilities. The fact is that if Adler's ethical idealism influenced his approach to history, it is also true that a larger dynamic sense of historical variety made changes in the ethical teaching given in his school.

Ethics teaching for the young children in grades 1–5 remained pretty much the same in approach and method, and not far apart in spirit from the views Adler set forth in chapters 6–10 in *The Moral Instruction of Children* (1892). Chapters 6, 7, and 8 of that book discuss the use of folklore, fairy tales, and fables in marking moral issues in childhood. Chapters 9 and 10 discuss "family relations exemplified from *Genesis*," social and personal relations illustrated in the *Odyssey*, and growth of "helpfulness and sacrifice" through examples taken from the "*Bible*, history and literature."

What was regarded as a new view of young children was developed in the Normal School, which trained teachers for the Kindergarten and in the child study groups which read the works of G. Stanley Hall. There were few new developments in ways of regarding this age group until the influence of Freud began to affect education in this country.

"The Grammar Course. Lessons on Duty," as described in chapters 11–17 of *The Moral Instruction of Children* (ages c. 11, 12, 13), changed a great deal during Adler's life. In this book Adler was still teaching a system of duties to "self" and "others" rather closely following Kant's tabulation in his *Tugendlehre*. This position may not have been far from rather general middle-class ethics of the mid-nineteenth century. But it did not take into account rapidly developing new problems and the changing situations and experiences of the students.

Dr. Adler's developing regard for historical situations and changes began around the turn of the century to have a major effect upon ethics teaching in the upper grades and especially in the four years (ages c. 14–17) of the new high school division. Ethical discussion became much more related to student growth in the specific social contexts about to confront them. The following outline (evolving 1900–1904) gives evidence of this.

Ethics teaching in the high school division
Grade Alpha Age c. 14
> As a link with results obtained in the Eighth Grade teaching from Roman history, a summary of principal provisions of the Penal Code of the State of New York. Ideas to be prominent: Social stability; ethics of wealth; slavery and poverty; the negro problem; the inalienable worth of every human being.

Grade Beta Age c. 15
> The school and the family as social organisms, with emphasis on right relations toward superiors, equals, and inferiors. Problems of authority; of understanding; of sex relations; of rivalry—in adolescence.

Grade Gamma Age c. 16
> Centers around the subject of vocational ethics, with discussion of selected vocations and of their interrelations. A discussion of friendship follows and of comradeship in preparing for the work of life.

Grade Delta Age c. 17
> The State is the principal subject, having for its ideal aim the unification of the various vocational groups and the expression of the national

character and genius. The various forms of government are compared; a kind of short catechism of political ethics, e.g., ethics of loyalty, of party, of taxation, of relation to religion and church.

It must be said, however, that after 1900 new associates were as much responsible as Adler himself for changes in the teaching of ethics. New candidates for leadership in Ethical Culture—John Elliott and David Saville Muzzey who came in the nineties, a bit later Henry Neumann and others—were actually teaching more ethics classes in the school than Adler himself. And despite the latter's authority, each of these teachers was allowed to relate ethical alertness to current life in his own way.

Adler observed, meanwhile, that, "Education in Life Problems would be a better term . . . education toward a life purpose of a kind as shall give lasting satisfaction. . . . The very word 'moral education' as pointed toward performance of external acts without an inspiring motive is repugnant to the finer perceptions." General attendance in the ethics classes was expected in Adler's school but no marks were given in the subject and the once a week meetings evolved into discussions rather than lectures.

The whole system of ethics teaching, however, has always had its critics, some of whom doubtless shared John Dewey's reservations. Himself a moralist with interests similar to Adler's in many specific reforms, Dewey nevertheless questioned a separate program of ethics classes. Except as it arose in actual conflicts among students, emphasis on the ethical threatened to be too self-conscious, Dewey believed, and perhaps largely verbal. Yet for a number of years several of Dewey's own children attended the Ethical Culture School. He appreciated the ability of certain teachers, with their initiative and their understanding of growth in the young. "If they have teachers like that," Dewey is reported to have said, "I guess the ethics classes can't do much harm."

For his part Adler never regarded the school's ethical aim as depending on this one source. He believed, on the contrary, that all development of truly human powers—in science, art, social organization and religion—yields ethical insight, energy, and life.

Ethical instruction is but one of the factors which must pervade the entire school for its supreme object of the moral development of its pupils. Other factors are: the school environment and atmosphere, the general spirit, the personality of the teachers and principals, the public opinion of the school, the reaction of the pupils on one another.

Adler and Dewey agreed in general on treating children as active rather than passive recipients of learning. But they differed in that Adler never gave up an "Ideal" of ethical perfection as universal and permanent. Moreover, he also thought, rightly or wrongly, that he was attending to the more lasting individual capacities of his students, while Dewey's "projects appealing to their interests" might be more ephemeral.

Percival Chubb, whom Adler brought in to head the high school division, had been educated in England but had taught in various schools in New York City, including the new Manual Training School, and had also lectured on the history of education and psychology at the Pratt Institute. New York school boys gave this cultivated and poetically fervent Englishman some hard times, but he found a more encouraging response when he gave some lectures for the Ethical Culture Societies. Thus he was pleased to accept Adler's invitation to join the staff of the school both as head of the secondary school division and as a teacher of English. Many students who read Chaucer, Shakespeare, and Milton with Chubb recall the experience with quite exceptional delight and gratitude. In his own way Chubb pursued Davidson's object to reanimate society through building the spirit of an uplifted company. In his way of doing this he made much creative use of drama and of festival, establishing distinct traditions in the Ethical Culture Schools and to a lesser extent in the Ethical Culture Societies as well. In 1911 he left the school to take up the leadership of the St. Louis Ethical Society.

Felix Adler held that education must be concerned with mentally mastering nature and with glorifying life in art and consecrating it in morality and religion. This still suggests Kant's threefold division of the Mind's rulings.

Dr. Henry Kelly was also a leading teacher and one who not only encouraged a strong development of the natural sciences but also related the sciences to other studies and imbued them with Adler's human aims. Kelly's special field was biology, but it was said of him:

. . . Dr. Kelly in his course on Biology and Human Life . . . has selected
. . . facts and principles that help a student majoring in euthenics to
understand herself and others; and in a way to form something of a
tentative philosophy of life. By its many-sided treatment of man, his relations with the lower animals, his geological history, his development of
a social life, his differentiation into races or types, his embryological development, the laws of his heredity, the problems of eugenics and euthenics, his emotional and intellectual development, he has made extraordinary progress in finding teaching material of great value. This
work, with its excursions and its laboratory procedure seemed particularly significant for the non-verbal type of girl. . . . Moreover, by bringing into his course pediatricians, psychiatrists, and anthropologists, by
clinical work and by bringing these concrete experiences to bear on large
general problems he has contributed toward a sound and liberal education.*

It is impossible to mention here all the other teachers who were
important associates in teaching the sciences. But among those
who furthered the connective spirit as well as pursuing precision
in their respective fields one thinks of Augustus Klock in physics
and Joseph Jablonower in mathematics.

What Felix Adler called a "classical" school did not mean one
concentrating on ancient culture, but more inclusively on the
study of any literature of lasting interest. Latin and Greek, however, both came to be notably well taught by teachers such as Su-
san B. Franklin and Alberta Newton, who exerted a memorable
personal influence on their students as well as teaching them the
classics. In literature classes the excerpts contained in standard
readers were early abandoned in favor of reading whole original
works. The study of foreign languages and literature, begun with
German and French, was extended and deepened with the
growth of the high school division.

The tradition of dramatic festivals promoted by Chubb, with
the warm help of Emma Mueden and others, frequently expressed the school's ethos in free-style ceremony. Though never
myself a student in the school I felt truly included in its spirit
when attending some of these festivals. A wealth of song was also
cultivated in the school. Peter Dykema developed choral singing
of much good music that many students long remembered. (They

*Letter to General Education Board from V. T. Thayer, November 1934.

say a scoffing opponent at a game once exclaimed: why didn't Ethical bring its basketball team instead of its chorus?)

The school was thus realizing a lively balance between general learning and variety with special emphases. Nevertheless, there were problems. Among those that arose with enough frequency to engage Adler's special attention was the following: there were students who showed strong interest and capacity in one or more of the arts while their work in other subjects lagged. These students did not always regard college as the best step for themselves after graduation. There was indeed such a case in Adler's own family. So he came to imagine that somewhat special programs could be built to support and enhance the artistic interest without neglect of other essentials to a liberal education.

Such planning occurred even before 1913, though it was eventually formalized in what was called the Arts High School in that year. It was not a separate school but a differentiation of study programs selectively adapted. Adler described it as follows.

Students who have an active interest in art are given a wider and more thorough training in that subject than their classmates and are taught to perceive that their special interest is closely related to their general course. In history, for instance, they find themselves studying the political activities that made possible the Parthenon. . . . Their course in literature makes them acquainted with poems and plays that filled the minds of the Athenians; and some little reading of Plato and Thucydides helps weave the courses in art, in literature and in history into a living Kulturgeschichte.

We do not confine the history and literature to those phases which possess only an art interest. . . . We make use of the special interest to illuminate and vivify a study of history and literature no less liberalizing than the general courses given to students who do not specialize.

Again, where the general student experiments with formulas of the chemistry textbooks, the student in this art course analyzes the pigments that he is using in painting, the clay and glazes of his pottery, the aniline dyes with which he colors his fabrics, the mordants of his etching. In this process he comes to understand scientific accuracy while learning to be a better craftsman.

It has been our experience that the graduates of this course are technically far more expert than most high school graduates, and in general culture and breadth of interest certainly not inferior.

In its conception and execution the Arts High School program proved broadly educational rather than specialized and technically constraining.

Such appreciation of the differing talents and capacities of students went back to the early days of the elementary school and had continued as an underlying assumption of the program for the high school division. The Arts High School program carried these basic principles one step further toward the ideal Adler had proclaimed at the World's Columbian Exposition.

World War I and its aftermath for a time drew Adler's thoughts and writings primarily to political and economic questions. He was deeply saddened by the war and though he rejoiced at the end of imperial rule in Germany and the dissolution of the former Austro-Hungarian Empire, he was disturbed by various elements of the postwar scene. Given his opposition to colonialism, it was inevitable that he would deplore the strengthening of the British and French empires by the peace settlement. And given his dedication to democracy, it was inevitable that his momentary satisfaction at the downfall of the Tsar would be replaced by opposition to the excesses of Bolshevik communism. In these situations he saw no advance for democracy in the world at large.

In 1921 Adler turned seventy. Recoiling from events which he continued to protest but could not alter, he now dreamed another dream for his school. Basically it was not a new dream but a new attempt to forward a vision he had long harbored. The Ethical Culture School had become an exemplary one in several of the directions he had outlined in his Chicago speech of 1893—in its classical and scientific programs. Other schools had instituted in growing numbers what he had referred to as technological, commercial, and evening programs. But for his own school he wanted still another program. He had remained a man who thought in universalist terms for the good of democracy, and he was not content to have his school serve only the scholarly elite. He remained concerned with how the school's broadly humane and ethical bearings might be enhanced.

It should be acknowledged that personal experience continued to play some part in the direction that Adler's thinking took during his seventies. The much hailed freedom in American colleges impressed him as rather wastefully aimless. His own youthful years in Columbia College had not seemed to him solidly profitable. What followed more productively for him in Germany (1870–73) was actually an education along liberal prevocational lines. So fifty years later he was still thinking of how his school might usefully serve some more differentiated objectives than merely preparing students for college. He believed that the fact that more than 90 percent of the school's graduates aimed to go to good colleges exerted too strong an influence on the selection of entrants to the school in the very first grades.

To counter such influence, Adler decided to add at least two more special programs to the school curriculum, one for students intending to go into business, and one for women looking toward homemaking as their vocation. He spoke of such possible lines of study as prevocational rather than as precollegiate. The prefix "pre" was intended to treat them all as connected branches of a general cultural education rather than to have them isolated vocational studies per se.

Four specialized programs—in arts, science, business and homemaking—were thus envisaged by Adler as desirable possibilities within the future Ethical Cultural School. He could rejoice in finding large and speedy financial support, including a sizeable grant from the Rockefeller Foundation of some $400,000 plus a supplement. It is evident that this support was due to the already high reputation of the school as well as to the appeal of the innovative concept of a prevocational education. Ethical Culture resources brought the funds available to more than a million dollars and permitted construction of a group of new school buildings on a beautiful old farm site in Fieldston in the northwest corner of the city. Adler's proposals thus became known as "the Fieldston Plan." In a memorandum on "the large new educational experiment on which the School is launching forth," he offered the following explanation.

How can a human being be so educated as to be deep and progressive in his speciality, and at the same time have a grasp on the interests and activities of his fellowmen in departments outside his own? This is the problem which the School sets itself to begin to solve. Is there any educational experiment more important and more vital than this?

Briefly, the line of solution is as follows: discover the major bent of the pupil by about the age of sixteen, if possible sooner. Train him along the lines of his paramount faculty and interest. This interest points to one or other of the various vocations—science, technology, business, art, etc. Create a like number of prevocational schools, covering the period of from sixteen to twenty years of age, and linking up directly with the professional schools of the university.

He laid further stress on "the contact points between the chosen vocation and all other vocations. . . . No vocation can be practiced in a large human way, worthy of the dignity of the human personality unless the effects upon other vocations be mastered." This was a crucial issue for him.

Neither Adler's age nor health allowed him now to supervise as closely as hitherto the administration of the school, let alone to develop new branches. Yet he succeeded in promptly engaging new helpers of distinguished quality. In the person of Dr. V. T. Thayer he found a man of high character and a well-prepared educator caring much for people. In 1928 Thayer became educational advisor and later educational director of the Ethical Culture schools. After Adler's death he was also appointed a member of the Board of Leaders of the New York Society for Ethical Culture, so that the leadership of the school and the Society would remain closely connected.

In the late 1920s and early 1930s Dr. Adler, Dr. Thayer, and others all wrote to explain and advocate the new programs intended for Fieldston.* Dr. Thayer sometimes preferred to use the term preprofessional instead of prevocational. From Antioch College came Dr. David Hanchett who spent several years at Fieldston planning and outlining a program of studies for those expecting a career in business. His prebusiness studies included: (a) introduction to economics, and to the efficiencies of various commercial and industrial practices; (b) history of the commercial classes and their relations to the life and culture of various eras; also to the "psychology of nations" (an Adlerian touch); (c) ethics dealing particularly with industrial relations, and joining with studies in history; (d) special work in English and foreign language; and (e) science and art courses related to the history of commerce and industrial development. Simultaneous with such planning, Algernon Black for a time conducted a group of students in the experience of running a school store.

*For an introductory statement of these new programs, with many endorsements, see "A New Departure in Education" (New York: Ethical Culture High School Building Fund, 1927).

Mrs. Daisy Koch, a teacher of history at Fieldston, worked out plans for prevocational home-developing studies for women. It was proposed to include in these: (a) a course in the history of women in different stages of civilization, with appraisal of present problems and opportunities; (b) ethics of marriage and family relations, but also of women's roles in other vocations and in the state; (c) studies in physiology and psychology, especially (i) developmental and child psychology, and (ii) study of character, including group psychology; (d) history of educational movements and systems; and (e) domestic science (food, diet, household arts and economics) including hygiene, chemistry, and physics as affecting both the home and the outlook of the present.

But as these plans went forward, the Great Depression intervened to impose years of retrenchment instead of freedom for experimentation. "The effects upon the Schools," Dr. Thayer later recalled, "were devastating. Not only did it dry up private contributions for expansion, but the collapse of heavy investments drastically reduced the endowments for scholarships which, in the past, had been an important source of enrollments in the Arts High School and were now, hopefully, a potential source to aid young people who might enroll in the new prevocational courses. . . . Some reductions in staff" and occasional heavy deficits could not be avoided.

Moreover, tuition payments from families who could afford to have their children go to college became increasingly more rather than less important for the school. Whatever Adler's personal feelings about the preponderance of this group might be, Dr. Thayer could unquestionably advise trustees that "this is where financial support of the school is coming from." The number of graduates wanting to go to college was approaching 100 percent, and indeed the time was near when it would become a truism that "you have to go to college nowadays to get a job at Macy's."

Given these conditions and trends the number of students expressing any interest in entering the new prevocational programs proved minimal. Under the circumstances, principals and faculty, engaged in maintaining high college entrance standards, found little energy and inspiration to develop radically different and still untested patterns. Some, perhaps including Dr. Thayer, wondered whether Dr. Adler was not wrestling with problems more natural to the college than to the high school years. And even Adler himself considered at times whether his proposals implied that the high school course at Fieldston should be extended from four to six years to accommodate the new studies he recommended.

In large outline the familiar ways of the school continued. And within them there were under Dr. Thayer's guidance certain important phases of progress. Specifically the psychological guidance of students who had emotional problems was amplified with help of psychiatric counsel. The study of international relations and of foreign cultures received more attention. Controversy continued over the teaching of the ethics classes. One may say that more teachers of the regular faculty gave time to such courses, although the Ethics Department continued to be headed by a leader of an Ethical Culture Society.

At Thanksgiving time in 1931, at the age of eighty, Dr. Adler spoke to the students at Fieldston at some length. Though not so intended, it turned out to be a farewell speech to them. And it is interesting that although he dwelt on his lifelong pursuit of the ideal of diversified studies to suit a universal public, Adler made no specific reference to his most recent proposals for prevocational education.

Joseph Jablonower, acting principal of the high school, noted in his introduction that the school had been through life "a darling interest" of Dr. Adler's. To which the latter replied:

I can not tell you how troublesome the darling was. Many a time I would wake at nights because the baby squealed and would not let me rest. There was something wrong with it. Sometimes it was lack of food. There were not enough funds to keep the School going. And sometimes it was the School which did not behave right. There was something the matter with the students or the teaching was not right. So, for over fifty years I have had this child on my hands. It is now grown up to be a fairly sturdy person, no longer just a child.

Thanksgiving is coming the day after tomorrow. I remember the first Thanksgiving in the history of the School which was in 1878. I then started the Kindergarten with three hundred dollars in pocket. I do not know whether you are aware how enormously the expense of keeping up the School has grown. It is now nearly three quarters of a million dollars a year. When the children in the Kindergarten were old enough, I wanted to start a primary school for them. Not having the means, I approached one of the wealthy people who wanted to give money to the Ethical Society, and persuaded him to give it for the School instead. Because I felt that in the School something vital and great could be done that would be more permanent than could be accomplished even by fine meetings on Sunday mornings.

What I had in mind, and what my friends believed in, was a better world. . . . I felt that what is wrong with the world is that so many talents and gifts are going to seed, not used, and that one of the things to remedy it was to cultivate more talents of people that were allowed to run wild. It occurred to me that the students who have no talent for language or mathematics or some other usual subject, might have mechanical talents or artistic gifts to make things with their hands. So instead of setting one standard for all, we said, every human being has some talent—that was the ethical seed—and the thing to do is to cultivate these various talents.

The School does not advertise itself as a school to get you into college. If we can do it, well and good. It does not advertise that it will make you successful in business; that is an incident. We do not want you to be unsuccessful. We do not want you to be inefficient. But what the School is for is to make a better world. And it counts, as Mr. Jablonower said, on me, on the faculty, and on you. We are all cooperating. You are partners with the faculty and the founder, and the many unnamed founders of this School, in doing something big, in helping to make a better world. In order to do that, to make yourself fit for such an undertaking, it is necessary that you should make something of yourself. You must cultivate your best talents in relation to those of others.

This talk to his students clearly states one side of Adler's educational philosophy, that which asks for individual dedication to "making something of oneself." But it does not speak explicitly of the concomitant subject of relatedness, of the social bonds between individuals and between essential groups. However, this side of his vocational idealism belongs inseparably to the personal development Adler stressed.

It has been said that the establishment of the High School of Music and Art and the Bronx High School of Science as part of New York City's public school system shows that Adler's proposals of prevocational programs were neither untimely nor idiosyncratic. Yet in reply Dr. Thayer points out that these schools still aimed at college preparation and did not think of their programs as presenting strongly alternative aims. Moreover, the emphasis on intervocational relations so important in Adler's view did not become particularly evident in these public high schools.

However criticism may run in detail, Adler surely had reason to see the relations of vocational and general culture as a major issue for the future. He did not experience the advent of the nuclear age. He assumed that advances in technology were and would be largely positive and he had no reason to expect unfortunate ecological consequences. The Woman's Liberation movement, some early phases of which he had himself supported, would be amused today by his proposed course in homemaking. In the realm of business education, too, relevant preparation has become highly complex as a consequence of economic and technological changes. Yet the educational future is likely to bring literally myriad interweavings of general and vocational learning at various levels of development.

Dr. Adler had sufficient strength of mind to be characteristically definite and distinctive in his specific proposals. But he also had the range of spirit to be aware of great potentials yet unborn and undefined, as he made clear in dedicating the new school buildings at Fieldston:

This place is an educational temple . . . to train for the growing life of the world. We are erecting here an altar to the Unknown God, the unknown, unpredictable, inconceivable divine things that slumber as yet unborn in the bosom of mankind.

[12]

PROSPECTS FOR ORGANIZED
DEMOCRACY: 1892–1922

THERE WAS MUCH unemployment and hardship in the United States during the long depression of 1893–96. Two great strikes attended by sharp violence drew general public attention. The Homestead strike of the Carnegie Steel workers in 1892 involved pitched battles with armed strikebreakers. And in 1894 the Pullman strike of railroad men in Chicago was broken by the intervention of federal troops despite the pleas of Governor John Peter Altgeld that the state of Illinois was capable of maintaining order. The right and the ability of labor to organize for collective bargaining was emerging as a crucial issue, with much of the American public still little prepared to accept, let alone approve, it.

In the same decade Populist campaigns were spreading through rural America a broad political challenge to the financial leadership of the country, with demands for free coinage of gold and silver, grain credits, an income tax, and public ownership of utilities. The moral outlook of American populism was largely in harmony with the traditional individualistic ideals of the country.

By the turn of the century, debate over the course of the economy was further complicated by developments in our foreign affairs. The Spanish-American War and its aftermath posed the question whether the United States should acquire overseas possessions. Expansionists, with Theodore Roosevelt as an ardent champion, reacted with an emphatic "yes"; but many eminent Americans were strongly anti-imperialist, cherishing, as they did, the democratic ideal that government should be of and by, as well as for, the governed.

Amid the pressure of these events Felix Adler felt compelled to question the prevalent moral standpoint of individualism. He was, indeed, inclined to doubt that democracy could survive if it did not transcend its reigning individualistic norms and habits. An important development of his ethical thought came with his efforts to envision democracy as socially reorganized to advance justice and freedom, both at home and abroad, amid new cultural and technical conditions. His idea of "organized democracy" had its theoretical roots. But it took more concrete shape amid the practical struggles of organized labor to become a reorganized and vital organ of American society, and also in the course of his warning against American entanglement in imperialist rivalries.

During the mid-nineties there flared up also, in world literature especially, a widely voiced radical challenge to bourgeois ideals of marriage and family life. The spokesmen of this revolt were sometimes among the exponents of Socialist thought. But in matters of sex and marriage an extreme individualism was now widely advanced as a vanguard cry of emancipation.

These simultaneous moral challenges—concerning the future of industrial labor, of family life, and of our national aims in expanding foreign relations—all stirred Felix Adler deeply. This chapter and the next two will consider, in turn, how his views matured in each of these areas. And they will describe how he regarded the prospects of democratic society through a needed reorganization.

The Labor Movement

From early manhood to the end of life, Adler had an idealistic vision in which the upward struggling industrial workers appeared as pioneers of a new social order and of a more just type of civilization than the world had yet seen. But he was also realist enough to face with genuine understanding labor's actual situation in the ruthless competition of the expanding American economy after the Civil War, when the labor market was often glutted by great waves of immigrants. He had to maintain a dual perspective upon the raw actuality and the ideal possibility, hoping to find ways for their better convergence. The immediate demands of labor for better hours and wages, vital as they were, could in no way define the scope of what was at stake. Industrialism was producing a new social order and achievement of full dignity for the workers, and the forwarding of their economic, moral, and mental development within this order made the labor question the "chief moral question of the day."

Viewing the labor movement not merely as the concern of a single class for itself and its future but as a means of raising civilization as a whole to new levels, Adler became at once an unflinching advocate and a radical critic of labor's progress. Not blind to values of a competitive economy, he recognized the workingmen's need to organize for a due share of *power* in the market. He was a man who could indeed give battle himself. But in his ideals for society, including commerce and industry, cooperation stood above competition as the more basic and higher social value. He had identified himself early in his career with several cooperative projects, and with the conclusion that labor as well as business needed to learn *social dedication* to inclusive rather than to narrowly self-seeking aims. Yet he was not satisfied with the programs put forward by the Socialists.

Basic contrasts in the programs and leadership offered to American labor in the 1890s come to mind at the mention of Samuel Gompers, Eugene V. Debs, and Daniel DeLeon. Debs and DeLeon were both Marxists and became heads of the Socialist party and of the Socialist Labor party respectively. Both wanted to organize labor in comprehensive industrial unions with political aims of revolutionary scope. Debs (working to achieve an inclusive American railway union) would emerge from militancy and arrest during the Pullman strike to become the U.S. presidential candidate of the Socialist party in five elections beginning in 1900.

During the same period Samuel Gompers had been engaged in bringing many diversified trade unions into a new American Federation of Labor. His policy was to guide union leadership away from political attack on the existing social and economic order to bargaining with employers in what were essentially business terms. When it came to immediate tactics, Adler stood closer to Gompers than to the Socialists, but his view of desirable social and political change went far beyond Gompers's aims. Despite this difference, Gompers publicly voiced appreciation of Adler's aid to the cause of labor. Indeed Ethical Culture's outlook, in respect both to religious liberalism and to active interest in better education and working conditions, moved Gompers to join the New York Society for Ethical Culture.

Though he would return to the subject often in later years, it was in the summer of 1894 that Felix Adler offered the first extended statement of his mature views on the labor movement within the large social context, in a series of twelve lectures at the School of Applied Ethics in Plymouth, Massachusetts. That year the directors of the school had decided to "concentrate all lectures of the present session, whether in the department of Religion, Ethics, or Economics, upon one great subject, the so-called labor question."

It was a timely decision. That April some 20 thousand unemployed men, known as Coxey's Army, had marched to Washington to voice their distress and ask for jobs. And now in June and July federal troops had been sent to Chicago to intervene in the Pullman strike. Thus the discussion of economic and labor problems at Plymouth that summer took place in an atmosphere heightened by these disturbing events.

The *Boston Transcript* reported that this "third annual session of the School of Applied Ethics finds a larger attendance of students than in any previous year. . . . There were nearly a hundred listeners to Professor Adler's opening lecture. . . . There was an impressive spirit of solemnity, in view of the grave need of the hour for just the service which the School this year aims to give to the problems of the day. . . . Plymouth is granting the free use of the High School, in which all the lectures will be given."

The meetings at Plymouth were conceived less as popular forums than as an opportunity for experienced people, trained in different disciplines, to confer on new questions of general moral consequence. Those registered for the sessions were expected to have had experience, either in teaching or in advanced study, in civic or in social service posts, or in church work. The lectures were in the main given by university men. And among these in 1894 were the following from the fields of economics and social and political science: Professors H. C. Adams (Michigan), J. B.

Clark (Amherst), J. W. Jenks (Cornell), F. H. Giddings (Bryn Mawr), E. B. Andrews (Brown), R. Mayo-Smith (Columbia), E. R. L. Gould (Johns Hopkins), Woodrow Wilson (Princeton).

Amid this company of teachers and students, Felix Adler conducted himself wholly as the ethicist, educator, and advocate of social reform that he was. Though alert to current affairs, he did not pretend to the role of a labor leader, a business executive, or an economist. But the twelve lectures he gave that summer were really his first, sustained effort to discuss the labor question in the framework of a general theory of society and of social ethics. This involved his considering not only the labor movement and its immediate concerns, but also the reconstruction of other institutions, such as the schools and the democratic state, within industrialized society. After 1902, when Felix Adler was appointed Professor of Social and Political Ethics at Columbia University, he would further develop his ideas on all of these topics.*

Adler's involvement in the Plymouth lectures was profound. Indeed, he avowed: "There is nothing I have ever done in my life in which I am so deeply interested as in these lectures, and in their aim to vindicate the power of ethics and to do it in scientific fashion."

That statement surely needs comment if one is to go beyond Adler's fervor to understand his conception of purpose. Could he have meant to demonstrate ethical judgments by a scientific analysis of social conditions? Or vice versa, to arrive at knowledge of society by implication from ethical ideas? One would come nearer to his logic in supposing he wished to show that scientific knowledge of the facts revealed necessary functions of ethical ideas to achieve a sufficiently comprehensive and reasonable response to the situation.

To grasp this position more precisely one must recall that all through the 1870s and 1880s Adler had viewed the labor question, not as one of special class interest, but as "the chief moral question of the day," because of its bearing on all the other great questions. Now he felt able to present this view writ large in a

---

*See his *The World Crisis and Its Meaning* (1915). chs. 5, 6, and 7; *An Ethical Philosophy of Life* (1918), ch. 5 of book 1 and book 4; and *The Reconstruction of the Spiritual Ideal* (1924), chs. 4 and 5.

greater range of social data and in less piecemeal fashion than heretofore. People needed to clear their thoughts on what tactics were acceptable in the contemporary labor situation. But the long-term reach of social and political transformation latent in the labor movement was also at issue in the confrontations of 1894. Adler's lectures that summer addressed themselves to definite conclusions both on the immediate and long-range levels, but it is clear that he was most interested in the latter.

He had always been inclined to a more cooperative economy, and he remained so although not on the pattern of either Marxist or state socialism. He gave strong support to the current development of labor unions. Yet in doing so, he declared: "They are indispensable parts of a largely bad system; for they are educating labor in the business ways of bargaining rather than in a vocational spirit of service."*

Right organizing, Adler held, is a vital part of true ethicizing. And he never wavered from the conviction that in the existing competitive system the labor unions have an indispensable role. He attacked the then-prevalent idea that the economy would be better off without them. They are needed to make work more secure and more rational by insisting on "standard rates, a normal day and normal working conditions."

Among acceptable rights of labor unions in the present system is the right to strike for reasonable objectives. And among the reasonable objectives of strikes is recognition of the union and its discipline as a bargaining agent. To insure "right organizing" of a labor union, as Adler meant it, a capacity for bargaining is not enough. Beyond this there needs to come: (a) a function of effectively helping to make industrial relations more socially advanced, and (b) eventually in this same spirit the power of labor to *govern* those relations as worker-owners of them. In the responsible dis-

---

*Adler's lectures at Plymouth in 1894 were devoted to (and in most cases titled): "Opening Exercises; (1) Economics and Ethics; (2) Continuation-Boundaries of Ethics & Economic Science; (3) The Economic Principle; (4) Unionizing of Labor; (5) Individualism; (6) Socialism; (7) Influence of Industrial & Social Conditions upon the Family; (8) The Ethics of Remuneration [critique of labor theory of value]; (10) Organic Education [Adler's own idea]; (11) The State and Economic Progress; (12) The Church & the Labor Question." These lectures exist in typescript only; the numbering of lectures 5, 7, and 8 is my own (HLF).

cipline of labor organization Adler believed new social virtues would replace inadequate individualistic ones.

He sought to be fair rather than one-sidedly partisan in his appraisal of labor practices, many of which were still poorly defined and evaluated in law. He made some rather broad generalizations, for example, about boycotts and sympathetic strikes. Boycotts are usually unacceptable weapons, he argued, since their harm is apt to spread too indiscriminately to the innocent. Sympathetic strikes are also suspect of involving the same party and its friends in the role both of judge and prosecutor. He approved peaceful picketing but cautioned against its too easy involvement with intimidation and violence.

In 1894 (the very year that Adler was expressing these views in Plymouth) the Wisconsin economist, John R. Commons, circulated a questionnaire on labor problems. One question which he addressed to labor leaders asked them to rate religious and professional groups in the order in which they supplied the best and most persistent "advocates of the cause of labor." The reply of Samuel Gompers, president of the still new American Federation of Labor was:

1. Members of Ethical Societies
2. Unitarians
3. Non-believers
4. Catholics
5. Protestants
6. Jews
7. Ministers
8. Physicians
9. Lawyers

The top and bottom of this list have some interest; but one must remember that Gompers was himself an early member of the New York Society for Ethical Culture and was joined with others there in combating sweatshops and poor working conditions.

However close they were in some efforts, in his hopes and aims for radical social transformation through the labor movement Adler looked quite beyond Gompers's ethos of competitive business and its bargaining. His radicalism, however, was also distinct and different from that of the class-struggle radicals and labor revolutionists.

Samuel Gompers would not have defended trade unions by calling them "indispensable parts of a largely bad system." But since Felix Adler did use this expression, it was incumbent upon him to say what was bad about the existing system and to evaluate proposed alternatives. This led him beyond measures of immediate relief to a critique of rival social programs and ideologies. In the 1890s both socialism and populism were acutely challenging traditional individualism.

In the years from 1894 through 1896 Adler addressed himself to all three ideologies—Individualist, Socialist, and Populist. Though he found none adequate as a comprehensive outlook, he did recognize some points of permanent importance in each. And he wanted to do more than to reject, he wanted to propose a fourth view which appealed to him as more whole and truly constructive. At first he often used the term "Vocationalism" to designate this, but eventually (by 1916 at least) he was referring to it as his view of the needed reconstruction of what he called "Organized Democracy."

Adler's estimate and critique of Individualism had been rather consistent from his earlier years before his lectures at Plymouth in 1894. But ever more keenly he felt that under an individualist, laissez-faire economy, democracy is doomed to fail in the control of an advancing industrial order. At Plymouth in 1894 he said of Individualism:

> As a system of life it has fallen into deserved disrepute, yet the world remains under a permanent debt to the individualist philosophy. It made men realize as never before their individual rights, and the importance of protecting those rights. This message can never become obsolete.
> But what Individualism covers up with its doctrine of a hidden harmony flowing from enlightened self-interest is the fact that men are not equally able to protect their rights. The wolves are thus allowed to run away with the sheep.

Inequalities of gain and power follow from unequal ability to protect oneself in a laissez-faire economy under an individualist philosophy. Also, production falls into an anarchic kind of direction or lack of direction. Inequality of purchasing power leads to high demand for extravagant luxuries at one end of the scale, and for cheap necessities and stimulants at the other. The efficiency of machines used with insufficient regard for social consequences results in frequent depressions and severe unemployment.

Since such points are close to the criticisms of the existing economic system emphasized by Marxists, the question promptly arises: Is not socialism the answer? Adler indeed granted that Marx pointed to the gravest human and moral fault of our industrial society in noting that the workers become "alienated," divorced from vital control over their work. But, while he also agreed that radical changes of organization are needed to correct this condition, he was unconvinced that the Socialist call "to expropriate the exploiters" would prove the effective road to real worker control and a more humane industrial order.

Adler differed from the Marxists on other issues as well. While they saw economic revolution as a necessary precondition of better education for the masses, Adler had concluded that a fitting education was a necessary prerequisite for a true liberation of labor. And he saw difficulties in the underlying assumptions of the Socialists. In a Socialist state, he pointed out, "the citizens must possess . . . an enlarged and enlightened intelligence, a willingness to be determined by remote rather than proximate ends and universal disinterestedness of the most sublime order."

Adler's criticism of socialism came both in his lectures at Plymouth in 1894, and again the next year in several addresses at Carnegie Hall for the New York Society for Ethical Culture. A passionate appeal to throw off oppression and to liberate labor by mass action was readily understandable, he said. Yet it seemed to him to harbor a great illusion and oversimplification. Psychologically he called it an appeal to "mass egoism" that did not do enough justice to diverse relations and creative interests. If labor is viewed simply as an unpropertied mass, its discipline to manage a complex industrial life will be impossible, he predicted, without prolonged coercion under dictatorial leadership. Yet the world of commerce and industry should not and need not be abandoned either to raw competition under unregulated individualism or to coercive regimentation under "proletarian" dictators.

Adler's fear of Socialist bureaucracy was rather immediately conditioned in 1894 by the spectacle of America's corrupt politics, as when he asked his audience to consider how

Our "bosses" and "rings," our professional politicians, have made our name a reproach to us among all nations. . . . Consider what would happen if these same bosses and rings and professional politicians should gain control not only of post-offices and departments of public works and police departments, but of all the manifold industries upon which the sustenance of the people depends.

His immersion in urban affairs and lack of familiarity with the farmer's problems shows in Adler's far stronger concern with the labor movement than with the contemporary waves of populism. Yet, in fact, his own views in favor of a "mixed economy" led him to an independent endorsement of some measures that Populists were advocating in the 1890s. He had been speaking for income taxes, largely to support education, ever since the 1870s. And as for utilities, he was now inclined to favor some features of "municipal socialism" and even some broader measures of public operation. A special vocabulary which he used in 1894 to advocate a "mixed economy" held that state regulation (or possibly ownership) was needed for "homogeneous" industries, that is for such as provide a uniform resource or service in great quantity, e.g., water, power, light, transportation, and mail. The need here was to assure common availability on equitable terms as against discriminatory rates and combines. But in "heterogeneous" industries the desirable variety in production, experiment, and risk should be fostered by freer conditions. A socialized uniformity imposed here could have deplorably deadening effects. Indeed, Adler's argument in favor of legislative control of public utilities was put largely in terms of freeing the rest of the economy from uniform authority and direction.

Adler was not sympathetic to the radical financial demands of the Populists for free coinage of gold and silver. When coinage became a national issue in the election of 1896, he was moved to speak out strongly against Bryan's campaign for free silver. Explaining that he himself was far from being an uncritical spokesman for high finance, he nonetheless believed that Bryan was fostering a dangerous illusion in recommending easy money as an aid to the people. Much given to graphic parables, Adler likened

Bryan's proposal "to knock the bottom out of the standard of value" to "an impulse of resentful steerage passengers who would cut a hole in the bottom of their ship underneath the first-class saloon—thereby to destroy their enemies."*

Adler not only rejected "free silver" as a remedy for the ills of the day but also questioned other proposed solutions. "I am astonished," he said, speaking at Plymouth in 1894, "that the labor question is so often stated as if it were merely a question of securing a more equitable distribution of wealth. To my mind the main point is to secure a more equitable distribution of men among the various callings." In this statement, and the explanation that followed it, Adler was at last striking the fundamental note that dominated his own view, which he then called Vocationalism, and which he maintained was the key to the kind of Organized Democracy that was needed. Yes, labor must bargain collectively for shorter hours and better wages (it is shocking to recall what was then customary). But he believed that the long-run labor problem was to get rightly qualified men into the right jobs for the world's work. And insofar as they helped forward this end, the labor unions would be serving not just a special class interest but the universal cause of civilization.

Insofar as labor's rights had become identified with helping "to rationalize the world both in its production and consumption," Adler contended that an ethical charge is placed upon us all: "Interest in the best discharge of social service . . . brings into line the ethics of the market with the ethics of family, of citizenship, and harmoniously relates the industrial life with the intimate sanctities of the human heart."

Adler's ideal of Vocationalism made a close connection between the labor problem and all high ethicism. It implied the following essential conditions: (a) fitness of the worker for the particular task in which he engaged; (b) value of the task as a means of real human growth; (c) right relations with fellow-laborers in the same

---

*Nevertheless, in the national election of 1900, Felix Adler voted for Bryan rather than McKinley. Adler had not dropped his opposition to Bryan's espousal of a free silver policy, but he felt even more strongly about the issue of imperialism which had come to the fore after the Spanish-American War, and here his views accorded with Bryan's.

calling; and (d) right relation of each calling to other callings. As to the last point, Adler sometimes expressed it by saying the "laborers are to understand the *science* (i.e., the interrelations) of their calling."

His ideal being of this kind, Adler could well declare that "the elimination of poverty is not the end" (at most it is only a beginning of the labor problem). The end is "to sustain the laborer in proper exercise of his function, to have the function of his calling performed in the best possible way." Explanations of this sort are found in Adler's Columbia University seminar lectures (e.g., 1906, 1908, etc.).

In essence, the purpose of Vocationalism was to offer a social alternative both to Individualism and to the absolute sovereignty of the state or any other single institution. In this line of thought, sovereignties were absolute, if at all, only for specific agents in their special fields. In their elaborations the Columbia seminars include frequent detailed criticism of many absolutists and individualists with a quite considerable variety of shadings.

Vocationalism as Adler preached it was clearly a professional man's ethic. It demanded a scientific preparation for excellence in one's work and it called for putting social service ahead of self-serving. These were the points that he regarded as too little stressed in most talk about "the human factor in industry." It is not rest, food, and shelter that decisively raise men above the brutes, but mental and moral activities. To respect the human factor in industry must mean to regard and respect the worker as a responsible and creative person, as a whole man concerned with the thought, the method, and the consequence of his work.

Yet an obvious doubt attended the idea of applying so high-pitched a vocational ideal to the current labor problem. Could one really expect workers on the assembly line to think of themselves as following a vocation? No, said Adler in 1894, no one can be blind to "the gap that now separates factory labor from the requirements of a vocational theory." The answer is that the existing factory system must be transitional to

one which would impose more and more of the drudgery upon the machine itself and take it away from the man, that would distribute the remaining drudgery as a toll to be paid by many in as few hours as possible, and would find more and more room for supplementary work to counteract the monotony of machine labor.

And beyond this, Adler put a further stress on education for the workingman in the whole range of his human capacity. Vocationalism thus linked industrial reorganization with general humanistic advance. It bade both labor and business to promote a more thorough and humane education with respect to the economy and to polity in general.

Adler declared that his vocational view of industrial relations was "a song of labor not yet sung." In both the competitive bargaining of AFL unionism and the revolutionary thrust of the Socialists he missed a controlling emphasis upon organizing specialized excellences for comprehensive social development. Perhaps his own concentration on this point can also be questioned as an overrationalized ideology of a professional man. Intended to be comprehensive, perhaps it does not allow enough for what is fertile within the confusion and hurly-burly of society.

Yet it was with this kind of professional ideal in mind that Adler, when speaking in 1901 on "The Highest Hopes for Humanity" in the new century, outlined the following hope for the labor movement:

The working classes must realize, I think, that the goal before them is not just to secure the advantages which other classes already possess, but rather to secure for themselves, and to confer upon others, benefits which no class as yet possesses; in short, that their true mission is to be the harbingers and the pioneers of a social order with a loftier type of morality than the world has yet known. This new, broader, truer, social morality will be at once the condition and the reward of their real success. The working class can rise only on the condition that they raise us all with them, and that they lift us up where it is most needful and most blessed for us to be exalted, namely, in our moral part.

The Role of the State

In one of his Plymouth lectures, entitled "The Relation of the State to Economic Progress," Adler had developed several ideas that would be crucial in the evolution of his notion of "organized democracy." The ownership of property, Adler declared, should be suitable to function and purpose. And with this in mind he distinguished three types of ownership. Private ownership is appropriate, he said, to goods held directly for individual consumption, such as food, garments, and homes. Public or state ownership, per contra, is suited to serve certain very general common needs. Thus, in 1894 Adler spoke favorably of state control and eventual ownership of what he called "homogeneous industries," such as "the mail service, railways, telegraph, etc. that enter into and affect all industrial activity whatsoever . . . so that in the interest of an increasing diversification of production, it is required that the homogeneous class of services shall not be withheld from any member of the community." The battle to outlaw discriminatory railroad rates illustrated that point. But Adler wanted to stress still more the importance of a third type of ownership, which he called "group ownership" of the properties involved in pursuing specific "heterogeneous industries" by those engaged in such a line of work or calling.

Adler mentioned the aim of diversifying production and of encouraging "the freest functional activity" as a reason for preferring group ownership of such industries over state ownership of all the means of production. But this preference was also grounded in his vocationalist ethical ideal of developing strong, responsible personality through shared and knowledgeable control of one's work. "Group ownership," he said, "is to favor the ethical ends of a calling. Every worker is to have an interest in the business, and is to be encouraged to contribute to the advancement of the calling."

Adler recognized that what he advocated could not be immediately practiced except in pioneer instances. Still he wanted to indicate a direction of industrial development that seemed to him more salutary than the existing order of private control or than general socialism with direct public control. He urged individual business leaders to share governing responsibilities and profits with their workers. And he advised that labor unions should aim to become employers themselves and achieve group ownership and organization of industries for public service.

In the language of a later day (the 1960s) Adler was advocating "participatory" democracy in his thoughts on group ownership and control of industries. But he believed it was crucial that participation be connected with specific qualification. Under the existing pattern of individualistic democracy, suited perhaps to agrarian life, the politics of a complex industrial society failed to connect specific qualification and participation. He came to doubt that representative government, where the individual citizen cast his one vote simply as a resident of a district, could produce democratic control of advancing industrial society, with its immense web of interdependent special tasks. Adler's active experience with city politics during the 1880s and 1890s too frequently revealed boss control of parties and party manipulation of helpless electorates. "Our system of government," he came to conclude, "may be described as a system carried on by professional politicians, in league with powerful special interests, intermittently modified and sometimes irresistibly directed by the force of public opinion." By the turn of the century his doubts were enlarged by a sense of growing crisis for democracy. And the engaging of democratic states in imperialistic conflicts and wars (e.g., the Boer War, the Spanish-American and Philippine wars), resulting in dominion over unrepresented peoples, deepened Adler's sense of gathering crisis.

So, besides wanting to see the people in an industry develop greater participation in its control, Felix Adler also became receptive to suggestions for restructuring representative government of industrial states. His thinking on this matter was reinforced by current discussions on government, including a book published in 1897 by a French writer, Charles Benoist, *La crise de l'état moderne. De l'organisation du suffrage universel.* In this work it was proposed that universal suffrage should be organized so that members of legislatures would be elected to represent vocational or functional groups rather than geographical areas. Otherwise, Benoist argued, the voter would in effect be represented only as a victim of the professional politician. This was very much Adler's own conclusion.

He continued to propound the idea of vocational representation throughout subsequent years, as a device for improving the quality of democratic government. Yet he looked for political reform to come only gradually, out of free development within the organization of industries and professions, rather than by legal imposition from above or revolution from below. In *An Ethical Philosophy of Life* (1918), where Adler described most explicitly his view of "vocational representation," he stressed that he did not want it "regarded as a mere device in the mechanism of politics."* It appealed to him as a step in advancing the ethical purpose of society and of the state in the upbuilding of people and their relations.

Although many disappointments, above all World War I, with all its attendant horrors, had sobered Adler's hopes, he still maintained in 1918 that if a reorganizing of industry in the vocational key could actually be realized, it would be "a world reformation greater than any other." It would introduce a higher type of civilization than the world had yet seen.

And in his seventy-first year, in an address to the Society on January 15, 1922, he looked back again at his course, and recalled:

> The Ethical Movement was started with the labor situation in view as one stinging motive. The desire to contribute to the evolution from an unjust society into a just society was present at the initiation of it. That interest has never ceased and must never cease. . . . Ancient civilization was founded on the conception that culture depends on maintaining the privileged few, and there never has been a time when the world was otherwise arranged.
>
> But "No" say the ghosts of plebeians, peasants, Chartists, the millions of the past that trail behind the labor unions of our day. The workers of today are but the present column of a great procession that has been marching, marching for ages. Civilization, they say, the real, the true civilization depends not on the maintenance of privilege but on the abolition of privilege. . . . The labor movement, so far as it stands for that, is an ethical movement, and I am with it, heart and soul.

Testing in Action

In his work for a better organized industrial society, and for labor's due share in democracy, Dr. Adler did not confine his efforts to lecturing. Important as his 1894 lectures at Plymouth were in articulating his ideas, he wished to forward their application in action, and occasionally participated in the arbitration of

---

*See also *The Reconstruction of the Spiritual Ideal.*

specifié labor disputes. He further attempted to educate himself and others in these matters by bringing together at small gatherings in his study men of various callings to discuss leading issues in economic and political ethics touching on the personal concerns and activities of those present.

Another man who became deeply and significantly involved in these crucial issues of business ethics and practice was the then rising Massachusetts lawyer, Louis D. Brandeis. Brandeis was a second cousin of the Joseph and Regina Goldmark children, and in 1891 the relationship was compounded by his marrying Alice Goldmark, a younger sister of Mrs. Adler, in a ceremony performed by Felix Adler. It was not the case, however, that either Brandeis or Adler led the other in his economic thinking. Brandeis lived in Boston and was not a member of Adler's discussion circles, nor do they appear to have corresponded much upon economic questions. But the ideal of what Adler called Vocationalism, emphasizing excellence of work and social function above self-serving, was independently convergent despite some significant differences with the spirit of Profession that Brandeis was recommending as a guideline to both business and labor.

A significant day dawned in the labor relations of the garment trades with an industry-wide strike in New York in 1910, involving some 75 thousand workers. Both Brandeis and Adler (at first through some of his followers on both sides of the conflict) became centrally involved in the efforts at reconstruction.

In *The Promised City*, Moses Rischin, basing his comments on research in the Jewish literature and journals of the time, asserts "the Ethical Culture Society led the way in seeking a settlement of the strike." While this is a role that the Society as such could hardly claim, it is true that members of the Society, and eventually Adler himself, were prominent on both sides, first in arbitrating the dispute and then in helping oversee the subsequent working out of the agreements made in the course of settlement.

One such man among the manufacturers strongly interested in new policies toward labor was Max Meyer, who prized much in Adler's teaching on the labor movement. So also, though with a difference, did the lawyer engaged as counsel by the Manufacturers Association, Julius Henry Cohen.

On the other side, living among the garment workers, was

Henry Moskowitz, who had been active in starting the downtown Ethical Society which later became the Madison House settlement on the Lower East Side. By 1907 Moskowitz had also joined the leadership of the main New York Society. He and his future wife Bella worked hard and without cease toward fruitful negotiation of the strike. The chief legal counsel for the labor interests was Meyer London.

A crucial point of disagreement was the union's demand for a closed union shop, which would make union membership a condition of employment in the industry. The manufacturers were not ready to relinquish control of hiring and firing to that extent but the unions were adamant in pressing this demand.

As this impasse developed, someone suggested that Louis D. Brandeis might be the ideal man to arbitrate in the strike. Those who wanted to open a new path with labor felt that his record for industrial statesmanship could help build a needed bridge with the unions. And up to a point it did. (It has been said that A. Lincoln Filene, a leading Boston merchant whose department store trade was being damaged by the strike, was urged by Henry Moskowitz to persuade Brandeis to work for a settlement.)

Brandeis found the manufacturers would not settle, and he himself thought they should not settle for "closed union shops." Instead he made his famous proposal of "preferential union shops," by which agreed-upon union standards would prevail, where discrimination against union members would cease; and, given equal qualifications, preference in hiring workers would be given to union members. At this point, according to Moses Rischin, a dispute over terminology put the proposed settlement in danger:

[Julius Henry] Cohen's "treaty of peace" upset union leaders as much as [Meyer] London's "collective agreement" disturbed employers. Finally, Jacob Schiff, ever jealous of the reputation of the Jewish community, summoned Louis Marshall to break the deadlock. Marshall solved the semantic difficulty by suggesting the word "protocol."*

The Protocol brought a package of crucial new decisions. Among the lines of reorganization in the industry projected in 1910 were: cooperation with the unions to maintain and improve

*Moses Rischin, *The Promised City* (Cambridge: Harvard University Press, 1962), p. 252.

standards of employment and work; a Board of Arbitration for the industry with supplementary grievance machinery in the hope of doing away with strikes; and establishment of a Joint Board of Sanitary Control for the advance of health standards in garment manufacture. The last of these proposals was given extra force by widespread public reaction to the tragic Triangle fire in 1911, in which 146 female shirtwaist workers lost their lives and many were badly injured because of a lack of safety provisions.

Further progress lay in the advance of education for the entire range of operations in the garment or needle trades. Such education was indeed a key element in the vocational concept of work that Felix Adler was advocating. And the development in this instance was one in which Max Meyer took prominent, creative part, including the launching of the High School of the Needle Trades.

A forward step in labor relations though it was, getting the preferential union shop policy to work was beset with problems. Louis Brandeis agreed to become the first chairman of the industry's new Board of Arbitration. He hoped that occasions for formal arbitration would be few. But wrangling over interpretations and breaches of agreement abounded and though the number of strikes was reduced they did not, as had been hoped, cease. The more radical union leaders wanted to square the preferential union shop with the circle of their control. Brandeis tried to convince them that the preferential shop principle would allow them to achieve full union shops on the basis of merit instead of by coercion of employers and employed.

After some four or five years, many business and even some union leaders began to feel that attempts to apply the garment trade protocol, in matters of hiring and firing especially, were causing harassment and frustration. New individuals came to the fore who were impatient of "uplifters" and conciliators. Some even made deals with racketeers for protection against obstructive opponents. A depressed economy around 1913 made the going harder.

In 1915, with the Protocol truly imperiled, a Council of Conciliation was appointed by Mayor John Purroy Mitchel in an effort to save what had been hailed as a great advance. Julius Henry

Cohen and now Morris Hillquit, as counsel respectively for the manufacturers and for labor, both recommended that Dr. Felix Adler be chairman of the proposed council, and he was so appointed. This was indeed a high tribute to his long and balanced interest in labor problems.

The council's task was not that of arbitration; its role was to hold hearings and make recommendations on the conduct of the industry. This it did, calling many witnesses to its sessions, which were held from July 13 to July 23, 1915. Brandeis was a member of this Council of Conciliation and shared Adler's view that both business and labor should cultivate a professional commitment to excellence, integrity, and service.

In the recommendations accepted in August 1915 by both union and manufacturers' representatives, there was this synoptic statement:

The principle of industrial efficiency and that of respect for the essential human rights of the workers should always be applied jointly, priority being assigned to neither. . . . Peace and progress depend upon complete loyalty in the effort to reconcile them.

If one understands by the term "industrial efficiency" the somewhat larger concept of excellent work, the above statement can stand as a limited application of Adler's vocational and of Brandeis's professional ideal for organized industries.

Yet there was also a significant difference between the positions taken by the brothers-in-law. Brandeis was more concerned than Adler with protecting and preserving fair competition and bargaining within society as a whole. He distrusted bigness of organization and, as far back as 1904, had said "Prolonged peace and prosperity can rest only upon the foundation of industrial liberty." Adler had always looked with strong hope toward a harmonizing of interests in the economy and a trend to cooperation. Such expectation was expressed, for example, in his statement at Plymouth in 1894:

Let the different classes that make up society stand face to face with one another, and they will not only come to terms, but to a clearer understanding of their mutual interdependence; and the consciousness of their unity which is at present dim and ineffective will more and more become a felt and living power.

Widely varying judgments have been expressed about the effect of the Council of Conciliation, which Adler chaired in 1915. A biographer of Brandeis has said that it left the conflict-filled situation virtually unchanged. Pressures moving in the contrary directions of fuller union control on the one hand and fuller liberty for management on the other still continued. Yet the reconstructive efforts of 1910–16 in the garment trades projected principles and aims that exerted a profound influence beyond that industry.

Though practice and application remain very uneven, recognition in principle of a preferential union shop policy, and of the educational and welfare roles of unions, became widespread in subsequent years. Still the situation with regard to "industrial liberty" is far from realizing the fair dealing that Brandeis associated with that concept. And Adler's ideal of harmonious interdependence is far from satisfied in the kind of relationship between unions and management that has developed in many industries since that time.

[13]

MARRIAGE AND FAMILY IN
ORGANIZED DEMOCRACY: 1876–1927

THAT INDUSTRIALISM IN ITS advance would effect many changes in family life was a belief Felix Adler shared with some of his contemporaries, but he resisted the view that these changes must bring a loosening of family ties or, indeed, an end of the family's role as a major agency of social cohesion, ideas which had become widespread early in the twentieth century.

For his part, Adler hoped for and believed in a future that would bring new strength, rather than a decline; a renewal of the family's importance to society as well as to its individual members. His conception of its enduring role was interwoven, not only with his religious view, but also with his vocational prospect for social organization. Conservation and progressive features were thoroughly joined in his thought of the family's future, but he was unable to imagine a viable society without the vital contributions of family life.

He observed that the family had always taken some special shape from the larger social frame in which it existed. Thus it had often been designed to preserve particular castes or feudal inheritances of property. It was Adler's thesis that there was now a pressing need to reconceive its role within the context of industrial and democratic society, since no adequate grasp of its functions in that setting had yet become clear. We may expect family life to bear still finer fruit, he declared, if the way of falsely conceiving democracy along purely individualistic lines is overcome, and we advance "toward higher and truer definitions of the democratic idea." In this belief his hopes for the family were inseparably part of his total outlook on social development.

Despite all his strong critique of individualism as a general philosophy, he always defended individual freedom in the choice of

159

mates and protested against parental interference with it. "There are certain intimate rights of moral selfhood," he said, "over which each one is bound to stand guard, and which no one has the right to relinquish, and the right of idiosyncracy in the choice of a marriage partner is one of these." Such a position clearly sets a fundamental limit to parental control of the family, whether that be exercised for worldly advantage or out of religious conservatism.

But whatever his vision of desirable changes, it was from first to last "the monogamic family, with an expectation of exclusive and permanent bonds" between husband and wife that actively concerned Felix Adler. He did not, of course, overlook the fact that many very different forms of the family existed both in the past and in the present. But he held that historical experience established some moral results beyond question, and the strictly monogamic family he viewed as one of the assured, indubitable achievements of human development. Indeed, as a young man, at the start of his public career, his rhetoric hailed this type of family as "the noblest invention of human genius . . . and the foundation of all morality."

For more than a decade after the foundation of the Ethical Culture Society in 1876, Adler encountered no controversy because of this belief, since it expressed the prevailing sentiment of his public in those years. Later on, in the course of the 1890s, when debate over Victorian family ethics became widely joined, Adler was drawn repeatedly to argue in hot defense of the proposition that:

There is no doubt, in the mind of all who think justly upon such matters, that the permanent, the—as a rule—indissoluble union of a single wedded pair is the highest type of marriage which has been evolved, and that, whatever future developments may take place, the continuance of it must be assumed, and all changes must be in the direction of more perfectly realizing the ideal of monogamy, which at the present time, is still an ideal to which the practice of the world has by no means been thoroughly assimilated. [1899]

This stance had mixed consequences. In his ministerial capacity Adler was, of course, much consulted for family advice, and not a few people were put off by counsel which they found intolerably confining. Others were ever grateful that their home relations had been saved and strengthened because Adler had personally helped them deal with severe trials. In the more open forum of ideas he could also be appreciated, and was so, for presenting a conservative view of the marriage tie that did not appeal to supernatural fiat and sanctions. But at the same time there were critics who felt that he had actually deserted the liberal cause by teaching a family ethics that failed to realize the freer choices in personal relations made possible by new conditions and insights.

Such criticism may too easily dismiss Adler's efforts as nothing more than rearguard actions in defense of the Victorian family. For this would overlook the important ways in which, from the outset, he worked to change the conventional mold in favor of an ampler design for the family. As long as Victorianism was a dominant climate, he had no call to defend the basic principles of the monogamic family, but was free to focus upon what he thought this institution needed for its further "perfecting" in modern democracy. Right from the start of his public career he stressed three points. There should be, first of all, a more equal partnership of men and women. Adler was a steady advocate of educating women, beyond social "finish," to a stature fully complementing that of men. But closely tied to this was a second, sustained care for more light on the development of children, an understanding of childhood that would better nurture "humanity in the young." He was not a man to disparage instinct and feeling in woman's "natural vocation to motherhood," but he believed that these would not be enough. So he urged women to equip themselves also with a "professional expertness" by scientific study of child growth, and he saw great promise of progress in this.

A third objective, perhaps still more distinctive of Adler's inclusive ideals, was that there be more active interplay between family life and other community interests, so as to modify "family egoism" and the overvaluing of artificial luxury too prevalent in the upper middle class. An effective mitigating of family egoism and narrow interests must, of course, involve all the relations between a family and other groups in the wider spheres of life. Yet near the beginning of his career (and before his own marriage in 1880, be it said) Adler raised the question whether a direct assault upon this problem might be advantageously made through the experiment of a number of families, perhaps five or six, undertaking to live "cooperatively" in adjacent homes with certain quarters and facilities in common.

Each family would have its private sleeping, dining, and reception rooms; but there might be a common kitchen, laundry, garden, kindergarten, and "art-room." The value of the idea would lie partly in the esthetic prospect of making gardens, spacious halls, and ceremonious living possible to families with moderate means, but still more in the educational advantage of bringing a group of young children together without necessarily separating them from the supervision of their own mothers, who would themselves be the "kindergartners." Also, the plan could prevent the duplication of household chores, and would permit of making domestic service a more independent profession with less personal subservience. Finally, each group of families living in such cooperation might undertake the rearing with them of one or more "neglected children."

This whole description combines beautifully the different aims and the spirt animating Adler's other cooperative proposals in his early ventures toward humanizing industrial society.

For a moment, just after the marriage of Felix Adler and Helen Goldmark, it seems that they and some of their artist friends (the Douglas Volk and the George de Forest Brush families among them) may have contemplated such an experiment in combined family living. Though it was not pursued, Adler occasionally referred to the idea in later years. As late as 1918 in the chapter, "The Family," in his *Ethical Philosophy of Life,* he says:

The question may be raised whether the single family should remain the primary social unit, or whether a group of families united in close cooperation would better fulfill the purposes for which the family exists. . . . One great advantage would result if care were taken to include in the group persons belonging to different vocations—scientist, scholar, architect, lawyer, artist. Young persons as they mature would then have the benefit of contact with those who are intimately familiar with different lines of vocational activity, and would be helped to know their own mind as to their future career better than they commonly do now.

This last remark is typical of the constant joining of domestic, vocational, and educational considerations in Adler's thought on the family.

But nowhere were the conservative leanings and the progressive features of his thought more fully blended than in his ideas on what might be the functions of women in better organized democracy. The great majority of women should build up in new scope, he thought, their "natural vocation to motherhood." In this he gave little pleasure to the new feminists, who were bent on opening many careers to women. Adler sent two of his daughters to Smith College in preference to Bryn Mawr—which had been attended by his sisters-in-law and later also by nieces—because he though that Bryn Mawr education under M. Carey Thomas emphasized vocational interests that led away from homemaking.

Yet, in this attitude Adler was not advocating a narrow *Küche, Kinder, Kirche* concept of women's sphere or of their capacities. Let there be equality of opportunity, he said, for the higher education of women in "colleges, professional, and post-graduate schools. It is equality alone that will make woman mature for the appreciation and exercise of liberty." He discussed this subject in public addresses at least eight times between 1878 and 1883, and from years thereafter some twenty or more such lectures have been preserved. In 1883 he declared:

Every girl should fit herself to render some service to society by which she may gain the means of self-support, and this independently of the question whether her parents are wealthy or not. . . . The true independence of woman demands that she should be able to maintain herself.

Nevertheless, in the progress of events it became clear that Adler's interest in the higher education of women did not have the primary aim of encouraging them actually to follow many diversified careers. Yes, they should have a hedge against economic dependency. But mainly he hoped that the great majority of women would apply their better training and broader outlook to what he considered to be three major and consummate ends of life—to their becoming "more complete partners of their husbands, more intelligent mothers of their children," and vital agents for a more humane integrating of society at large. Specialization in our advanced industrial culture brings with it a danger of reducing life to role-playing, to becoming a "repertory of various parts"; a great society needs, besides efficiency in specific functions, to care for the quality of its human wholeness.

As has been seen, Adler laid much emphasis on the importance of vocational excellence as a mainspring of future society. In fact, he believed that with industrial advance democracy could only survive if it were "organized" to assure greater influence of vocational expertness dedicated to social ends. But a balance, an integrating or harmonizing of specific productivities must also be achieved, if society was to uphold, and not disfigure, a true and generous version of human life. In large part such integration must be a concern of citizenship, a function of the state. But Adler believed that it must also be deeply nurtured in close relationships that are primarily intent upon "total persons" rather than upon specific roles. To give this essential nurture would continue to be, he thought, a chief contribution of family life. For the family, he said, is

a group numerically small, and yet sufficiently diversified to include in miniature the (formative experience) of three-fold relation to superiors, equals, and inferiors; furthermore, the bond of unity can there be secured by strong natural feelings of attraction toward the total being of others.

[It can be] a perpetual hearth or laboratory in which the partial fruits of development derived from the other social institutions are worked into the unity of character. . . . It is not too much to say that all the social institutions are spiritualized in virtue of the demands which the family makes upon them.

Augmenting this conviction about the family, Adler also believed that women are especially fitted and indicated to be an integrating influence, caring for "total" or complete human fruition. And he thought of a distinctive feminine role of this kind as played not only within the close family circle, but as a factor helping to harmonize all social spheres to serve a complete human ideal. It was with such a role and perspective in view rather than a career aim that Adler advocated the broadening of educational opportunity for women.

It should be added that he did not come by this idea of a distinctive feminine vocation simply to meet the exigency of his social theory, with its need to find forces favoring a balance of interests and wholeness of development. But neither did he adduce impressive empirical evidence for his view of "woman's nature." It may be that socially integrating influences are more culturally than sexually determined, and that some men as well as some women have greater individual aptitude than others to serve in this way. But Adler undoubtedly took his view out of a legacy of romantic idealism. He took it from Goethe and Tennyson, perhaps with some harking back to Dante, and some later confirming by Lotze and others that

Woman has an "assembling faculty"—*das alles in einander webt*—she has intuition of the whole and Sibylline powers of divination. She has a psychic disposition to guard over the whole of particular lives entrusted to her, and a gift for intuitively grasping the totality of concrete effects, whereas man's aggressive strides to conquer new ground are necessarily one-sided and need her complementing.

If it came to an issue between "the new woman" and "the eternal womanly," Adler said in 1897 that he was decidedly on the side of the latter. Yet he added that he wanted to affirm as much as ever the need for removing artificiality from women's education, for opening up the professions (though factory labor by women should eventually be rendered unnecessary), and for replacing the assumption that "woman's reason is weaker than man's" by admitting her fully as a partner in counsel. Despite Adler's reckoning of an American attitude toward women as one of our "national greatnesses," there probably always remained in him an Old World element of distance between the sexes. Across this distance he built his rather exalted bridge of speculative generalizations about the nature of woman.

If his ideas on women had this romantic idealizing aspect, another side of his mind also came to the fore in the late 1880s. At that time the attention he gave to the facts of divorce in the United States and to its *legal* implications showed a capacity to join his ideals with realistic inquiry.

In 1887 the U.S. Bureau of Labor issued a first monumental *Report on Marriage and Divorce in the United States 1867 to 1886*. It appears that Adler studied the great compilation closely. The thousand pages of statistics and analysis in this *Report* documented the fact of an increasing and markedly higher rate of divorce in the United States than had yet been reported for European countries. This, of course, disquieted Adler. But he did not have to quarrel with the viewpoint of the commissioners, since it too aimed at strengthening the permanence of marriage.

Instead he could devote himself to studying the findings, which dispelled some explanations frequently given for the high divorce rate in the United States. And thereby his own thinking, especially on the subject of divorce legislation, became informed by the date of the *Report*. Eventually, in 1889, he gave his own views a new statement in two addresses before the Ethical Culture Society, entitled, respectively, "Marriage" and "The Divorce Law." Although the address on marriage came first, his thoughts on the law of divorce may properly be considered first, since it was the problem of divorce that was now in special focus.

Adler commended the government's *Report*, which showed in much significant detail the bearing on divorce of deep-reaching social factors, such as wars, poverty, and special occupational conditions. It also suggested the importance of "physiological causes," by pointing to the high incidence of divorce around the fourth and after the twenty-first years of marriage. To these conclusions Adler added a comment that certain other features of American life—migratory habits, the higher position accorded to women, and individualistic conceptions of freedom—were probably also increasing the rate of divorce.

By contrast, such popular explanations as intemperance, the unequal laws of divorce in the different states, the laxness of law and administration, were discredited by the statistics and were seen as giving too much weight to what were merely superficial influences.

A basic conclusion that Felix Adler drew at this time was that repressive legislation, namely more uniform and strict laws, would not be an effective or desirable way to try to reduce the incidence of divorce. Moreover, he declared himself able to recognize the following as admissible *legal grounds* for divorce: adultery, willful desertion, incurable insanity, habitual cruelty, incurable intemperance or depravity, and conviction of felony (this last especially after a first imprisonment).

But in recognizing these various admissible grounds for divorce, Adler made clear that it was specifically "the divorce *law*," the legal treatment and not the ethics of divorce, that he had in mind. The laws, he observed, could not go too far beyond prevailing moral standards and still work effectively. Yet current morality, by its relevance to law, did not thereby acquire the authority of the ideal. *In the ideal of marriage,* he declared, *divorce is to be rejected,* and hence ethical effort must aim to reduce its prevalence. Among measures that might be positively helpful in such effort, he now suggested there should be better opportunity for acquaintance between the sexes than present city life affords. There must be better teaching and counseling for marriage than the churches generally offered. We must depend on advancing right views of "conjugal duty," he said, with convincing reasonableness about the functions of marriage and family life.

As an ethical teacher Felix Adler felt a special appointment to this last task. And in his 1889 address, "Marriage," he began to approach it with a new thoroughness. Describing three current theories of marriage, the contractual, the sacramental, and the romantic, he found none really adequate in the growing context of democratic society. Kant's view of marriage as a contract to regulate sexual rights, whatever its historic pertinence, now had an offensively narrow and illiberal emphasis. And in any case, when its aims are more broadly considered, marriage is much more than a contract, for the parties entering into it are not free to make the terms whatever they will, nor is the essence of their relation enforceable by law.

Turning next to the sacramental theory, Adler said:

The ideal content of the sacramental theory of marriage we should willingly accept, for we too believe that it is a divine power that brings them together and makes them one. . . . But we mean thereby the higher power of unselfish love working in the human soul. . . . Whereas the theory that God is a third partner, a silent partner in every marriage, has proved a stumbling block in the way of a rational treatment of this subject, and we can not adopt it, but must set it aside. . . . It would give us a scruple, not a reason, against severing of the marriage tie whatsoever, and it is this scruple which explains why the Catholic Church has always consistently opposed divorce in any shape.

This passage, especially by its appeal to "the power of love working in the human soul," would seem clearly to associate Adler with the romantic theory of marriage. Yet he wanted now to make an important distinction, correcting some of his earlier expressions on the subject. Henceforth by "the romantic theory" he would mean such ideas as that of "the grand passion," of "elective affinity," and of perfect soul mates achieving "a complete union" in marriage. He had himself sometimes spoken of a complete union of persons as the marriage ideal. But now he said that such romantic expectations must be rejected as illusions, which in all but the rarest cases are bound to end in disappointment. A more "ethical"—as distinguished from a "romantic"—view of marriage must indeed presuppose in each partner a love for "the total person" of the other as an initial condition, but it does not presuppose either the perfection of the lovers or of the harmony between them. Instead, the conjugal duty and commitment "may be summed up in the words: we take each other as we are, to the end that we may make each other better than we are."

This direction of marriage—toward "mutual growth and mutual furtherance, in closest intimacy and equality between husband and wife"—remained basic always to Adler's view from that time forward. The way he interpreted it in the ensuing years was much affected by controversy with the radical critics of permanence in marriage, and by the development of his own religious outlook. Both influences led him to a surprisingly strict rejection of divorce as contravening the ethical idea of marriage. His counsel to couples in great difficulty now became: "separation, without right of remarriage," yes, but no divorce. Why? because he took the initial marriage tie as a joining not to be *wholly* cast off or crossed out by another marital pledge. Acknowledgment of the original pledge as a permanent tie could be some way maintained through separation without remarriage. But Adler seemed to assume that divorce and remarriage *must* imply a discarding of respect for the mate as a unique person to whom one has become uniquely related.

In any case, in his ministerial practice he declined to officiate in the remarriage of divorced people. There were some, of course, even in earlier years and later an increasing number, who wanted an Ethical Culture wedding ceremony to celebrate a second marriage. They had to get colleagues of Adler's to officiate—which was possible, because he did not insist that they join him in his rejection of divorce as part of the ethics of marriage.

Adler's strictness over divorce and marital ethics led him into particularly vehement battle in the years 1895–1905, due to rising criticism of conventional middle-class views of marriage and family. Was it compatible with an expanding economic and social freedom to insist on the permanence and exclusiveness of the marriage tie and its obligations? How far were the usual standards still honestly believed in? A veritable burst of incisive questioning appeared in the literature of most Western countries. Ibsen, Meredith, and Samuel Butler were among those who had been heard; they were followed by Georg Brandes, G. B. Shaw, H. G. Wells, Havelock Ellis, and many more as the Victorian era ended. Freud was also beginning his psychoanalytic probing, although his influence, especially in America, was not widespread until after World War I.

Felix Adler became extremely excited over the issues raised. It was his habit to devote a series of Sunday lectures at the beginning of each year to a subject of uppermost concern. It is a sign, therefore, of how strongly he felt that each January for several years, beginning in 1896, he delivered four or more addresses on problems of marriage and the family from his Ethical Culture rostrum at Carnegie Hall in New York. In all these lecture series he sounded a note of alarm, declaring on the first occasion, in 1896, that "the monogamic family probably faces the most severe crisis of its history." The following January he said that "those who attack the marriage institution are to be regarded (though they know it not themselves perhaps, and intend it not) as the worst enemies of the human race."

In 1897, in addition to the January lectures in New York, a series was also given in February at the Lowell Institute in Boston. A letter from Charles W. Eliot, president of Harvard (signed as well by eighteen professors and leading men of the community) invited Adler to give his lectures there on "the Effect of Modern Industrial Development on the Family" and on "Socialism and the Family." Although Adler did not confine himself to these topics, he must have been pleased that the invitation showed understanding of the context within which he addressed the subject of the family.

In January 1900 came the statement quoted more fully near the beginning of this chapter.

There is no doubt, in the mind of all who think justly in such matters, that the permanent, the—as a rule—indissoluble union of a single wedded pair is the highest type of marriage which has been evolved, and that . . . all changes must be in the direction of more perfectly realizing the ideal of monogamy.

And in January 1900 he declared: "All laws, all customs, and all opinions which tend to relax among mankind the conviction that the marriage bond should be permanent are to be reprobated, rebuked, refuted, and repressed." In 1905 two lectures published in a booklet entitled *Marriage and Divorce* brought a recapitulation of Adler's views in this period of debate, together with a fresh statement given in January of that year on "The Illusions and the Ideal of Marriage."

After this his statements on the subject became less heated and more carefully argued and self-possessed. It was not that his basic convictions changed, but the new climate of world opinion was now more familiar and he had to meet it with less blast.

It is not easy to decide whether Adler's peremptory utterances more than seventy years ago were a rather representative shout from conservative ramparts, or to what extent they also involved some special personal prejudice in matters of sex. The trouble was not a lack of passion, nor was he the kind of rationalist who failed to credit impulse with positive value. The trouble was that a responsible dealing with sexual impulses was somehow judged to be possible in just one marriage pattern. Deviation from fidelity in marriage was attributed to the seduction of a lower kind of happiness, extramarital sex relations must be "licentious." Impermanence of marriage appeared as seduction too from highest regard for the partner. Such views seem to imply if not mistrust, at least a serious limitation of trust in people's ability to resolve these matters in more than one worthy way.

In his Hibbert lectures given in 1923 at Manchester College in Oxford, England, and published under the title *The Reconstruction of the Spiritual Ideal,* Dr. Adler devoted a chapter to "Marriage." It is probably the best deliberated and most perfected expression of his ideas on the subject to be found in print. It gives a beautifully rounded summation of his major contentions, stressing their positive meaning for his total outlook on life and avoiding harsh polemics. The theses are the familiar ones. In marriage the "objective" end of child development, as representing the interest of future humanity, should take priority over the "subjective" happiness of husband and wife. But, even aside from care for children, the ideal husband-wife relation requires a lifelong devotion of each intent upon the other as a whole and unique person. Marriage should be permanent because "an intimate knowledge of the spiritual life as it exists in one person—such knowledge as can arise only in life-long companionship—is the necessary condition of the knowledge of the spiritual life in general."

Nevertheless, the writer Margaret Deland, to whom Adler had given a copy of the book, felt "daring" enough to offer some criticism in a letter full of response to the high ground taken and the beauty in Adler's pages. Yes, she agreed, the "objective"—the interests of the child, of future humanity—this is "more important than the happiness of the man and woman." And yet, she asked with regard to a permanent relation making the best of a bad bargain: "if they *do* hate, what will a wincing endurance avail?"

The importance of the family was not limited, as Adler saw it, to its meaning for individuals, but included the effect of its interaction with other social institutions. He kept thinking of its functions for the development of "organized democracy" rather than in an individualistic perspective. The multiple professional and vocational concentrations that give modern industrial society its productive efficiency need to be counterbalanced by relations that move toward genuine human wholeness. Such an effect should be expected from the way that family life and its natural interest in "total persons" impinges upon more specialized groups and helps to direct their expertness within a general humanizing context. This expectation is strongly emphasized in the notes for Adler's seminar on the ethics of the family given at Columbia University in 1915.

There too he returns explicitly to his idea that women, given broader education, are especially indicated to advance this humanizing, social role of the family. And by 1918, with the victory of the woman's suffrage movement in the United States, the part of women in society again became an important preoccupation. In several addresses Adler gave voice to large hopes for a growing influence of women in the issues of public as well as private life. But he confessed that he still doubted whether the vote, now given to women, would prove an outstanding channel of beneficent results, since he had so little confidence in the election system of individualistic democracy, whereby each citizen voted on every kind of matter simply by virtue of being a registered resident of a geographical area. He was still unconverted to the "new woman" type of feminism which seemed to him bent on "imitating men," even where they had gone wrong!

Women now had the civil right to use the vote as they pleased. That could not be denied. But Adler's hope for progress rested rather on the chance that democracy would thrive through an increase of vocational expertness and dedication. With this perspective he kept dwelling on functions to which he thought women were especially called by both a fitness of their nature and by social need. First was the study of children and their development; and this would relate to better knowledge of human character generally. A concern with science in its bearings upon living might be expected from women, he believed. By their "assembling" or integrating faculty they were fitted to develop standards of criticism, and to engage in lines of management affecting persons and groups broadly. Their influence should count on the side of human unity against warfare and for national unity against civil strife. In religion, with a waning belief in the finality of Scripture, Adler cherished the hope that freely educated women would help our age in its spiritual need for reconciliation of heart and head.

Late in life, in January 1927, Dr. Adler was given a particularly appealing opportunity to express such views once more. He was invited by Smith College to give the first lecture of the new William H. Baldwin Foundation. He had a great admiration of Baldwin; they had worked together in civic affairs with a common high idealism, and he seemed to soar with the memory of it. He chose as his subject for the lecture, "The Distinctive Part of Woman in Creating the Civilization of the Future," and he drew a picture of modern life in the vast range of its problems and opportunities in every sphere. Whereas many forms of society had entrusted leadership to special groups—priestly, military, literary—charged with an assumed "supereminent function," democracy, he said, could not so regard any single function as supremely privileged. This caused our society to flounder. All the more did it need to be guided by principles and capacity to regulate the relations of functions. Saying this, he then unfolded, with many applications, his view of woman as a furtherer of such integrating principles in all walks of life. It would be difficult to find a casting of woman's potential part upon a more far-reaching and exalted plane. No wonder the Smith College students asked him, as his notes record, "Are women fit for the immense role ascribed to them?"

No, he hardly meant to place the future into the sole charge of women! But the idea of differentiated powers, as heightened and organized to advance a democratic type of civilization, was at stake in Felix Adler's quarrel both with the individualistic critics of the family and with individualistic feminism. The issue seems to be one that never can be resolved once and for all. As conditions change, democratic society must again and again accommodate both individual freedom and the needs of its vital institutions. Neither one of these two requirements can represent the whole aim. Individuals will continue to need protection with new allowances of freedom from social pressures, including those of the family. Yet society will also continue, one may predict, to give families special encouragement, support, and guidance in matters such as child rearing, health care, house and neighborhood planning, and recreation because of these and other enduring functions that family groups, however subject to change, will still be likely to fulfill.

[14]

NEW COMPANIONS AND LEADERS: 1893–1933

I NEVITABLY, over the years, there were newcomers to Adler's circle and to the leadership of the Society. Between 1893 and 1933—the second half of Adler's life—some sixteen people were added to the Ethical Culture leadership in addition to the original four colleagues discussed earlier. And besides these there was George O'Dell, who although not named an associate leader until the age of seventy in 1944 (after Adler's death), had for some ten years in England and some thirty in America, managed business for the Societies that did much to enable the officially named leaders to keep going.

Of the sixteen added leaders, eight committed their remaining lives full-time, while the other eight served either part-time or only for a number of years. Five of the new leaders became active in the decade between 1893 and 1903. In age they were between Felix Adler's own generation and the next. The first two, whom I count as giving of themselves full-time during the years noted, were John Lovejoy Elliott (1894–1942) and Percival Chubb (1899–1932). David Saville Muzzey (1898–1951) served more years as leader than either of these two, but since he taught at Columbia University he gave only part of his time. During this period there were as well Anna Garlin Spencer, who served as a leader for ten years, from 1903 to 1913, and Professor Nathaniel Schmidt, who served part-time from 1900 to 1939.

Each of these leaders came to the movement in his or her own way. John Elliott first heard Adler speak at Cornell during his sophomore year in 1889. He was still unsettled about his own career, but Adler's idealism appealed to him. Upon his graduation, while he was still in his early twenties, he followed Adler's advice and went to Berlin to do graduate work. Elliott stayed there for

174

two years, taking a Ph.D. with a thesis in penology. A visit to Elmira Reformatory, while at college, had aroused his interest in this field.

It was in 1894 that Elliott came to work with Adler in New York. He at first did every kind of chore, thus beginning a working relationship which endured for the remaining thirty-nine years of Adler's life. The companionship of Adler and Elliott was closer than that which Adler enjoyed with any of the other leaders. The two men worked so closely together that not a few members acquired the habit of thinking of the New York Society as jointly run by Adler and Elliott as leaders. Adler and Elliott were constantly in touch; Elliott enjoyed many summer retreats in the Adirondacks at the Adlers' home, and they took several trips together.

While he found important directions of his own, Elliott remained deeply dependent upon Adler and though they were joined in a basic sharing of many life-aims, they pursued many of these very differently. Their upbringings and their bearings toward people were distinctly different. Fortunately these differences proved in total effect more complementary than hostile. Both worked for greater democracy, but in feeling Elliott was closer to a larger range of people, while Adler was more admonishing and critical. Elliott in his youth had had experience of farming, of animals, and of poverty—all absent from Adler's life. On the other hand, Elliott had had slight acquaintance with ideas, and especially with their German philosophic elaboration. Yet Elliott recognized the power of ideas, and his attachment to Adler was pervaded by regard for the latter's ability as a thinker and his capacity for making use of his thinking.

Both men favored the development of women; yet Elliott advocated woman's suffrage while Adler opposed it (probably because of the faults he saw in our electoral system rather than because of faults he saw in women). People felt that Elliott, though he could be critical, was easier-going with them than Adler. We can only speculate whether this was an aspect of Elliott's pacifism, which Adler did not share. It could well be that Elliott's trust of people was more impulsive than Adler's.

I suggest that each affected the other at least slightly for both good and bad. Adler strengthened Elliott greatly in significant purpose, yet in doing so perhaps imparted some of his assertiveness with a dogmatic touch. Elliott on his part, though he genuinely raised questions for Adler, probably had as much effect in confirming the latter's *ipse dixit*ism as in modifying it.

At the same time, John Elliott made many contributions by the reach of his own nature, extending the orbit of Ethical Culture in several big directions. Looking to student life in the school, he also built up the New York Society's youth groups, including its Children's Sunday Assembly, areas in which Adler had done little. But a definitely original move was his decision to live in the Chelsea district among the longshoremen and other workers. Though quite at home in polite circles, he felt a too confined humanity among the higher middle class of the Ethical Society. He brought some of the latter a wider rapport. But what he accomplished by organizing and running a settlement house, the Hudson Guild, in a sturdier Chelsea neighborhood led Mayor LaGuardia to designate him as "good neighbor number one." His promotion of self-government within the Hudson Guild was of influence in the settlement movement at large. From 1919 to 1923, he was "annually elected president of the National Federation of Settlements." John Elliott's interest in prison problems also remained active. He spent much time helping young men to keep out of jail and to survive when they were in.

Percival Chubb had been quite active in English ethical circles before he came to serve in this country (1889–1932). He had helped organize the London Ethical Society in 1886, and before that had been influenced by Thomas Davidson's Fellowship of the New Life. To begin with, Chubb had been raised in the Church of England by parents who imagined a clerical vocation for him. As he later recalled:

The brightest memories of my boyhood cluster about the beautiful London church of St. Mary, Stoke Newington, where I was an infatuated chorister for three years. . . . I learned more about music than about religion.

We have already seen that after coming to the United States, Chubb spent several years teaching English in New York City's high schools before being chosen by Adler to head the newly forming Ethical Culture High School and to teach English there. Chubb had a spirited nature and was very well read in current English literature. He had the gift of sharing the relevance of his views with students and adults in dramatic form. In both the Ethical Culture schools, and in the Societies as well, he established a long-lasting tradition of dramatic festivals. In 1905 he was named an assistant leader of the New York Society, but in 1911, some years after the death of Walter Sheldon and in Chubb's own fifty-first year, he became leader of the St. Louis Society, a post which he held until 1933. In my view, Chubb did not match the philosophic strength of Davidson and other teachers. Among the group of Ethical leaders I see him as remaining an enthusing "chorister"; his addresses were engagingly songful and increasingly free. These qualities worked to maintain the strong congregational life-note in the St. Louis Society.

The third new leader to enter in this same time period, David Saville Muzzey, was in certain major respects quite different from Elliott and Chubb. He was and remained a university scholar, and served only part-time rather than full-time as an Ethical Culture leader. Also, as it happened, he was the only one of the three with a ministerial degree, a B.D. from studies at Union Theological Seminary and New York University, as well as further work in Church history undertaken in Berlin and Paris in 1897–99.

Beginning in 1899, David Muzzey taught for a number of years both in the Ethical Culture High School and occasional classes for adults, the latter on historical phases of Christianity. In the high school he at first taught classics, but by 1905 he shifted his main attention to American history, and in the same year he became an assistant leader in the New York Society for Ethical Culture. In this latter role, he served only part-time, as he taught also at Columbia University. Yet he continued giving Sunday lectures for the Society now and then for a great number of years, indeed until 1951. For many years it was customary for him to lecture on the Sunday closest to Lincoln's birthday.

Both in religion and in his social views, Muzzey may have been a bit more conservative on some issues than his colleagues. Yet he enjoyed writing fluently with rather scornful humor of much accumulated rubbish in traditional observances and beliefs. This tone is strong in his book of essays, *Ethics as a Religion*, which despite its merits may now seem dated in its general account of church thought.

An important service of Muzzey's scholarship was to encourage the leaders to assume a broadly critical rather than a narrowly patriotic attitude toward American history. In his widely used textbook on the subject, he gave careful attention to the British as well as the American case in our revolt from England. This drew upon him some ugly ire, in Chicago especially, where one of the papers called him "a rat undermining the Republic." Report says that his classroom manner was dry; which is odd because he was at the same time accounted to be an unfailingly witty master of ceremonies. Those who knew him in leisure also remember him as a steady Yankee baseball fan.

Anna Garlin Spencer met Felix Adler in the Free Religious Association during the 1880s. She became an associate leader of the New York Society for Ethical Culture in 1903. From 1908 to 1912, she headed the Summer School of Ethics in Madison, Wisconsin, and for four years was executive secretary of the American Ethical Union until she resigned in 1915 to resume her ministry in the Unitarian Church in New England. She died in 1930 at the age of seventy-nine.

Another scholar who gave part-time to lecturing for Ethical Societies was Nathaniel Schmidt, Professor of Oriental and Semitic Languages at Cornell, and an archeologist as well. A friendly and lively person, brimful of information on Near Eastern affairs, he gave Adler and his followers studied accounts and moving stories of that tangled area. His intermittent relations with Ethical Societies occurred between 1900 and his death in 1939.

Another group of leaders, a generation younger than Adler, came into the movement between 1905 and 1915. This included two men, Henry Moskowitz and Henry Neumann, both Lower East Side children of New York, whose first activities with Ethical Culture lay in building the "down-town society," later named Madison House. In politics they both Socialists, though Adler's relations with Neumann became so personally pastoral that it was sometimes difficult to remember the latter's public commitments.

Organization of the National Association for the Advancement of Colored People (NAACP), a great event of 1909, involved several Ethical Culture initiators—Dr. Moskowitz, John Elliott, Anna Garlin Spencer, and William Salter.

Moskowitz's part during the garment strikes in New York, 1910–15, has already been given attention. Though serving as an associate leader in New York (1907–14), and teaching in the school, "most of his effort went into reform work on the East Side." In 1915, when an opportunity came to take a post with the newly elected city government of Mayor Mitchel, he accepted and resigned his Ethical leadership.

Henry Neumann's part in Ethical Culture leadership, on the other hand, grew steadily more extensive and intense. He began teaching both literature and ethics in the school, and indeed continued to be a builder of the ethics teaching program through the years. After assisting Moskowitz for a time with the downtown group, in 1911 he became leader of the Brooklyn Ethical Society and remained so until 1957. In 1933, without giving up this task, he also became a member of the New York Society's Board of Leaders. Henry Neumann was a staunch pacifist, and through this position as well as by personal appeal he enjoyed rapport with many people.

Alfred W. Martin joined the Ethical Culture leaders in 1908 and served for twenty-five years. With graduate degrees from Harvard, including the Divinity School, Martin found that the Unitarian pulpits which he occupied briefly in the East and West did not give him the freedom he desired. He had been influenced by leaders of the Free Religious Association and went on to found "Free Churches" in Tacoma (1893) and in Seattle (1899). But he felt isolated and friendless in these ventures, and looking to the East, he came to see Felix Adler in the Adirondacks in 1907. Each being satisfied as to dominant ethical purpose and independence, a joining of Ethical Culture leadership resulted, Martin avowing this to be "the only religious organization today that meets the test of a truly free fellowship." A special contribution Martin made was to hold a Sunday evening series on the history of religions, displaying a free spirit and critical resources in the search for truth.

Several Englishmen took posts as leaders of American Ethical Culture Societies later in the twentieth century. Their interest in the movement had been in part developed in England by Stanton Coit and others. In this particular group, the earliest and probably the most telling was Horace Bridges, who led the Chicago Society from 1913 to 1940. J. Hutton Hynd, a Scotsman, succeeded Chubb as leader of the St. Louis Society in 1933, the year of Adler's death. And only in the following year did Edwin Collier become leader in Philadelphia (1934–54). Collier distinctly shared Coit's inclination toward symbol and ritual but this had small effect in Philadelphia.

These men from Great Britain were all articulate and maintained a notable integrity in what they said. Horace Bridges was sufficiently outstanding as a speaker to hold a relatively large audience in the Chicago meetings. He and Collier, however, did little to push the social reform interests of the American movement. Yet Bridges did continue the legal aid provisions adopted by the Chicago Society.

George O'Dell, whom many thought deserving of a leader's position long before the end of the thirty years he served in an executive capacity in the American movement, had a role unique and apart. Before he came to this country (near the end of World War I after serving in the Canadian army), he had had long experience and plentiful activity in the English Ethical organizations. His active note and thought about American matters was too full and various to be summed up here but one may suppose that he wanted to see the plain man's influence enlarged in contrast to that of money power.

In the early 1920s an Englishman, Henry J. Golding, came to this country. He stirred Adler with a special spiritual appeal; this was in part due to Golding's taste for philosophy and his devoted study not only of classic thinkers but of more recent authors on the Continent as well. Adler's other colleagues were not impressive in this particular respect which Adler himself regarded as an essential condition of Ethical leadership. Henry J. Golding had not worked in England professionally as a leader in the Ethical movement, but he had been a member for some twenty years. After being rejected by the admiralty on medical grounds, he had attained a high place in the insurance business. But he was increasingly absorbed by his philosophic and moral interests. After reading Adler's *An Ethical Philosophy of Life* (1918) and conferring with him, Golding came to the decision to devote his remaining life to the work of a leader, if possible, in Ethical Culture. The choice involved for him a financial sacrifice that was itself somewhat extraordinary. But Adler was the more impressed by the inner terms, and understanding of his own position, with which Golding expressed his reasons, as when he said, "not sympathy, nor utility, but reverence, based on a profounder conception of man's nature and needs, could alone yield an adequate motive for the moral transformation of society. It deepened the sense of responsibility, individual and collective, and kindled morality to a personal religion."

Golding was in his forties when he and his wife came to America in 1923. Two years later he became a member of the New York Society's Board of Leaders. Very unfortunately, his remaining time in his vocation proved all too short as he succumbed to scarlet fever in 1931. Adler felt his death as a great loss.

Two years later, Frank Swift, a young man who had been chosen to lead in Boston, was killed in an auto accident.

It was of much importance, even if not sufficing to compensate for these losses, that several more new leaders were added during Felix Adler's last decade. Of special moment was the addition of V. T. Thayer, who became principal of the high school in 1922, after the retirement of Henry Kelly, and in 1928 was appointed educational director of the Ethical Culture Schools of New York. To continue a coherent relation of the schools and the Society, despite Adler's decline and death, Dr. Thayer became (1928–47) one of New York's Board of Leaders.

The youngest of those approaching leadership during Adler's lifetime was Algernon D. Black. He taught in the schools, principally ethics, from 1924 on, and ten years later became one of the New York Society's Board of Leaders. He occupied this office most actively and fruitfully until 1973.

Robert D. Kohn, the architect of the New York Society's Meeting House at 64th Street and Central Park West, was never a leader though he was chosen to be a member of the Fraternity of Ethical Leaders. In 1910, when the New York Meeting House was dedicated, Felix Adler spoke of him and his work:

He was asked by us to attack a problem entirely new, one that had never been even attempted. It was laid upon him to try to grasp an entirely new idea and to find the means of giving it truthful expression with the resources of his art. No one could have even approximately done this unless he had imbibed the spirit of the Society into his heart and mind and very soul; had lived and moved in the aims for which the Society stands; at the same time possessing the fertility of conception, the artistic sensitiveness and training, to translate the breath of our ideal into line and proportion.

[15]

WRESTLING WITH AMERICAN
GROWTH: 1895-1933

W̶E ARE TOLD THAT in 1901 a diplomat in Washington remarked:
"I have seen two Americas, the America before the Spanish
War and the America since." And to this we may add the feeling
expressed in the fall of 1898 by John D. Long, secretary of the
Navy, who though he continued to serve in McKinley's Cabinet,
confessed:

I really believe I should like to have our country what it was in the first
half of this century, provincial, dominated by the New England idea, and
. . . going along in the lines of the Fathers. But I cannot shut my eyes to
the march of events—a march which seems to be beyond human control.

Both of these remarks were no doubt made with foreign policy
and the expansion of the United States into world power relationships principally in mind. But this development cannot be sepa-
rated from the internal growth of the nation, its rising population
by birth and immigration, its westward push and the addition of
states, and its great industrial drive. Before the mid-1890s, Felix
Adler did not talk much about American foreign relations and
policies. He was intent instead upon the labor problems in our
cities, upon education, religion, and family life with freer growth
for women and children.

It is somehow strange that Americans could speak so often of
imperialism as a new and un-American phenomenon. Throughout our history expansion had been a powerful reality at the expense of the Indian tribes and it was conspicuous also in the Mex-
ican War. But the spread of the United States on the sparsely
settled North American continent was hardly viewed as a venture
into foreign dominion in the same sense as our overseas acquisi-
tions following the Spanish-American War. Indeed, the Monroe
Doctrine was seen by Americans as a barrier to European impe-

rialism rather than as an expression of self-aggrandizement by the United States.

It was the appearance in the United States of a more imperialist tendency—not an American but a world condition—that aroused Adler's explicit concern with foreign policy, war and peace, race relations, and world order. Through much of the 1890s, as has been said, the country was restive with energies pent up by business depression and economic conflicts, that came to a critical head in great strikes and in the Populist movement. A series of incidents in the same decade brought waves of jingo excitement— aggressive, patriotic—to the surface. One such occasion was the strident tone in 1895–96 in our notes to Great Britain threatening to intervene in her boundary dispute with Venezuela. Our surprisingly high war temper abated when Britain, diverted by mounting trouble with the Boers in South Africa, agreed to settle the Venezuelan boundary by arbitration. At the same time, beginning in 1895, Cuban resistance to oppression by the Spanish government raised the question in some quarters of American intervention there. And presently, the Boxer Rebellion in China showed how universal imperialist power problems were becoming. In the Chinese situation, the moderate indemnity asked by the United States, and the "Open Door" policy advanced by John Hay as against exclusive claims in treaty ports, were generally cited to show our nonimperialist attitude. Yet interest in American participation in East Asian affairs was already rising to a new, steppedup level.

To begin with it was politicians, historians, and publicists, rather than business leaders, who made the case for imperialism in this country. And the expansionists, who held that the nation's future demanded naval power, militance, and empire, found a brilliant and effective leader in Theodore Roosevelt.

The Spanish-American War and Anti-Imperialism

The Spanish-American War, in its onset, if not in its results, was widely accepted by Americans as a war of liberation rather than of expansion. When we went to war with Spain in 1898 (after the mysterious sinking in Havana of our battleship *Maine*), it was not with a popular clamor for empire but to liberate the oppressed Cubans. But our swift victories both in the Caribbean and in the Philippines not only fanned an expansionist temper but created problems of military control by the victors from which it was difficult to withdraw.

The fighting had begun in April 1898 and by August Spain was suing for peace. The chief portent of the war was not that it took place, but in the American success that it brought. For as a consequence not clearly foreseen:

We acquired nearly a million subjects of Spanish and Negro blood in Porto Rico. We planted our flag in islands of the Pacific. We became the masters and protectors of seven and a half millions of people in the Philippines. [Senator George Hoar of Massachusetts]

Simultaneously Hawaii came willingly and independently of the war under our flag in 1898. It was the overseas implications of these events and the enthusiasm with which they were hailed that brought protest against our "new" imperialism from some quarters. "Kings can have subjects; it is a question whether a republic can." The nation was suddenly obliged to face this question in new concrete applications.

Prominent among those to protest against imperialism was the New England Anti-Imperialist League, although groups of similar mind sprang up in other parts of the country too. The New England League was organized in Boston in November 1898, when Spain had already been suing for peace for some months. The aggressive terms the United States was proposing for a treaty of peace (especially control of the Philippines) did much to mobilize anti-imperialist sentiment, which concentrated at first on opposition to the terms of the treaty with Spain. The U.S. Senate adopted the treaty on February 6, 1899, but by a majority of only two votes. The anti-imperialists thus lost the immediate issue; and in the fall McKinley was reelected with the fervent expansionist, Theodore Roosevelt, as his running mate.

But the controversy continued during the next several years as many eminent Americans campaigned against empire in an epochal debate over our foreign policy. They included the philosopher William James, Charles Eliot Norton, Charles Francis Adams, William Graham Sumner, E. L. Godkin (then editor of both *The Nation* and the *New York Evening Post*), and Edward Atkinson, who published his own polemical journal *The Anti-Imperialist*. Among statesmen and politicians there were Carl Schurz, Senator George Hoar (one of only two Republican senators to vote against the treaty with Spain), Speaker of the House Thomas Reed, and former President Benjamin Harrison. There was also Andrew Carnegie, espousing ideas of peace not common among his fellow industrialists.

Following ratification of the treaty, American military action in the Philippines became the chief target of the anti-imperialists as the United States fought to suppress the island's rebellion and sought to establish control there. How could such coercion be squared with the principle of government "by consent of the governed?" And what provision is there in our Constitution for the ruling of foreign subjects? But our military conquest continued unchecked, and in the course of 1902 resistance to it was crushed. At that time Senator George Hoar of Massachusetts expressed the grief of the anti-imperialists in these strong terms:

We changed the Monroe doctrine from a doctrine of eternal righteousness and justice, resting on the consent of the governed, to a doctrine of brutal selfishness looking only to our own advantage. We crushed the only republic in Asia. We made war on the only Christian people in the East. We converted a war of glory to a war of shame. We vulgarized the American flag. We introduced perfidy into the practices of war. We inflicted torture on unarmed men to extort confession. We put children to death. We devastated provinces. We baffled the aspirations of a people for liberty.

It has been observed that a good many anti-imperialists among the political leaders were already in their seventies or eighties, and that many were of distinguished native families bred in the ideals of an earlier America. By 1906 over half of the above-mentioned leaders were dead.

Felix Adler, although approaching the age of fifty in the year of the Spanish-American War, really took a place among younger adherents of the anti-imperialist cause. He was not a native son, and he was indeed rather new to counseling on foreign policy matters. His protest could have little immediate influence, but it was important as the beginning of the stance he took later on international events relating to World War I and its aftermath. What distinction there was in his anti-imperialist position came because his thinking was turned forward toward a growing industrial future rather than back toward our more rural past.

His public declarations on the issue (1898–1903) began, however, in a rather typical way. On the eve of our going to war with Spain over Cuba, he supported those who found the war justified. In a speech on April 10, 1898, he explained:

I admit that, as a rule, non-intervention is safest and best. And yet, I maintain with equal strength of conviction that there may be exceptions; that a case may arise where a nation having no mandate from other nations, acting solely on its own motion, may interfere on behalf of outraged liberty and justice in the affairs of another nation, if, namely, the offense is flagrant, violent, persistent, and so far as human foresight goes, incorrigible through any efforts which the afflicted people themselves may make, and if the intervening nation comes into court with clean hands, if it is absolutely certain of the rectitude and disinterestedness of its own motives.

In only a few months our posture as victors, and especially our insistence on sovereignty over the Philippines and Puerto Rico, showed that we now were not in the war with hands entirely "clean" in this disinterested sense. Adler still stuck to his April 10 dictum that "so far as the bulk of the American people is concerned, there cannot be the slightest doubt that they were not moved by the desire for territorial aggrandizement." Yet before the end of the year, on October 23, 1898, he felt obliged to discuss "The Good and Evil Results of the War." And now the jubilation rising as a result of our military victories led him to say, "I cannot sufficiently express the anxiety with which I believe an imperialistic policy should be viewed by everyone who really cherishes the traditions of the Republic. The very word 'imperialism' has something about it that should make us hesitate, because it suggests un-American and alien ideas."

This note became dominant for Adler in a speech on March 12, 1899, just a month after American ratification of the treaty with Spain. His subject was "The Duty of Civilized Nations to the Uncivilized," and while he began with our "anomalous" Philippine situation, he went on to the question of empire in general, to Britain and to the duty of American democracy.

Adler wanted to criticize the idea of the "white man's burden" assumed under the aegis of a war god. Rudyard Kipling's "Recessional" (first published in 1897 for Queen Victoria's Second Jubilee) had just had a new printing in America. With some unfairness Adler passed by the penitent refrain "lest we forget" in Kipling's poem and dwelt instead on the opening lines:

> God of our fathers, known of old,
> Lord of our far-flung battle-line,
> Beneath whose awful Hand we hold
> Dominion over palm and pine—
> Lord, God of Hosts, be with us yet,

Now the Filipinos, he exclaimed, who but yesterday were hailed "as patriots struggling for their rights" against Spain, have suddenly become "the rebels against United States sovereignty!"

And Christian ministers in this city are just echoing Kipling. . . . He has kindled in the minds of men a certain idea . . . to my mind, all wrong, all false. Yet Christian ministers are voicing these martial strains, justifying the smoking gun and the dripping sword, because of the purposes which these ghastly tools are expected some time to bring. Are we not yet sick of those tools?

In this same address Adler stressed next that he was not "an advocate of mere isolation." He decidedly wanted to acknowledge a positive duty of "civilized nations to the uncivilized," but not one of "forcing upon them importations from without and from above, downward." The problem is one of a more subtle pedagogy; for "the greatest good that can come to a people is not good government itself, but the process by which they can arrive at self-government . . . the broadening of their mental and moral horizon which is incidental to their efforts to work out their own welfare." Education, based on understanding from within a people, not their subjection to government from without, must be the method of civilizing.

In this same speech Adler also dismissed the notion of an "election" of specific peoples (e.g., the Anglo-Saxons) to the role of civilizing the world. A year later, in March 1900, he returned to this theme, and it remained thereafter a basic point in his view of international society. The aim, he declared, should be

not one civilization regnant at the cost of the extinction of others, but as many types flourishing on this earth as possible; the individuality of peoples to be cherished and held sacred as the individuality of persons. And not the external benefits of government are to be prized above everything, but rather the awakening and the training in the masses of men, the world over, of the power to become self-ruling. Rather let there be less of the actual benefits if they are to be received at the hands of aliens; and instead, the slow growth on the part of the people of the power to attain these benefits through their own efforts, to work out their own salvation.

During the next years, when speaking both in Boston and in New York on "What to Do with the Philippines," Adler's interest was not to increase anguish over the immediate situation, but to develop the case for making United States control of overseas possessions temporary. He showed concern for the Filipinos' future independence, but equally for "the influence of Asiatic dominion on the future of the American Republic." In a speech on "Anti-democratic Tendencies in American Life," he confessed to shock at finding respected leaders among the men who had advocated introducing Chinese coolie labor into the Philippines. Adler denounced this proposal as virtually reviving "a modified form of slavery" upon American territory, and he backed his contention by describing conditions of coolie labor in the colonies of other nations. He feared lest the nature of such rule over aliens abroad would impair the spirit and the standards of democracy at home.

The contrast with which William James and Felix Adler protested empire over subject peoples deserves note. James, nine years older than Adler, had a well-established berth in America's life and a heritage of predominantly individualistic moral ideals. Adler's family had lived less than fifty years in this country. Although influenced too "by the New England idea" he was not "going along in the lines of the Fathers" like many of the anti-imperialists. Adler was seeking a social ethic for rising phases of industrialism. James could better appreciate "the uncivilized" as they were; he usually showed warm acceptance of human types and conditions of men as he found them, with less will than Adler to urge responsibility for what they might still become.

In a letter of November 18, 1898, to William Salter (Adler's colleague who had married a sister of Mrs. James), James questioned whether the talk of "raising and educating inferior races"—to which Salter like Adler was given—was "mere hollow pretext and unreality." But for Adler "the duty of the civilized toward the uncivilized," though not to be met by subjecting the latter to government by the former, was also not satisfied by simply leaving each alone unto themselves. Better ways of a "joint development" of people were the yet unsolved problems which engaged Adler's efforts.

Anti-imperialists, defeated as they were at the time, adjusted their thinking in various ways. To Edward Atkinson and to Andrew Carnegie, for example, "an empire of the marketplace" without military rule seemed an eligible policy aim. One of the views of Herbert Spencer, the British sociologist, now seems to have been prophetic, namely, the belief that industrial progress would in time substitute a peaceable type of economic leadership and control for world governance by military power. But in 1898, given the Spanish-American War, the Boer War in Africa, and still other colonial conflicts, he confessed to second thoughts. In a letter written in July 1898 to Moncure Conway, he predicted sadly:

Now that the white savages of Europe are overrunning the dark savages everywhere; now that the European nations are vying with one another in political burglaries . . . the universal aggressiveness and universal culture of blood-thirst will bring back military despotism, out of which, after many generations, partial freedom may again emerge. There is a bad time coming, and civilized mankind will (morally) be uncivilized before civilization can again advance. Though I believe still there is a good time coming, it now seems to me that the good time is very far distant.

Felix Adler also foresaw a bad time coming unless society and its policies were radically redirected. But rather than advocating a return to Spencerian individualism, he hoped for a new organization more free and productive than either socialism or the old liberalism.

In 1908 a special opportunity came for Felix Adler to express himself at length about America when he was appointed to lecture in Berlin as Theodore Roosevelt Exchange Professor. President Roosevelt had instituted these professorships to encourage good relations between the United States and Germany through mutual understanding and, perhaps, to foster a softening of Germany's martial posture. As he wrote in a letter to Felix Adler:

I have very high regard for the German people and the German Emperor. I am certain that you will with great success dedicate yourself to the great mission of strengthening the bonds of mutual good-will, of mutual respect, and of mutual service, which should unite Germany and America.

The program, though essentially one of education, thus had a quasi-diplomatic flavor. The exchange professors and their wives were abundantly entertained and even received at Court. Adler also recalled a conversation with the Kaiser that went deeper than official politeness.

As the general theme of his lectures, which began in the fall of 1908, Adler chose "American Ideals." By way of preparation he devoted his Columbia University seminar that spring to "American Democracy" and the effect of American "pre-suppositions in respect to equality and liberty." Moreover, as early as January 1908, he had also given two Sunday lectures at the New York Society for Ethical Culture entitled, "Our National Shortcomings and Our National Greatness."

In the Columbia seminar, Dr. Adler worked to develop a central thesis of his social theory and its ethics.

The point I call attention to is that the nation is not simply an aggregate of individuals. It consists of groups. These have dissimilar as well as common interests. And the public interest or welfare consists not only in promoting the common interests but in adjusting or harmonizing those vital diversified interests that are also essential.

Government and the State are indeed concerned with common ends, not as sole ends, but as conditions and as part of the larger office of adjusting the different functions performed by groups—farmers, manufacturers, scientists, artists, etc.—in such a way that each in advancing its functions may advance those of all the rest.

Adler called this an "organic" view of democracy, and added it does not mean that all are "equal or like in endowment," but "it does mean equality in obtaining the requirements for playing one's part."

When lecturing on "Our National Greatness" Adler claimed that Americans are titans bent on production more than on money. Among our country's strengths he stressed specifically: freedom from caste, absence of gendarmerie, care for childhood, schools for all, esteem of women, abundance of philanthropic activity, and focus on continuing future development. These, he said, amounted for Americans almost to articles in a "religion of democracy." As to national shortcoming, however, he declared that the ideal of individual "efficiency in immediate material results," with no contrary group standards to offer check, produced a "lack of discipline" with a shrugging of shoulders at unscrupulous methods, such as the adulteration of products, false advertising, watering of stocks, unfair rebates, tax evasion, and bribery of government officials.

Lecturing in Berlin, Adler felt confronted with a popular impression of rampant individualism in America, freely released for money-getting. It seemed important to describe various cultural phases that had historically entered into forming American views of liberty and equality. Beginning with the Puritans, Adler discussed later periods, including those of the Revolutionary and Civil wars, and finally came to current issues. Though in the ranking of our ideals he put liberty above equality, he did stress the absence of a caste system and the assumption that "supreme excellence can come from anywhere and needs no external badges" as a fundamental feature. He argued that earlier attitudes of laissez-faire freedom from government were changing to more positive ones, citing concern for protection and justice for labor, for children, and for women. And he did not omit his favorite point that American freedom must forward the fitness and social motives of functional groups as well as care for the rights of individuals.

Both in his Berlin lectures and in reporting on them in New York, Adler emphasized a desirable learning of both nations from one another. Many of the American shortcomings might be alleviated by growth in vocational efficiency and in government standards of corporate responsibility such as the Germans had.

On the other hand, without the free initiative and experiment in voluntary organization that Americans enjoyed, the prospect for a strongly democratic future in Germany was hardly convincing.

Adler received much acclaim for eloquence and penetration in these lectures. And he himself was impressed by the close attention given them by many students in his audiences. Toward the end of his Berlin lectures, on February 23, 1909, Dr. Adler gave a farewell dinner to seventy guests. Then, before returning to America, he visited and lectured at least briefly in several places, but especially in Vienna where there was an Ethical Culture Society (Die Ethische Gemeinde) of about fifteen years standing. The reception accorded him here was one of great enthusiasm and his visit was much publicized.

The course of world events, and the help needed by the International Ethical Union, drew Adler's attention to the relations among peoples and nations and to international problems. In the compass of his ethical outlook, he always remained a universalist but he never became an advocate of uniformity or of dominion for any single civilization. "The individuality of peoples," he said, "is to be cherished and held sacred as is the individuality of persons."

It is the inalienable right of a people to be ruled by those who understand them, who speak their speech, who observe their customs and their religion, who feel the sorrows and joys of life as they do. The humble masses feel this primary craving for independence, even when they bow their necks and accept the yoke. It is seen in savages. It does not forsake man as he ascends the steps of culture.

Besides having this regard for self-government, Adler preferred diversity to uniformity of civilization because he thought it afforded a greater expression of humanity than any single culture could. And especially did he press his anti-imperialism against the ambition of any one group, Anglo-Saxon for example, to subordinate and guide others with a claim to its superior institutions and lifestyle.

The extent to which Adler took a parallel position on American attitudes to our own ethnic divisions is not to be missed. He attacked our hypocrisies in regard to giving full citizenship to the "Negroes, the Indians, the Filipinos" and other minorities. He consistently argued that any attempt to keep them permanently as inferior classes, to hew wood and draw water, without opportunity to rise to full participation in government, occupations, and public affairs would eventually spell the doom of our democracy. At the same time Adler's conception of Americanization was not that of "the melting pot;" it meant rather a give and take, a new harmonizing of differences. "True Americanization," he said in 1909, "means that the best qualities of the foreigner should be blended with the best qualities of the native." To be sure, in the same address he explained more specifically that:

The foreign-born if he is wise will not dispute the hegemony of the native-born in the matter of language. He will not attempt to substitute any other language for the English tongue, and he will recognize the laws and traditions and institutions, especially the political ones of Anglo-Saxon origin, as the pre-eminent decisive framework of this nation. But he will also recognize that he, the foreign-born, has elements from his own tradition to give, to be grafted on to the main stem, and that this is not an English but an American country with the American type still in the process of making.

The climate of concern with racism has changed greatly during the last half century, stirred by such events as the war against Hitler, the return of Israel to nationhood, and the 1954 U.S. Supreme Court decision making school segregation illegal. It is not easy for us to recover the sense of the times or to appraise fairly the attitudes which characterized Felix Adler's thinking about the prospects for Jews or blacks.

Adler rather early came into touch with General Samuel C. Armstrong, who shortly after the Civil War established the Hampton Institute in Virginia. The emphasis of Hampton on vocational education fitted well with Adler's own early interest in the education of workers. A similar focus was continued at Tuskegee Institute in Alabama in the educational work begun there in 1881 by Booker T. Washington, a graduate of Hampton. Felix Adler became a rather regular visiting lecturer at both Hampton and Tuskegee.

Adler also wanted some black students, we would say too few, admitted as pupils in his own school. He invited both Booker T. Washington and later W. E. B. DuBois to speak at meetings of the

Ethical Culture Society. And there is no question that he consistently professed the desire to see blacks participate fully in American citizenship and civilization. At the same time, I judge that his activity on behalf of the advance of blacks mostly took the form of visiting and formal championing rather than of more thorough involvement.

He did, as Mrs. Adler notes, occasionally do extensive visiting and speaking in cities of the South.

In 1902 and in 1907 an occasion came for closer contacts when he was invited to join a company of educators, ministers and social workers by Col. Robert C. Ogden, who traveled to the principal cities of the South, visiting Negro colleges and addressing large audiences in Atlanta, Richmond, Birmingham, Chattanooga, Knoxville, etc.

Besides many other prominent travelling companions, Adler was accompanied on one or more of these trips by his good New York friend and frequent associate, William Baldwin. Among the personal results Adler himself mentions the gaining of a much better knowledge of blacks. But in speaking of this, he also reports a definite mixture of feelings. In March 1885, he wrote to his wife from Richmond of "surprise (judging merely by the Negro population of New York) of what fine intelligent expression the colored face is capable of. I had seen the most interesting heads and some of the children are positively lovely." He then mentions conversations on experiences of the blacks. In a later letter of 1902 from Tuskegee, however, he confessed "I have never felt such a sinking of the heart at thought of the immensity of the problem."

The need of the blacks for education was apparently foremost in Adler's thinking about the problem, and his habitual approach must seem to our time to have been excessively paternalistic. He was hardly a leader in actively stimulating the economy and politics of the blacks for directing their own futures.

Nevertheless, he did make a move to promote a more enlightened level of thought on the relations of peoples by proposing a "Races Conference" in terms of advanced experience and inquiry tending toward more cordial and understanding relations. It appears that Adler first made the suggestion on July 3, 1906, at a meeting of leaders of the International Ethical Union held at Eisenach. During the next five years, the practical organizing of a "First Universal Races Congress" devolved upon an independent international executive council predominantly British in leadership. The congress was held at the University of London, July 26–29, 1911. Its president was The Right Hon. Lord Weardale, while Mr. Gustav Spiller of London was its organizer and secretary. In the latter role, Spiller collected some sixty papers of the congress in a volume entitled *Papers on Inter-Racial Problems,* published in 1911 by P. S. King & Son, London, and The World's Peace Foundation, Boston.

"Encouraging between the peoples of the West and those of the East, between white and so-called colored peoples, a fuller understanding, the most friendly feelings and a heartier cooperation" was the declared "object of the Congress." And the executive council noted:

When it is remembered the Object closely trenched on politics and was liable to be misinterpreted, . . . it is very gratifying to find among the patrons, who belong to no less than fifty countries, thirty-five Presidents of Parliaments, the majority of the Members of the Permanent Court of Arbitration and of the Delegates of the Second Hague Conference, twelve British Governors and eight British Premiers, over forty Colonial Bishops, some hundred and thirty Professors of International Law, the leading Anthropologists and Sociologists, the Officers and the majority of the Council of the Inter-Parliamentary Union, and many other distinguished personages.

Those attending did indeed represent high orders of authority and of scientific and moral concern. The estate of the British Empire at the time, and the coronation of King George V in 1911, also obviously had their effect upon attendance.

It is not ready-made solutions or unanimity of specific views that should be emphasized. What was of crucial importance was the sign of growing resources and a critical spirit for understanding the relations of peoples as an alternative to blind acceptance of race prejudice. Perhaps the congress might have been better called the "Universal Peoples" rather than "Races" Congress. The prevailing hopeful spirit appears in "two short Resolutions unanimously agreed to at a meeting of the Government delegates":

That this meeting of Government delegates favors the introduction into all schools—and also into all institutions for the training of diplomatists and Colonial administrators—of teaching which emphasizes a just appreciation of different peoples and races, and which commends friendly relations, both personal and public, between them.

That this Congress begs the Governments and Parliaments of the world to consider the advisability of eliminating from their legislation and administration all distinctions of race and religion between citizens of the same country.

In his own speech to the congress (Spiller, pp. 261–67) Professor Adler opened a session on "The Modern Conscience in Relation to Racial Questions" by remarking that the attendance and the papers showed the congress to be much more than only a matter of good will. He hoped for the creation of an International Institute to pursue productive objectives. He criticized a number of attitudes toward race relations that impressed him as either harmful or unreliable. One was to assume "that the forces making for peace and goodwill were about to triumph," so that one needed but "to swim with this great current." Adler was more pessimistic. In fact, he suggested that the contemporary sensitivity to race relations might be due to the realization that "nearly everywhere there was the determination to satisfy greed and the lust for power." Another criticism was, of course, directed against the dominance of particular racisms, as in the "conceit of one's culture such as inspires the Pan-Slavists, the Pan-Teutons, the Anglo-Saxons." Less obviously he also criticized the attempt to amend race relations by attending to common interests only. Instead he urged that world conscience must mount beyond selfish interests to mutual care for the distinctive strengths in peoples other than one's own. This regard for significant diversity within the greater unity of humanity appeared repeatedly as a major point in Adler's social ethics.

Today one cannot fail to ask whether his judgment on the Jewish people and their renewed national hopes, especially since Hitler, was consistent with his general position. As has just been remarked, Adler's general position treasured distinctive national vitalities. And he was always very decisively convinced that the ancient Jews in the prophetic ethics of their religion had conferred upon humanity one of its very greatest and permanent blessings. Yet shaped in his youth by early Reformed Judaism, Felix Adler viewed Jewish nationality as a thing of the past. Nations could die and still have their immortal legacies continue to be potent in the world without their national existence. This he believed to have been the case with the ancient Greeks as well as with the Jews.

But in his early career he had also said that nations can be "resurrected." And a question therefore persists whether events since his death in 1933 would have changed his views on Jewish national hopes. Adler says that his attention was first drawn to Zionism by Emma Lazarus, who died in 1887. But neither she nor others, including Brandeis, could persuade him to become identified with Zionist aspirations. It is, of course, not fully provable that a renewed racism directed against the Jews might not have worked a change in his attitude. Dying as he did only a few months after Hitler took command in Germany, Adler saw only the beginnings of Nazi persecution of the Jews and its world-wide effects. To my knowledge, the furthest he ever went after the Balfour declaration of 1917 was to entertain the idea of a "homeland" for those Jews who wished to go to Palestine, but not an Israelite nation or state. If such was his outlook, he hardly envisioned the rapid decline of the Western imperialist presence in the Middle East.

Adler developed several theses as thoughtful supports for his not engaging in Zionist hopes. One of these was his claim that both in the past and the present the creativeness of the Jews was strongly interwoven with their relations with other peoples (Egyptians, Mesopotamians, Greeks, West Europeans) as well as being shaped by their own Jewish traits. He harbored doubts whether Jewish contributions could be as great on the basis of Jewish traits alone. This is, to be sure, a controversial point and one that projects Adler's own building upon a variety of cultural sources. Another way in which Zionism ran counter to his feeling was that without a state or nation the Jews helped to modify the exclusive nationalism in the social order as well as the reliance on guns. So I rather doubt that Adler's judgment of Israel as a national state would have changed.

The outbreak of war between the major powers of Europe in 1914 overwhelmed Americans with shock. "A great cloud has settled on the world. . . . Since the world began there had been no such war." Although Felix Adler used these expressions in public at the time, he was in a sense less unprepared for the turn of events than many other people, for he had been talking since the beginning of the century about "the world crisis" that pointed toward war rather than peace. Amid the piling up of unprecedented fearful armaments, he spoke frequently about illusions in the peace movement. And as close to the war as May 10, 1914, he had said:

I had nothing but wonder tinged with a feeling of compassion for those childlike optimists who believe that in the twinkling of an eye, by some device such as arbitration or the like, war shall presently be abolished and universal peace among nations become an actuality. Not that I desire universal peace less than they do, or rate the benefits it will bestow less highly, but that I realize the interval that lies between it and our present state. Tremendous forces will have to be encountered and overborne.

Throughout World War I and its official settlement, Dr. Adler found himself quite out of line with much prevailing thought about causes, basic issues, and remedies. He had to deal with many tensions and differences among his usual followers as well as with people more remote.

The line along which our public thought was officially cast was to think of militarism and autocracy as the causes and issues in World War I. To get rid of the Kaiser and to curb the power of militarized leadership were the war aims popularly associated with the saving of democracy. Granting them some immediate relevance, Adler's addresses of 1914 nevertheless pointed to basic flaws in these views. First, it was important to recognize that autocracy and military rule existed on both sides, in Germany and Austria but also in Russia and Japan, which joined the Allies later. But at a deeper level than this was the question of whether the more representative democratic governments were any less aggressive in foreign policy. Whatever was gained by checking the Germans, Adler could not see the world made safer for democracy by an expansion of British and French imperialism. These views were not, of course, the prevailing ones and set Adler apart.

A second obstacle to the achievement of peace seen by Adler was the tremendous dynamism of science and industry underlying modern weaponry. Under these conditions, the powers for war could be quite rapidly rebuilt given the disposition for it. The vital question was what formed this disposition, what led nations to employ so much science and industry in armament races as compared to their use for peaceful cooperative world-building?

Adler's answer to this question was that the militant rivalries of the greater powers were chiefly fueled by their aims to dominate and exploit the weaker peoples of the earth.

The chief European nations are at bottom engaged in mortal combat at home for the sake of dominion abroad. Though the conflict is waged on European soil, the prize lies outside of Europe, in the East. The struggle we are witnessing is a struggle for the maintenance or achievement of world dominance, or of a share in it. The apple of discord is dominion over the weaker races.

Germany and England today are the protagonists in full view. [Then noting that Russia, France and Italy were likewise engaged, Adler continued:] The British Empire is increasing by leaps and bounds. It furnishes the most instructive example of successful imperialism, of silent and incessant territorial aggrandizement.

The wickedness which the civilized nations have exhibited toward the weaker races of the globe . . . I believe to be the fundamental cause of the present world strife.

Felix Adler had held this view ever since joining with the anti-imperialists at the time of the Spanish-American War. And he believed that only a new world conscience with a fundamentally different attitude toward the weaker people would disengage nations from their addiction to war and to preparation for war.

At the beginning of World War I, Adler hoped that the United States might play a role in bringing about such change because it was free from special imperial interests. As he expressed it:

The United States is the one great nation not embroiled in the present conflict. . . . When the time for settlement comes, its counsel will be called for and will carry great weight. . . . We must clear our mental eyes, so that we may correctly discern the radical flaw in our civilization that has made possible this huge debacle.

When the time of settlement comes this plea for a new colonial policy, in my view, should be our counsel. And we shall have the right to speak this word, because we have been true to our faith in Cuba, we have resisted the temptation to disturb the integrity of Mexico, and we are preparing to give full expression to the policy of "the Philippines for the Filipinos."

Adler explicitly contrasted this view with that of dyed-in-the-wool imperialists, like Lord Cromer of England, whose pronouncement "masters we are and masters we intend to remain" he rejected "as little short of blasphemous in the light of the ultimate destiny of every member of the human race."

After the sinking of the *Lusitania* and other German submarine atrocities, Adler came to approve arming our merchant ships to deal with such dangers. But he held off from advocating American entrance into the war. Yet he was not a pacifist. He believed that force may be justly used to prevent one's destruction. And moreover, his opposition to anarchism was such that in 1917, when a sovereign decision for the United States to enter the war had been made, he favored supporting it in action even if one were doubtful about its being a right cause.

Along with this, however, he did uphold freedom of thought on the question of right or wrong in the war. Not only were there pacifists among members of the Ethical Culture Societies, but several of his colleagues as leaders, to wit John Elliott and Henry Neumann, were so minded and were welcome to remain in their leadership. One prominent member, Oswald Garrison Villard, urged Adler to commit the Society as such to pacifism, but this Adler refused to do.

In an Easter address, "The National Crisis," April 8, 1917, Adler began as follows:

Unswerving and undivided allegiance to America, a readiness and eagerness to fulfill all the obligations of loyalty, the country demands of every good citizen. And to that call we respond.

But how heavy are those obligations and how soul-searching to some of us at this time, it is the object of my address to consider.

However loyal Adler felt to the country, inwardly he remained in anguish, declaring later in this address that he personally could not total up the right and wrong in this war. Some critics accused him of pro-German tendencies. And at least he never ceased to press the question, if German expansion is attacked, what about British imperialism? His private hope was that a disentangled, neutral United States might give a new turn in world politics. Yet he experienced nothing less than a crucifixion of spirit since he could neither in good conscience oppose resistance to German aggression nor join in the cause of downing Germany as *the* guilty party.

One thing became ever more clear as our nation turned to intervention, and that was Adler's radical disagreement with Woodrow Wilson's interpretation of the war. He could not subordinate or replace his own perception of the war as a conflict between rival imperialisms with the idea that it was truly a war to save democracy. Moreover, he believed that Wilson held essentially to the individualistic form of democracy which Adler had been criticizing throughout his life. Wilson, with his doctrine of self-determination, was now applying this outlook to nations. That doctrine presupposed a legal and moral equality of nations (as of democratic citizens) but overlooked the actual fateful inequality of national powers and experience. However far Wilson may have been ahead of still less liberal elements, Adler was convinced that Wilson's plans would fail, not only because of reactionary opposition but because they did not really face the problems. American democracy as interpreted by Wilson was not yet safe for the world.

With prophetic awareness, Adler exulted in the deposition of the Tsar shortly before his April 8, 1917, Easter address. In it he predicted:

The Russian revolution is the miracle of the ages. Nothing like it has ever happened in the immense populations affected and in its far-reaching consequences. . . . It is not the Russian revolution—it is the beginning of a great convulsion that will shake the earth.

You will see before the end how the repercussion of this movement is going to affect America and all the countries who are in advance of Russia in the matter of democracy. . . . I venture to predict that this movement is going to be felt in the countries that are more advanced politically. It is going to shake very much more than the thrones.

Do you think that the principle of hereditary power in the House of Lords in England is going to survive? Do you think that real home rule can be withheld from Ireland? Do you think that the state of India will be the same after the war as it has been? I believe that that upheaval is going to be felt in democratic countries in the direction of a far more genuine democracy than has yet been attained. It is going to be felt here.

So the downfall of the Tsar, and the belief that the Russian Revolution came from within, encouraged Adler to think that long-range advances for freedom were bound to be in the making. He said at once that he did not favor military action against the revolutionists, and his initial hopes were clearly that out of this upheaval would come gains for human development in a more dynamic, cooperative society.

His persisting conviction that democracy needed profound change and growth also helps to explain a stand of Adler's that perplexed many, including some of his close followers, namely, his unwavering opposition to the Versailles Treaty and the Wilsonian League of Nations. To him this combination amounted to a blessing of the old national rivalries instead of the making of a new beginning. This verdict was due not only to particular violations of "national self-determination" to which Wilson conceded, as in the cases of Poland, the Czechs, Dalmatia, the Tyrol, and Shantung. It was due also to Adler's belief that the League of Nations constituted a dominion of victorious powers to maintain an unjust peace rather than a free and inclusive congress of nations. The picture included much expanded British and French empires and monstrous reparations from Germany.

This should all be kept in mind when judging Adler's words in October 1919, entitled, "Moral Questions Involved in the Proposed League of Nations":

The very principle of liberty, in the sense in which liberty means the right to be free from foreign domination, for which we were told again and again the war was being fought, has been tragically violated in the compact of peace that concludes the war.

The League of Nations was to initiate a new world order, to secure peace through justice. If injustice is woven into the warp and woof of it, is it the right instrumentality for the end desired?

We all want a League—we want peace. But we want a League which shall secure peace through right dealing. Can we use an instrument which sanctions wrongs in the Covenant itself?

What I am concerned about is why when the wrong is as plain as a

pikestaff, many good men will not see it . . . nay, display a certain enthusiasm on behalf of this infected covenant, and cannot conceive that
ethically-minded men should not share their enthusiasm.

Adler was, of course, confronted by criticism of his rejection of
the League of Nations. Relatives who strongly supported Wilson
thought him to be wrong. The long barbarity of the war made
people feel it was imperative to *do* something corrective. Criticism
was not enough. It was urged that the steps now taken would not
be final, that they could be amended.

To this point on later amendment, Adler replied that if the new
beginnings aimed at peace and justice were themselves unjust and
unfriendly, the standards and levels agreed to at the start would
be harder to change later than to resist now. Later change might
aggravate rather than alleviate the trend of bad initial steps. But
he did agree strongly that something must be *done*. He was no
"isolationist." Not to try to change and to remedy conditions that
brought such a war would be intolerably inhuman.

The League of Nations was a league of governments, and in
Adler's view the powerful governments were largely directed by
commercial and militarist groups in competition with each other
for expansion and for control of weaker peoples and world resources. This to him presaged more warfare and oppression
rather than more peace and freedom.

What Felix Adler wanted instead was a fuller opening and effectiveness in all countries of broader popular will and activity.
For he believed that "among the people there is the will to a real
peace; they do desire the cessation of war." Yet he felt obliged to
add in 1922:

They do not desire to give up the practices which inevitably lead to
war. They want to eat their cake and keep it too.
I see no evidence that the ambitions and greeds which inevitably lead
to war have ceased to be powerful. Now there can be no peace in the
world until the goodwill to peace expresses itself genuinely and effectively. And as the goodwill to peace does not exist among the militarists
and the diplomatists that may represent the governing groups, with only
a feeble economic fear [of war], the world's peace must depend upon
getting out of the way. . . . the militarists and the diplomatists, and

bringing the people of the world on the scene—getting the people directly, through representatives elected by the people, and not executive appointees, to come together in council, because they, the people, have the desire for peace.

But how did Adler imagine such a change might be accomplished? For some years after World War I, he proposed that, as an alternative to the League of Nations, there be what he called an "assembly of peoples" and sometimes he spoke of a "Parliament of Parliaments." When he used this latter phrase, as he already did in 1916, he explained the members of such a Parliament are to be:

elected by all the legislative bodies of the different nations, with the understanding that all the different classes of people, the laboring classes, the capitalists, the merchants, the farmers shall be represented in the delegation that is elected by each parliament or congress. The object of this "Parliament" would be to take possession of the foreign relations of the people, to take them out of the hands of the exploiting groups, to put them back directly into the hands of the people through their representatives.

The Parliament of Parliaments will have the function of extending popular sovereignty, and will react necessarily upon the movement in the different countries represented, react in favor of putting the people themselves in control of their foreign policy with the end in view of excluding the special interest classes, the privileged classes that are now in control and hold back democracy in each country, expelling them from the control of the relations between people and people. But directly in command of their foreign relations the people will gradually perceive that their relations to one another are not foreign, because their interests are coterminous, because they are members of one another, because they are living components of the same great organism of mankind.

His faith in the possibility of such an undertaking had been stirred by his experiences in London some years earlier. As he recalled:

I shall never forget the impression made on my mind by the Universal Races Congress in London a few years ago [1911]. There I saw brown men, Hindus, splendid scholars from India, coal black men from South Africa, members of the African Parliament, negroes from the United States, Chinese and Japanese—men of all races, and the impression was one of astounding respect for fellow-beings,—an overpowering impression of the worth within these colored skins, a feel of the bigness of humanity such as I had never experienced before. It was the experience of that Congress that suggested to me what I have ventured to broach today [1916], the thought of a permanent Congress of Races, a Parliament of Parliaments.

Interest presses us to consider how these expressed expectations of Felix Adler's sound to us now in the light of world events since his death. Much of what he predicted in 1917 as likely to happen as a result of the impact of the revolution in Russia has indeed taken place. Yet with all the weakening of Western imperialism and the hopes for, and the rise to independence of new nations, the effects of change and revolution in our time upon popular sovereignty and democracy have been—to say the least— much more mixed than Adler hoped they would be. His age and his continuing duties in the 1920s precluded him from giving close study to the development of communism. But in a general way he, of course, observed the swing in its methods to new forms of dictatorship, including within them, no doubt, the influence of many old Russian habits.

But even closer to our immediate interest, whether more important to the world or not, is the bearing of changes (in World War II and after) upon the view Adler had of American ideals and our nation's fitness to give leadership toward a freer and more friendly world order. No doubt America has advanced in much that Adler could embrace as needed "corporate organization," but this has only in part extended popular control and freedom. It has also added to the exploitative strength of special groups. We have suffered the loss of some of those national "strengths" that Adler listed, such as the absence of "gendarmerie," and some of the "shortcomings" he noted in the way of corruptions have remained or grown worse.

One can indeed debate what has happened since Felix Adler's time: whether the rest of the world has become more like America in respect of "strengths" of democracy, or whether our country has become more worldlike in the direction of rivalry and coercive powers.

There is no reason to believe that events since his death would have shaken Adler in the religious poise he had found in his version of relatedness and mutual development. He had found his personal way of surmounting human misery and evil of which he had taken much account. He only wondered if he had really transmitted it to more than a few. On the other hand, the special sociopolitical hopes he expressed for America and its possible influence seem much more vulnerable now than in his time. I do not say that Adler would have had to forego his American ideals and hopes, but suggest only that here the course of events might have induced an altered trust.

It is, however, of some significance that his last seminar with colleagues, in his eighty-second year, was devoted to the subject of internationalism. He was recognizing the complex character of nations, and perhaps hoping to amend a too simple "personalizing" of their relations, but his final illness in the spring of 1933 prevented him from completing the trend of his reflections.

In any case, in this seminar he reaffirmed with new emphasis the view he had expressed as early as 1893 at Eisenach, that "the highest flowering of national character seems to us possible only within a morally organized Community of Humanity." He also underlined his ideas on the primary functions of statecraft: to protect the rights of individuals; to help obtain a just and well-working balance in the functioning of different vocations and productive groups; to uphold the distinctive spirit and moral ideals of a nation.

But beyond the arts of statecraft, Dr. Adler's prospects for internationalism were more fully and deeply connected with the growth of a more interproductive, less fragmented world conscience. How to press in many ways toward this greater humanity was, as ever, the heart of his endeavor.

As to the tangle of might and right, one often finds difficult, as did Adler himself, the experience that right often seems weak and wrong relatively strong; many indeed are the interpretations that may be given and that are given of this. If I now close with something that Felix Adler said about it in 1916, it is not in order to urge that this is *the* correct and adequate thing to say. It is just that what he said deserves a final stress as being so true to his own lifelong effort and concentration.

The right will triumph in the world the more it is conceived of rightly. Our notions of the right are imperfect. Therefore it is weak. The imperfect right succumbs to might. Right will triumph in the world more and more the more rightly it is conceived and understood. That is the thought, the main thought, which I have to offer to this intricate and difficult problem.

[16]

PHILOSOPHICAL PERSPECTIVE:
1900–1933

WHAT HAPPENED IN Felix Adler's thinking about man and the world is generally epitomized as follows. During his postgraduate student years in Germany (1870–73) he definitely abandoned the theistic and biblical principles of Reform Judaism and accepted instead a Kantian structure of thought as better suited to perfect an ethical view of reality. It is sometimes added that Hermann Cohen, who was then still a *Privat-Dozent* in Berlin and not yet the leader in Marburg Neo-Kantianism he became, probably directed Adler in some lines of his Kantianism. Relating exact knowledge of natural causalities to mathematical equations for energy transformations may have been such an influence. But later Adler came to view Cohen's interpretation of Kant as too intellectualistic and legalistic.

In general, this description of a shift to a Kantian thought-structure has large foundation and lasting explicit confirmation by Adler himself. And yet it may submerge or even conceal a development in his thinking that in my view has utmost importance. This is the fact that he radically criticized and revised Kant's ethics. Since Adler was bent on making ethics central, I do regard this change as crucial even though his map of man and world remained of Kantian type. As a matter of fact, it will be found that this map too eventually received some profound modifications in keeping with the changes in ethics.

Before describing these changes, it will serve us to note the chief respects in which Adler's philosophy remained of a Kantian type in its general thought-structure. The basic point that he accepted was the supremacy of Mind. As with Kant, Mind is a world-building power having "reality-producing functions" that transcend sense experience and order it in universally binding ways. In subjecting sense data to an order of causality, Mind brings about scientific understanding. It works for esthetic and artful structure through interpretive symbols and techniques. Yet its greatest work of all is to grasp an ethical and spiritual Ideal which is alone worthy to be the supreme organizing key to real perfection.

Thus Adler accepted Kant's three-fold division of Mind's rule in scientific understanding, in esthetic judgment, and in "practical," i.e., moral, reason. But he explained that the special appeal of Kant's philosophy for him lay in the supreme transcendence it gave to the Moral Law, the Categorical Imperative. Derived from the form of reason itself, Kant's ethical principle pointed to a more complete and universal coherence than the sciences could promise in terms of particular causalities regulating experience. Mind's "reality-producing" powers are not products of human choice *ex nihilo* though men must choose to operate with them. In so doing they participate in a rationality that infinitely transcends existing finite actualities. Man's using these powers of Mind to build a world marks the distinct dignity and creative freedom of his being.

So far Kant. Yet with this approbation of Kant's transcendent idealism, Adler soon had his doubts and increasing objections to the simple forms in which Kant developed his ethics of "practical reason." In his rationalism, the principle of duty was a matter of voluntary obedience by the individual person to precepts and laws that could be universally applied with coherence. "Act so that the maxims of your actions are fit to become universal laws," says Kant. In this formal universalism of duty, Adler came to see a one-sided emphasis with two major failings. It failed to recognize the moral worth of the individual's uniqueness, his difference from others, and it lacked emphasis on the relatedness of individuals in essential groups. Industrial society needed a social ethics stressing functional standards of groups and the interdependence of uniquely distinct individuals within them—both of them points that Kant did not develop.

Ethical principle, as sought by Adler, must combine both the "individualizing" and the "right organizing" of relations to elicit the energies of people at their best. For some years he seemed to expect that both these requirements might be served in a revised statement of Moral Law. But eventually he preferred to regard the ethical imperative in terms of an "organicist" (or "metaorganic") scheme of society. Kant was too taken by the physical model of conformity in phrasing duty as exemplifying universal law.

It may seem that Adler's ethics in turning from the form of law to a social scheme or pattern as an ultimate principle was a lapse from transcendence into immanence. But this was not the case. The social scheme he looked to as ultimate transcended every finite society as infinitely as any law or form of reason was ever held to do. And Adler could, when he wanted to, express it as abstractly—e.g., "the infinite unity of a boundless manifold"—as Kant could state the imperative principle. In Adler's first seminar at Columbia University on "The Philosophy of Ethics" in the spring of 1903, there is criticism of Kant, but also of Hegel and such neo-Hegelians as T. H. Green, for finding "the Absolute" immanent in social relations. A still fuller "Critique of Kant's Ethics" than is given in this seminar, or than I have here reported, was read by Adler to a group of philosophers in October 1900, then published in *Mind*, N.S., vol. 11 (1902), and published again in an anthology in honor of William James by his colleagues at Columbia University (1908).*

Adler's view of ethical freedom was distinctly more social both in meaning and grounding than was Kant's. Though more timely and fertile, it was not thereby more compelling. Kant had proclaimed free will on the ground of the allegedly simple fact of a universal sense of duty. But Adler's view of moral freedom implied a more explicit mutual regard for the moral freedom of others. Every person's own, uniquely best, self developed as he

*Whoever wants to examine thoroughly Adler's "critique of Kant" must read this essay as well as the relevant parts in his book, *An Ethical Philosophy of Life*. Besides such criticisms as I have stated of Kant's legalism and individualism, the essay expounds fallacies in Kant's arguments for belief in God, freedom, and immortality. Adler's strict ethicism finds singularly incongruous Kant's view that "God" rewards virtue with happiness. Let virtue be its own reward. The alleged universal sense of duty from which Kant moves to "freeedom" is also questioned as to whether it is a fact. But is not Adler's own "attribution" of a general moral capacity open to like question? As for "immortality," more will be said in the next chapter on Adler's religious caring.

advanced to realize the best as uniquely modified in the selves of his different fellows. Such was the base of Adler's inclusive maxim: "Elicit the best in others and thereby in yourself." Social freedom for Adler was not identified with the program of any party, state, or church. It meant what I choose to call the mutual maturing and developing of different persons and groups in effect upon one another.

To employ an ethical key to reality it is necessary, Adler repeatedly said, to give multiplicity a coordinate and equal metaphysical importance with unity. Here again is a main statement of highest abstraction. Religiously, as will be told, it meant substituting for a single "God" the "Divine Life" of an infinite "Spiritual Manifold." Ethically it called for elaborating an ideal of comprehensive relatedness. Adler did not think this ideal was to be projected *in vacuo*. It pointed to a potential foundation for rightness (however hidden) in every member of the social infinite. While the presence of this foundation could not be shown or proved in everyone, it had to be "attributed," Adler declared, to justify ethically one's own sense of worth. He did not suppose that any finite society could in actuality develop this foundation and realize the ideal except very imperfectly.

The seeds and roots of Adler's philosophy were pre-Darwinian but his thought developed during early responses to the revolutionary view of man as a creature of biological evolution. The idea of countless life-forms arising in a natural process stretching over millions of years was just too stupendous to be grasped all at once. Yet at the time a rash of suppositions about the destiny of mankind was promptly given alleged sanction by the evolutionary process, as guaranteeing, for example, "survival of the fittest" or alternatively the advance of Spencerian individualism. Somewhat later Nietzsche's will-to-power ethics and Henri Bergson's prospect of enduring novelty in "creative evolution" joined the array of these speculations.

Dr. Adler could not put his trust in any of these new "winds of doctrine." He saw that the moral conclusion in each instance had been arrived at independently and did not really follow from what biologists were saying about the evolution of life-forms. And on this point, indeed, he himself was in no different case; for he too had his predetermined ethical ideals. But he did question the rightness of looking to the process of natural evolution to guarantee or to serve as the sanction of his ideals.

As to the dynamics of biologic change, Adler looked for eventual instruction from the biologists. Meanwhile, he found Darwin's theory of natural selection a not unimpressive hypothesis by which to account mechanically instead of teleologically for organic adaptations. He was prepared to admit that the capacities of man's physical organism might thus have come about without there being a purposive trend at work in biological evolution. In a paper of 1904 entitled, "The Function of Teleology," in the *International Journal of Ethics,* he made no claim that the Ideal would serve to explain as a causal factor the changes of life-forms in natural evolution. But whatever those changes turned out to be, he was not ready to grant them the controlling voice in Mind's estimate of life-ideals. There is the function of *explaining* how things happen in terms of various causal and effectual orders. And there is the problem of *evaluating* what is and should be in terms of aims and purposes and ends. In his paper on teleology Adler upheld essentially Kant's view that, however paramount "ends" may be in evaluative judgment, yet in explanation they have only a "heuristic" role, helping to guide inquiry but not serving as the definite causes of natural processes.

Adler concluded that he should *not* base his ethics on assuming a purposive trend in natural evolution. Much of what was at stake for him is suggested in statements like the following.

Evolutionism applied to morals has for its chief factor survival and adaptation to given conditions.

Ethical idealism has for its object the creation of an ideal society, one that never was and in its completeness on earth never will be.

It is significant that Adler's pattern of "ideal society" and of the "spiritual manifold" emerges from reflection on interdependence within industrial life rather than from analogy with biologic organisms.

The classic motif of Western philosophy remained for him a firm conviction that a species with mental powers of human or higher level should cultivate a mind-guided life. One can grant the new evidence of biology that life-forms have changed and evolved without such guidance and that such evolution may be still unfinished, and yet maintain that humanity, having acquired the powers of Mind, should and can relate its life to an Ideal Order of its own discovery and choice. Man's freedom to guide himself by thought in building a more ethical world can mark his distinct human dignity.

Among Philosophers

In the *International Journal of Ethics* during the 1890s and elsewhere at the turn of the century, Dr. Adler began writing for philosophical readers. But response to printed papers is uncertain and often slow and Adler felt a growing need for regular and intensive exchange with thinkers more productively engaged in philosophy than were his colleagues in the Ethical Culture leadership. With typical initiative, he decided to gather a group for such discussion, noting in his private files: "I have great pleasure in repartee. It is very rare to find a partner in the game. All my life I have sought for minds congenial to my own in philosophy, in religion, etc. without being rewarded by finding them."

The first meeting of such a group as Adler proposed took place on February 28, 1900. His notes on thinkers attending the first meeting offer the following unpublished comments:

Professor George William Knox of Union Seminary, a predestinarian, an ex-missionary forced to learn western philosophy in order to talk to educated Japanese, Hindoos, and Chinese.

Dr. Vladimir G. Simkhovitch, a Pan-Slavist and follower of Schelling or Hegel who considers himself an orthodox Kantian.

Henry Rutgers Marshall, a religious nature with a hedonist theory in art but not in ethics, almost a Spencerian.

Nichols, a poetic humanitarian interested in reconciling realism with idealism.

Charles Augustus Strong, then lecturer in psychology, soon to publish *Why the Mind has a Body* (1903), with a father conflict against orthodoxy, influenced at Harvard College by James especially, Palmer and Royce, and committed to Matthew Arnold's "verifiable tendency" rather than to religion as a source of righteousness.

Charles C. Hall, president of Union Seminary, a skeptic at fourteen but back to denominational theology as a Christian pessimist influenced by Schopenhauer and humanitarianism.

The critical accent in these observations is rather revealing, in my opinion. Adler was considerably given, as he himself knew, to presenting his views over against those of others taken as "foils." He did in the course of years work out his own position but criticism of what he regarded as inadequate views always remained an important trait in his philosophizing.

Under the name of the New York Philosophy Club, the group achieved a permanence beyond anything likely to have been expected, for it still meets to the present day. Eventually a little etiquette developed of the club's meeting on the third Friday of each academic month: first, for tea; then to hear a paper by some member (or occasionally by an invited guest); then for about an hour's discussion of the paper (6–7 p.m.); and finally, for dinner together. This must have been the more socially interesting in the early years, when meetings were usually held in members' homes. With the spread of membership beyond New York City and a decline of home service, this became rare and meetings shifted mostly to the Columbia Faculty Club. I myself remember attending only twice in homes, once at Adler's and once at Wendell T. Bush's.

During the early years, membership of the club (about twenty-five at a time) came to consist mostly of professors teaching philosophy in eastern universities near enough to make the trip to New York City. Some theologians continued to belong. It had been Adler's intention to include more nonacademic people in the group also. In the years c.1904–29, when Adler was a participant, the Philosophy Club included a rather notable group of American philosophers. Some of the older members particularly memorable to me were Dickinson S. Miller, A. C. McGiffert, William Adams Brown, F. J. E. Woodbridge, John Dewey, William P. Montague, Wendell T. Bush, Morris R. Cohen, and Harry Overstreet, all from New York City. From outside of New York City were Charles Bakewell, W. H. Sheldon, Warner Fite, Charles Hendel, Arthur Lovejoy, Edgar Singer, and Wilbur Urban.

If what Adler desired was face-to-face exchange in matters of philosophy, he surely enjoyed much of this from these men. But as far as his further interest to find partnership with "minds congenial to my own in philosophy, in religion, etc." was concerned, the experience must eventually have brought him considerable disappointment. A goodly number of members, including Miller, Bakewell, Sheldon, Montague, and Cohen, had engaged in philosophical studies at Harvard with William James. The latter opened the door to explore "varieties of experience" more freely than was done in the Kantian tradition. Together with Kant, James recognized mind as active and formative but instead of linking this to mind's transcendent principles, he emphasized the "apperceptive mass" which individual minds acquire from time to time and use in the shaping of their experiences and views. This makes of experience and of philosophy a rather deeply biographical matter, an individual interpretation.

John Dewey likewise wanted to open the door of experience more widely, but he sought to discipline it by a "logic of inquiry" addressed to specific situations and problems rather than to three large types of experience in the Kantian tradition. The story goes that his Ph.D. thesis (long missing) contained a critique of this threefold architecture of Kant's system.

There continued to be "idealists" in the club besides Adler, but without their being imitators most of the members in the period mentioned were much influenced by the freshly empirical and critical directions pursued by James and Dewey. In varying measure, too, they were concerned to examine mind anew in the context of nature instead of as an independently sovereign power in the "idealistic" manner. Adler was already in his forty-ninth year when these philosophical meetings began in 1900. He was working at significant changes in Kant's ethics, but retaining the Kantian view of Mind's "reality-producing functions" and of its threefold distinct dominion in physical science, esthetics, and ethics. As long as he dealt with the themes in his papers on "Critique of Kant's Ethics" and "The Function of Teleology"—both read to the club—he could expect some encouragement and help from their responses.

But when Adler extended his approach from ethical experience into a metaphysical world-view, the meeting of minds was not the same. This was already apparent in Adler's comments on early papers (e.g., one on James's "Will to Believe," 1900, and one by Henry Marshall on "Psychology and Ethics," 1901). He criticized the taking of "experience" too loosely—"favorable to allowing miracles" for the theologians, but otherwise too personally relative and "naïvely lawless." In comment on Marshall he said he would trace the origin of morality to a "constant predisposition," but neither to instinct as acquired in natural evolution nor to habit engendered by environment.*

His own views, with some of their highly speculative as well as their down-to-earth reaches, received fully challenging expression in his paper, "The Relation of the Moral Ideal to Reality," presented April 20, 1911. Herein Adler gave the members a rather stiff dose of what he called "the epistemological foundation of ethical science." "The worth" of the individual person, he said, is not discovered in "the value" of his empirical conduct. He attributes worth to himself, but only as a unique member in mutual, constituting relation to the infinite number of other unique members comprising the universe's "metaorganic" whole. The worth thus attributed is transcendentally ideal, yet it is also the perfect reality of the interdependent selves. An exemplification of this worth in our finite experience is bound to be imperfect but should be striven for. "The impulse to organize our lives should derive from the moral ideal. To ethicize and to organize are synonymous terms," Adler here declared. He viewed the basic relations—of family, school, vocation, state, and church—not just as instruments for the individual's benefit but as essential conditions of personal self-realization. These relations, moreover, are seen as in living change, not as "survivals" only of culture and society.

Reactions at the club meeting were rather brisk. Professor Montague approved the distinction between "value" and "worth"

---

*Records make it likely that Adler read to the club on "Critique of Kant's Ethics" (October 1900); "The Problem of Teleology" (1914); "The Relation of the Moral Ideal to Reality" (April 1911); probably "Organization" (December 1915); and there was discussion of his Hibbert lectures at Oxford (October 1924). Brief comments by him on papers by others are also extant for February 1900, March 1900, October 1901, October 1911, November 1911, January 1915, January 1917, March 1917, and October 1920. It is not implied that his participation was limited to these times.

yet confused Adler by extending "ethical relations" to include the lower animals. The theologians Arthur McGiffert and Dickinson Miller argued for "sympathy" rather than the Adlerian "rational ideal" as a basis for ethics. Professor Lovejoy thought moral ideals "futile" if not closer to the realities of empirical value than Adler proposed. On this occasion only an English visitor, Leonard T. Hobhouse, expressed favorable regard for Adler's "metaorganic" ethical view of the universe, likening it to tendencies of his own.

The crucial philosophic problem here for Adler was to interpret the principle of ethics as the supreme principle of reality's "organization in the spiritual sense." That principle was presented as one of "reciprocal causation," an interdependence of each unique essential self upon every other. This ideal of personal interrelation was held to function as man's top clue to a best, most perfectly "organized" view of the world.

There were important points of give and take and of convergence between Adler's thought and that of some club members. Charles Bakewell, for example, was strongly influenced by Thomas Davidson and wrote about him. It is not surprising that Adler noted there was "a drift in Bakewell's thought in agreement with his own in assigning pre-eminence to the practical categories." Yet he noted too that Bakewell found himself still "vague about the nature of these categories." Morris Cohen, finding his way as a newcomer in America, was helped by both Adler and Davidson. More than the other club members, Cohen always stressed a debt to Adler for insisting on a coordinate dignity in the role of thought to unify and to differentiate instead of subordinating either function to the other. In his own thinking, Cohen gave this point some freer methodological application than Adler himself had done. Montague also, despite vital differences from Adler both in ethics and theology, expressed strong accord with the aim to free ethics from dependence on theological formulations.

Professor Sheldon of Yale, who habitually expressed himself ironically as baffled by the predicaments of his compeers, saw "the strife of systems as productive." At one meeting he went so far as to suggest that "round squares," while contradictions in thought, might very probably exist.

Professor Edgar Singer, whose ex tempore comments on papers were always music to the ear in the perfection of their statement, retained more of the Kantian three-fold types of experience in his own thinking on science, ethics, and esthetics than did most of the others. He, however, also sought a unity of direction which he designated as "increase of power," no doubt human power. Yet Adler remained doubtful how far this unification in Singer's theory may in some way have been congenial with his own revising of Kant.

There was no hesitation in the group about the honor due Adler as a public figure and a high-minded man. But he did not succeed in drawing strong cooperation on the philosophical concerns that most occupied him, and in turn he contributed but little to what were becoming main intellectual efforts on the part of the others. Through freer exploration of "experience" and sophistication of logical invention, what became ascendant in his philosophizing was an autonomy between the relations of ideas and empirical evidence rather than a compelling determination of ethical or other ideals from experience. Wendell T. Bush, a very open-minded man, offered the suggestion to me that Felix Adler and John Dewey might profitably be studied as two recurring types of moralist who agreed in many particular measures despite their contrasting ways in theory and method.

Adler found what he perceived as loose and varied conclusions drawn by club members from experience more disconcerting than the "naturalistic" emphasis shared by many. After all, he did not consider himself a "supernaturalist." But what he hoped to find was a "fulguration out of ethical experience" of "the mind's exigent requirements which alone satisfy the demand for certainty," its bent toward the Ideal of a unity and diversity perfecting one another. He did not regard this as "a transcendental deduction" of the Ideal in a strictly Kantian sense. But in any case he found no such common effort among his fellow-philosophers in the club. He was instead dismayed by the amount of disagreement and "subjectivity" among them, a condition to which many no doubt believed he himself added. In any case, as he saw it, "the ethical approach is attempted by none of the members of this group. It is not even recognized as possible [i.e., as giving principles of metaphysical primacy (H.L.F.)]. Their ethics, *per contra,* is an application of principles derived from elsewhere."

Despite this sharp sense of intellectual divergence, Felix Adler's public reputation for a significant career of teaching was such that in 1924 he was elected president of the Eastern Division of the American Philosophical Association.

"Ethical Energy" and Winning Relatedness

The expression "ethical energy" appears here and there with some frequency in Adler's *An Ethical Philosophy of Life.* It is obviously of serious moment, yet it is not expounded with special or systematic meaning. It could be used incidentally because Felix Adler himself had so much patent ethical energy and also because in one large aspect what he meant by it resembled common usage. Yet there was more of special character too in his full thought about it.

From a commonsense point of view to ask the question "what is ethical energy?" may well seem superfluous. The most likely answer would be that it is activity well-organized to accomplish good functions. And this clearly is a large phase of Adler's reflections, as in the following:

Such words as moral and ethical [he granted] . . . convey notions of repression and of old-time sanctions that are really quite foreign to our thought. We mean life.

Through right personal relations, that is where you get life; there are the springs of the eternal fountain. . . . The most vitality and effectiveness is manifested by the man who most emphasizes that which is peculiar to the human being and distinctive of him. That includes science, art and morality.

This statement begins by praising vitality and effectiveness and ends by calling attention to organized activities, like science, art and morality, that are distinctively human.

Much of Adler's social ethics as discussed in our chapters develops this emphasis on "ethicizing as right organizing." In this view, human energy becomes "ethical" when men use their powers well in their distinctive activities and relations, such as those of family, school, vocation, state, and church. Yet much as he made of this view, Adler became increasingly clear that it could not satisfy his full inspiration. A decisive reason for this was that all human organizing remained motley, imperfect, and limited even when at its best. Despite what he did for greater excellence in education, in the family and larger community, his awareness of persisting defects tended to mount, eclipsing his sense of gains. In late retrospective and private notes upon his career and experience, there are at times very dark passages. The following is perhaps one of the most extreme:

> I did not succeed in producing growth in the other; in fact, I had the greatest difficulty in abnormal situations to secure even a fair conformity to the normal type. . . . I found myself in a relation that was pitifully anti-climactical to the thing I had ideally conceived.
>
> I was forced to reflect, ponder, react, arriving at the conclusion that not the actual change produced in the other, but the effort to produce it was the essential thing for me, as far as it worked in my own nature (and outlook) certain spiritual changes.

So the sense of "frustration" was strong, as is frequent among idealists, but it was definitely not the last word for Adler. Call it religious or spiritual or what you will, from youth to age he continued against whatever odds to find life's greatest prize in a personal relation to, indeed in a personal partaking of, perfection. He struggled with traditional ways of assuring this, such as by obedience to an individually perfect God, as not being ethical enough. They infected human freedom with a posture of submission and much occupied people with anachronistic inherited *sancta*. The "Divine Life" in which Adler eventually believed he could himself partake of perfection more ethically was by a relation to his best self in mutual constitution with the best selves of all others. These all others would be what he called "an infinite society" or an infinite "spiritual manifold," meaning that besides all humans it would include other beings with whom communication could favor their and our own best natures. Of course, more will be said about this infinite map of ideal personal relations in the following chapter on Adler's religious caring. He did not think of this ideal as only a wishful dream of what might be.

He was the kind of idealist for whom it was a true dimension of reality, indeed a foundation in persons of their universal and greatest real being.

How did this transcendent world-map affect Adler's life purpose? Was it a truly ethical resource, or perhaps rather a mystical or only speculative vision? Speculative it surely was. As to being "mystical" as some interpreters held Adler to be, he inveighed often against the tendency in much classic mysticism to absorb the individual in the unity of The Ultimate One. But in debate he admitted to features of mysticism being present and vital in his relation to the unique individuality of each member in the infinite "spiritual manifold."

The salient emphasis of Adler was to connect ethical victory with winning relatedness of people in the development of each other at their best. "We grow and develop in proportion as we help others to grow and develop." But in the speculative reaches of his world-view, he extended this relation abstractly to a mutual maturing of infinite members. This extension, coupled with his Kantian reservation about any complete knowing of the individual person as a *Ding-an-sich,* introduced a vagueness into practical ethical relations. Adler needed the requirements of basic social relations, imperfect though they remain, to overcome this vagueness with content. He also needed some summative, perhaps mystical, sense of the ideal personality or character of individual people.

As to whether Adler's transcending speculations of a world-map of infinite society are truly ethical or not, I personally would reply in a way somehow resembling what Adler said when asked whether Ethical Culture is "religious." He said "it is religious to those who are religious-minded and who interpret its work religiously, and it is simply ethical to those who are not so minded." So I now say that Adler's transcending speculative world-view is "ethical" insofar as it strengthens anyone's ethical energy, as no doubt it did his own. But wherever it has no such effect, it is simply speculative.

Personal character is often complex and in even more cases perhaps plainly obscure. Yet there are those who in their relations with others behave with a distinctive manner and focus of their ethical energy. Heroes and saints are clearly not all alike and the same applies no doubt to less prominent people. The cults of saints, by the way, are not so much studies of their persons but concentrate rather on identifying and celebrating marked roles of their remembered energies in life. Their "immortality" is known in terms of their spiritual energy rather than by a fuller knowledge of their persons.

I have from the very beginning of learning his thought had difficulty in connecting Adler's abstract and open ideal of "infinite society" with his more specific proposals for family, vocation, state, and similar organized activities. He surely believed that ethical relatedness grew from both these sources, the more concrete and the more abstractly ideal. It does, and the more close to hand and the more outreachingly infinite can aim to be in keeping with each other. But it seemed problematic, if not impossible on Adler's terms, to judge the measure in which this harmonious relation is accomplished.

What I am here suggesting is that perhaps the observable facts of ethical energy, as developed both in social organizations and in distinctive relations of mutual maturing between individuals, can have some uniting power in ethical regard. Adler might have drawn closer than he did to his rising associates in contemporary philosophy had he pursued such a line of more unified thought. A continuing moral and spiritual development might be affirmed this way without proposing a world-map of the infinite spiritual manifold.

Yet could he then have been as true to himself? In offering his more complex outlook, not radically dualistic but in some effects so, Adler no doubt felt more profound and adequate to his inspiration that:

There is a kind of activity which you may exercise on the people with whom you live, and it is the highest kind, for it consists in making persons more valid than they would otherwise be, producing not a blending of euphonious sounds but a harmony of interacting souls.

You are but a tiny estuary, but when the tides enter your being you will feel the pulse of the infinite sea.

[17]

FELIX ADLER'S RELIGIOUS CARING:
A SUMMARY

How RELIGION IS or should be related to Ethical Culture seems
endlessly debatable. This chapter will explore only the connections between Felix Adler's personal religious outlook and his
view of Ethical Culture. Can it be taken for granted that Adler's
view of Ethical Culture and his own ethical religion were identical? Not a few would answer "yes"; surely Ethical Culture was his
religion. There is valid substance to support such a conclusion—
especially during the earlier phases of his public teaching. But in
time Adler explicitly emphasized a distinction which it is very important to understand. In the face of all that makes Ethical Culture difficult and even close to impossible, Adler's mature religious convictions distinctively supported and capped for him its
validity and feasibility. Religion "faces the wreck of worlds, and
prophesies restoration; she faces death, and prophesies life." Religion must offer an answer to evil.

Yet religious resource is a "wizardry" that proves too much for
many people. That Adler recognized this and formed a policy for
the Ethical movement in accord with it, is clear from such statements as:

The daring thought we had, in beginning the Ethical Movement, was to
unite in one group, in one bond, those who had religious feeling and
those who cared simply for moral betterment.

I want the advantage and the strength, the essential ethical strength, that
comes from touching hands with those honest people who are ethically-
minded, but who do not take the same religious view of things that I
myself do. I think it has been a great misfortune that non-religious persons have been compelled to try to be religious.

The Ethical Movement is religious to those who are religiously-minded
and to those who interpret its work religiously, and it is simply ethical to
those who are not so minded.

224

Although it has its critics, this policy continues to be observed in the movement. It declares ethical purpose to be the inclusive bond of unity for Ethical Culture and views "religious-mindedness" as a further point in feeling and interpretation. Without question, Felix Adler's personal religion strongly supported and magnified the meaning of Ethical Culture for him. But he clearly recognized and deliberately accepted the fact that many people joined the Societies for Ethical Culture with a religious support different from his own, or, indeed, without any that they would call "religious" at all.

How Adler Remained Religious

Remained is hardly the appropriate word because it does not suggest the changes in Adler's religious evolution nor the fact that in time he became more distinctively and explicitly religious than before. He himself distinguished three phases in this development. All three were effectively formative in molding Ethical Culture, but the third and last phase expressed his own religious consummation far more definitely than the earlier two. His eventual ethical lifeline for religious progress was only slowly elaborated, although from the start it had fertile roots in a reverence for the individual and his relations.

The phrase "remained religious" serves a purpose, however, because there was deep continuity in Adler's development reaching back into the Judaic heritage of his family. Here too was a religion putting "deed before creed," even though Reform rabbis, like Felix's father, maintained special Jewish traditions of observance and of providential care.

There is also a larger, world-wide continuity to be considered. For all its veils of meaning, much of religious language has crested into a great flood bearing "love"—the love of God and man—as its main tiding. Reiteration of any one word, as in the case of *love* risks vagueness, which persuaded Dr. Adler not to overindulge in its use. Yet it would be wrong to say anything against a truly high use of the word *love*. Religion, and especially one stressing relatedness such as Adler's, needs to embrace both the intimacy that love fosters between some and the inclusive scope of benign care that it can try to extend to all. While both these reaches of love's meaning are vital, they can lack a combining bond, and in some measure even appear in opposition to one another.

In trying to express a distinct turn in Felix Adler's view of relatedness, I have used the words *mutual maturing*, to suggest a helping of one another, both individuals and groups, to develop along their best lines. This may seem cooler than to speak of love, yet it offers two values: it puts a special stress on growth and it perhaps reduces the tension between intimacy and inclusiveness in love. For both reasons, I trust it conveys faithfully a sense of Adler's universalism.

However the language be taken, let it be clear in these pages how his religious views belong to and branch out from the world's great stream of reverence usually referred to as a love of God and man.

Matthew Arnold, in *Literature and Dogma*, wrote "the true meaning of religion is not simply morality, but morality touched by emotion." Now while Adler in *Creed and Deed* (1877) maintained that religion "has its roots in the feeling of the sublime, which the presence of the infinite in the thoughts of man awakens within him," he did not mean thereby that morality becomes religious simply by being touched with emotion. The sublime regard of the infinite he saw as a response of the whole man, including acts and beliefs about people and the world, even if these were not framed as a "creed."

Although it involved misunderstanding of Adler's character, it is not really surprising that in 1878 and the early 1880s some saw him as having abandoned religion in favor of social reform. To begin with, there was his concern with the labor question, city housing and politics, with family ties, child care, and education. Even more to the point was the absence of public prayer in his Sunday meetings, in itself sufficient to stamp him as nonreligious for a wide public. Replying in 1879 to charges of heresy, Adler called it "arch heresy" to deny the possibility of progress in fighting license, slavery, and poverty. To be sure, this is not what he meant in protesting at the same time that he "never was an atheist." What he meant was that he believed always in a more than human basis, a transcendent ground of duty. Yet it must be admitted that in the first years of his teaching he was pretty vague as to the nature of this. He referred sometimes to "the great All" and again to "the unknown God," expressions which before long were less than satisfying to himself.

During the controvery with Rev. Dr. Kaufmann Kohler of Chicago, Adler made a statement characteristic of his attitude in this period:

I believe in the supreme excellence of righteousness; I believe that the law of righteousness will triumph in the universe over all evil; I believe that in the law of righteousness is the sanctification of human life; and I believe that in furthering and fulfilling that law I also am hallowed in the service of the unknown God.

These words "the unknown God" reveal the manner in which Felix Adler in these early years avoided explicit formulas of theology. His religious position in this phase was one of reserve about the universe and its source, but of insistence on greater human responsibility for specifically needed social and educational reforms. Indeed, these latter were pursued with a near utopian zeal and live commitment that bore the character of crusading religion.

But focusing on specific reforms—though it entered lastingly into Ethical Culture—did not satisfy Adler's personal religious spirit for long. He would soon declare, "I myself have always been a religious person in the sense of being given to cosmic outreaching, and never a mere moralist." Yet this did not mean that he therefore intended to give up action for speculation. For he continued to profess and to bear witness that:

One cannot attain religion merely by trying, in his closet, to think out the problems of the universe. The symbols of religion are ciphers of which the key is to be found in moral experience. It is vain we pore over the ciphers unless we possess the key. . . . The essential faith is the product of effort, and is sustained and clarified by effort.

Success in specific reforms was not only fitful, but uncertain in its effects on the character and development of people. While keeping on with his active efforts for needed changes, Adler was outgrowing his youthful utopianism. Deeper effort and commitment, personal and social, were coming to outrank particular results as an ethical prize and aim. This change was also driven home by painful losses experienced early in his public career: the death of relatives and of several major supporters in his work. In a late retrospect Adler wrote: "At bottom my tendency was toward the transcendence of evil . . . and the divinity I needed was one that would strike into the life of mankind—a divinity that has power, eventually vanquishing evil."

A sober change was now perceptible in this second and middle phase of Adler's religious caring. A care for "free religion" was matched now, or perhaps surpassed, by one for a religious firmness that would fortify and sustain progressive effort. This middle period, calling for "the religion of duty," lasted a longer number of years than had the first phase, and also impressed its form upon Ethical Culture.

To preach the supremacy of The Moral Law was our business just as the theologians preached God. . . . The god of theology was gone, but something that was very real had taken his place, because The Moral Law was not conceived as an abstract thing, but as a power actually working in the world. And I and my fellowmen were installed as the agents of this divinity, to treat every man as an end per se. Thus there was transcendence at both ends—a transcendent power in the universe, and the transcendence of an evil and imperfect world through moral agency.

Devotion to one's rational duties, Adler claimed, would at the least oppose "the world's being a madhouse, though with its cruelties it often seems such."

Ethically, the meaning of "The Moral Law" needed to be freshly spelled out with new social and individual applications in an era in which industrial life with all its concomitants was expanding rapidly. Adler was not satisfied that reverence for The Moral Law could in itself make the world "less of a madhouse." He aspired further to the positive end of taking his best self to be a unique and indispensable member of "the spiritual universe"—a world (however mad!) yet with a divine dimension of life.

But how was this to become a persuasive conviction? In a late explanation of where he finally arrived religiously, Felix Adler said:

I draw a sharp distinction between divine being and divine life. The theistic religions insist on the existence of a divine being. They say, if you believe in that being, you are religious; if not, you are an atheist.

I draw the distinction, however, between existence and life. The endless attempts to prove the existence of an individual being named God—the arguments from design, evolution, and so forth—are foredoomed to failure. And if they did succeed they would not avail us. For the outcome of such arguments would be what Aristotle described, the proof of a self-sufficient, self-contemplating, self-enclosed perfection between whom and ourselves any relation is incomprehensible.

But it is otherwise if I anchor on the conception of the divine life. If the perfect life quickens in the universe, then it may quicken in me who am part of the universe. And of this life I can have actual experience. The uttermost secret of it, indeed, I cannot penetrate. But I can know its manifestations.

My ideal of the divine life is that of . . . a spiritual society infinite and composed of infinite members, infinitely diverse, each necessary to the whole and the whole necessary to each. It is this ideal of the perfect life in which I seize the symbol of the utter reality in things.

And the truth of this ideal I can discover in ethical experience, for this, as I interpret it, is nothing else than the endeavor to act toward my fellow-beings as a member of the infinite spiritual society would act toward his fellows—seeking to prompt and quicken them to express the eternal excellence that is potential in each and thereby making actual the eternal excellence that is in me.

What these paragraphs describe as "the divine life" is the relatedness of infinite members maturing one another and furthering their infinite society. This, instead of worshipping an individual God, was the religious vision that Adler reached in his maturity and held to as being the more ethical. He developed it thenceforth as the culmination of his religious thought.

In one regard, this view of the spiritual universe and its divine life can be seen as radically humanistic, because it takes its central clue from ideal potencies in human relations. And furthermore, in contrast to other religions, very little, if anything, is said here about features of the world apart from man. Nevertheless, Dr. Adler rejected being labeled a "humanist" as a provincial narrowing of the religious vision he intended to uphold. The "infinite society" he envisioned was not confined to humanity but embraced all beings capable of spiritual intercommunication.

Though as yet unknown to us, and perhaps forever to remain so, it was this infinite relatedness in mankind and with other possible communicants that Adler spoke of, not as God, but sometimes as "the Godhead" and more often as "divine life." For him this vision of inclusive ethical relatedness had an unfathomable reach and sublimity comparable to that of the *visio Dei* in more traditional religion.

While he professed not to be a metaphysical dualist, Adler's teaching made much use of the word *spiritual* and of contrast as well as relation to body. He occasionally expressed sympathy with the ancient Zoroastrian view of life as a battle of good and evil in which human choice could affect the eventual outcome. Yet he did not go so far as to avow a Manichaean world-view of Good Spirit contending with Evil Body.

It must be stressed that what his ethical religion attributed to people was a universal foundation for development in ideal relatedness rather than any exemplary attainment of it in finite life. Indeed, he increasingly insisted that finite society must be "frustrated" in respect to realizing the ideal relatedness. Yet his idealism continued to rank the need for social improvement above individual hero-worship. Can it be validly claimed that life gets nearer to the Ideal? This truly remains questionable, said Adler, but such frustration can be accepted as a necessary price for a truer vision of what the ideal dimension of reality is. And such truer vision is itself to be prized as a factual index of closer approach.

The traditional mystic rose surrounding a Single All-Great Luminary was not the physical symbol appropriate to Felix Adler's religious vision of the universe. It could more nearly be a Firmament of Infinite Lights in uncounted galaxies.

Questions of Belief and Practice

Adler's development had brought him to identify "divine life" with a maximizing of "ethical energy" through "infinite" interrelations with others. But this matured version of his idealism asked for right implementation, including adjustment to the defects in people. As has been evident, the faults and weaknesses in all, in-

cluding the best, impressed Adler ever more strongly. Yet he persisted in attributing a worth to every person, leaving out no one,
regardless of how he conducts himself. How was this attitude to
be combined with the reality of experience? The universality of
worth had to be a transcendent yet directive ideal; one could not
expect to see it actualized in any length of finite existence. Life
would ever involve a continuing battle for personal and social reconstruction.

At the very start of his Sunday lectures in 1876, Adler had devoted five sessions to the theme of immortality. Judging by the
considerable number of addresses he again gave to this subject in
midlife, there was some return to the question of how such belief
bore upon the problem of reconciling the success and failure in
human beings. Adler decided against reversing his early conclusions but it appears he added something to them. He would not
draw upon a life-after-death belief to suggest either a purgatory
of the kind envisioned in Catholicism, or an indefinitely long
progress à la Kant, in which to perfect human character.

What he now claimed, however, was another way of belonging
to eternity. In each person the true worth, the "crystal fountain"
of rightness, is uniquely present. And this unique rightness, a po-
tency in each person's character, was now viewed as an eternal
component of the "spiritual universe," as a lasting turn in its ethical energy that survives the individual's temporal life.

It is in this sense that I myself interpret what Adler says near
the close of An Ethical Philosophy of Life.

I do not affirm immortality. I affirm the real and irreducible existence
of the essential self. Or rather, as my last act, I affirm that the ideal of
perfection which my mind inevitably conceives has its counterpart in the
ultimate reality of things, is the truest reading of that reality whereof
man is capable.

I turn away from the thought of self, even the essential self, as if that
could be my chief concern, toward the vaster infinite whole in which the
self is integrally preserved. I affirm that there verily is a divine life, a best
beyond the best I can think or imagine, in which all that is best in me,
and best in those who are dear to me, is contained and continued.

To understand the practical meaning of words like these is sure
to be difficult. Yet some people who were critical of Adler's gen-

eral philosophy recognized a special distinction and strength in his memorial and commemorative speeches. This does not mean, to my mind, merely that he had a felicitous technique for honoring the departed or for composing what are called eulogies. Rather, it means that what he was able to say on such occasions embodied his whole ethical approach to human relatedness. He described what he had perceived of a person's (or a group's) relations to others and from this gathered his sense of their distinctive belonging to that great, inclusive community which eternally is "the spiritual Universe."

Adler wondered to what degree his matured religious thoughts penetrated his followers, for he was not unaware of difficulties in his ideas. First, there is something to be questioned in the conception that every person is unique, not only transiently, but by having in his nature (however hidden) a distinct component of universal ethical energy. And even more problematic may be the second thought, namely, that these components are all interdependent, providing a foundation for an ideal of "complete rightness or righteousness" to guide the efforts for improving finite society. Even though they are in line with many widely felt current causes, these convictions postulate a kind of "providence" in support of Adler's ethics that strains persuasion.

Even if it was less ethically girded, faith in an all-caring God was emotionally easier for most people than confidence in these new Adlerian presuppositions. He was carrying his idealism to a new height and an infinitely encompassing orbit. And one result was a greater sense of "frustration" with the small limits of any current progress.

The outbreak of World War I could only intensify this sense. During the wartime years, when he was writing *An Ethical Philosophy of Life,* Adler sometimes doubted whether the trend of his thinking was going to have any constructive effect even among his colleagues. In a poignant moment of opening his heart to them in 1915, when leaders of the Ethical Societies were at their autumn meeting at Glenmore in Keene Valley, he said:

My life has been—if I may perhaps make the statement in this intimate presence—singularly happy. I have had the marvelous felicity of being able to live out my life. On the point of being squeezed into the cloak of a Jewish rabbi, I escaped into the broad fields. I have been able to work out, as far as possible, the things that were most cherished. Now, in the last lap of the race, I have the additional happiness of finding myself here in a group of more and more congenial spirits.

And yet, if towards the close I now look back, I must say that in essential respects there has been absolute failure. I say it because I realize today what a religious teacher should be.

The little things which others commend, and which they would fool you about, appear in their true perspective. The whole scene fades and fades, and you find yourself at last lifting your eyes and asking—what has your life meant, and in view of that what does the whole world mean?

To answer his own question, he then used a phrase clearly intended to shake up his hearers. "The answer," he said, "is I have lifted mine eyes and seen through the darkness, and because of it, 'the Glory of the Lord!' " In using this expression he was, of course, not announcing any reversion to a traditional God-belief. But he was meaning to stress "the glory" of a clearer vision of perfection, of "divine life" as a dimension of experience, which he now counted the supreme boon despite the fading scene wherein one's effectiveness must at last look small. And seeing "through the darkness" of persistent evil was here seen as a condition of clearer vision of the divine.

The sense of "absolute failure" Adler expressed here surely calls for interpretation. Besides confessing genuine regret it was doubtless intended to prod his colleagues into awareness of new emphases in his thinking. Moreover, the sense of failure does not appear as a reflection upon his religious seeking but upon his small effect as a religious teacher. The statement to his colleagues in 1915 implies, after all, his having successfully found a deeper vision. But it seems to doubt what corporate role he still can give it. To make his own matured religious views a requirement for his followers was out of the question, of course, as affronting the freedom of religion endorsed in Ethical Culture. Yet Adler could well believe that his now more distinct religious views, had they been arrived at earlier, might have given Ethical Culture stronger support and deeper focus than did his vagueness in the beginning and his still merely derivative statements in much of middle life.

As I see it, Ethical Culture was formed, is still moved and needs to be, by all three stages of Felix Adler's thought. It needs to be stimulated to specific vital reforms ever and again as it was in the beginning. It needs to be regulated further by enlightened Moral Law. But in regard for Moral Law alone there can be a danger of Phariseeism. And a sole care for unique ethical energy in infinite members could forward a libertarianism. It is a tribute to Adler's practical wisdom that he never pressed for operating only on the basis of his own climactic religious thinking.

In the fall of 1912, Felix Adler's Sunday morning meetings were moved from Carnegie Hall to the new home of the New York Ethical Culture Society, built next to its school on Central Park West between 63rd and 64th Streets. This remains its present location. The architect of the building was Robert D. Kohn, son of a founding member of the Society and himself for many years its president. Adler conferred with him about several points he thought important for his meeting hall. He wanted a low platform so that he might talk in the midst of the people rather than from a high pulpit. The same end was greatly served by a semicircular seating which gave more width than depth and put no one too far off.

Behind the platform, in large golden letters, was inscribed: "The place where men meet to seek the highest is holy ground." *Religious search, together,* is the note stressed in this, and the same inscription has since been used in several other Ethical Culture meeting places. In the symbolic treatment of the hall, Robert Kohn had the attuned aid of his wife, Estelle Rumbold Kohn, a sculptor. Underneath his lettering at the back of the platform she created a low-relief frieze, in wood, of standing figures grouped in close companionship. Large figures, also carved by her, stand at each end of a balcony, an elder with a youth on one side and a man, woman, and child on the other. The symbols are thus all of vital human relations.

The meeting hall could accommodate some twelve hundred—a smaller audience than could meet at Carnegie Hall—but one it was hoped more cohesively organized in active membership of the Society. This hope was in a real measure fulfilled, though not in all the ways that Adler projected. In his stress on vocational ethics he said that "in each vocational group is to be worked out the specific ethical ideal of that vocation"; and added that a major function of ethical fellowship is to promote a harmonizing of these ideals in a complete way of life. Groups of teachers, lawyers, businessmen, a Women's Conference, and for a time also, a Workers Fellowship, all made special contributions to the life of Ethical Culture. But their efforts were mostly responsive to particular felt needs rather than productive of a stable organic role and effect for the whole Society, such as Adler had in mind. This is well illustrated by the Women's Conference which, though it achieved permanence and continuity in a number of valuable activities, did not have the suggested "integrating" result for the Society as a whole.

Adler had even indulged the thought that in the Sunday meetings vocational groups "should be allocated to different parts of the meeting hall." And with his belief that women are particularly fitted for an integrating role, he advised that

the vocational group of Mothers occupy the central place. . . . In close touch with the other vocational groups, women henceforth will take a deeper interest in the ethical development of human society . . . and their influence should be to draw the entire religious fellowship together into a coherent unity.

This idea of patterning the Sunday audiences was an artificial tour de force that could not and did not take practical effect. Adler's vocational emphasis had other consequences but little direct influence on the configuration of the Society's Sunday morning meetings.

During the last decade of his life Felix Adler, not unlike many others who have attempted religious innovation, seemed to waver in his feeling about the prospects for his steps to advance ethical religion. Emphatically he could say in public:

I have been very happy in the fulfillment of my duties despite all difficulties. And I cannot be sufficiently grateful to you who have protected me in the freedom to live out my own true nature—to teach religion, to speak on the highest subjects, and to do so not only without wearing a mask, without any equivocation, but without the necessity of conforming in the least particular to usages and predictions, or forms of language which are not wholly true to my convictions. This I regard as an inestimable privilege.

Yet about the same time his personal notes carried reflections like the following:

The actual formula at first for me was: pay homage to the other by service, and rejoice in the simultaneous service rendered to thee. The important change arrived when the formula became: promote the appearance of the spirit in another, and thereby release the spirit in thyself.

This change was, I think, the result of painful experience, namely appalling bafflings. I did not succeed in producing growth in the other; in fact, I had the greatest difficulty in abnormal situations to secure even a fair uniformity to the normal type. I certainly did not find in the object on which I lavished my effort anything like recognition of my worth, let alone the desire to further it. I found myself in a relation that was pitifully anti-climactical to the thing I had ideally conceived.

I was forced to reflect, ponder, recast, arriving at the conclusion that not the actual change produced in the other, but the effort to produce it was the essential thing for me, so far as it worked in my own nature certain spiritual changes. The principal one was no longer staking on the result the worth-whileness of my spiritual experience.

Spiritual experience is the seeking of a friend, of a spiritual companion. Connected with this is the acceptance of pain, the opening of the breast to it, as one sees in the literal pictures of the Roman Catholic Church the breast of Christ opened. . . . The great remedy appears to rise from the abnormal beyond the normal to the supernormal; that is, to see the relation, not as a happy one, but one that requires spiritual growth, constant attempts at more penetrating understanding, and then self-control, enduring the suffering due to friction . . . discovering the strength of the other and building positively on that.

In facing these severe counsels, one does well to remember what Adler said soon after the end of World War I. In his address on "Religion and the Joy of Life" in January 1919, he offered a reply to those who felt his great emphasis on frustration was discouraging:

Frustration itself is not the last word . . . . though it is necessary to correct our presumed ideals and to compel us to conceive loftier ones in their stead. . . . We must discover how it is possible with the unvarnished truth in view, to keep up our courage and hope and gladness of heart. We must be prepared for evil without becoming evil-minded ourselves, or desperate or lugubrious, losing the relish of mirth and things sweet.

Prospects for Ethical Religion

If he ever had done so—as he may have at the age of twenty-two in closing his one and only temple sermon—in his maturity Adler never committed himself to the prospect of a single world-religion. Not only the special cultural soils in which various traditions had their roots but different turns in faith and spiritual outlook were against it. Moreover, in Adler's judgment, no religion, including his own views, was perfect enough, or ever likely to be, to achieve universality in actual observance as well as in ideal. He wanted to acknowledge deep permanent contributions made by various faiths but he also continued to the end to speak against what he regarded as their weaknesses and errors.

The question of prospect for ethical religion, therefore, became one of whether enlightened and relevant ethics would receive growing support from religion in its multiple developments. On this question Adler in his late years made memoranda in the following vein:

From the great wars of our time I expect to see more of a recrudescence of superstition than a reawakening of religion.

Only in the longer reach of time does religious progress seem possible, and then as a consequence of long gathering forces that make
—for a better adjustment between religion and other aspects of developing society
—for the emergence of a differently and more broadly educated leadership in religion
—and for the growing interplay of the earth's peoples and civilizations.

The unity of mankind will never be in a single creed.

The religious temple of the future will be built not of stone, but of living humanity. Many nations will be in it, many chapels or diversities of spiritual insight. And the dome overarching it will not be Michelangelo's hovering cupola, but the broad vault of heaven itself, symbolizing with its myriad stars the infinite paths of light and truth.

Thus, just as no previous period of history had seen mankind united in a single religion, so it appears Adler did not expect our spreading industrial culture to bring this about either. Yet repeatedly the world's many religious faiths have taken on similar features in adjusting to widely experienced phases of social and cultural life, as in the ancient city-states, empires, medieval feudalism, and modern nationalism. In the same way, adjustment to industrialism has been producing common characteristics—an epochal resemblance—among many faiths in our time. And much of Adler's own lifework was directed toward achieving a greater coherence between religious perspective and the changing democratic character of modern industrial society. His idea that "better adjustment between religion and other aspects of developing society" can be fruitful for "religious progress" reflects a central thrust of his career.

"A more broadly educated leadership in religion" was stressed as another vital condition of progress. Neither the Free Religious Association nor the Ethical Culture movement found the means and the will to respond to his early proposals to establish an academy for the more adequate education of a "liberal" religious leadership. The fact that this challenge remained for all religious bodies to face, and has been partly met in the programs of leading "union seminaries," tended also to preserve distinctiveness in the plurality of faiths.

With regard to the aid to religious progress that Adler saw in "the growing interplay of the earth's peoples and civilizations," it must be admitted that he himself did not attend as much as he might have to features of Indian and East Asian thought. The strength of vocational ethics in India was marred for him by its connection with caste gradations. Furthermore, his estimate of the Eastern religions seems to have been dominated by the idea that individuality was lost in their mysticism, and that their often grand naturism was too pagan. He either did not know or else took little note of teachings in the East that viewed "individuality as retained in the grand communion of the universe." The desire to be free of *illusion,* he thought, had led the Eastern spirit into excessive resignation and fatality. Nevertheless, he did recognize that, in their "acceptance of what is hard to face," the Asian peoples had indeed shared in "mankind's on the whole wonderfully stalwart attitude toward life."

He ended his life in an epoch of very mixed and strongly opposing currents. The world crisis, aflame with war and revolution since World War I, stirred both assault and counteraction in the religious as in other spheres of life. Communists directed a propaganda for mass conversion from religious traditions on an unprecedented scale. But anxiety over dissolving ways and ties concurrently gave rise to efforts to restore the old faiths. In both Europe and America a plea that religion must regain its traditional base in *theonomie*, in recognition of God's sovereignty, came to be heard now from socially and politically progressive leaders as well as from conservative ones.

Since he died in April 1933, Felix Adler did not see this tide advancing strongly in America. But in world perspective he had already noted, during the 1920s, that

Among present tendencies we find retrogression toward orthodoxy in all departments, as toward Catholicism and ritualism, and then on the other hand, attempts to carry out individualism to its furthest conclusions in free-love, anarchism, and in Nietzsche's doctrines; then again, relief from individualism is found in nationalism and other political mass movements.

Although, as noted earlier, he criticized communism as an overreaction to the injustices of capitalism, he also remarked that he feared that the likely backlashes to it might become even more dangerous to progress.

In his last decade, there was a memorable afternoon in which Adler shared his thoughts on "the state of religion" with a company of students and colleagues in the Ethical Culture leadership. On this occasion, he held that the relatively low influence of religion, including his own views, was due less to the inroads of modern science than to religion's not taking its own life-shaping tasks dynamically and constructively enough. In short, religions were acting too defensively toward "God's citadel, instead of expanding spiritual truth to transform human society more ethically."

Of Judaism, and of a religious implication in Zionism, he said in particular that day:

The prophetic teaching thundered that Justice, Mercy, and Humility were above all what Jahweh required.

In this the prophets caught a glimpse of the spiritual that is true for all time.

But they failed in that they prophesied its fulfillment in time. Jahweh would bring to pass his purpose in and with Israel historically, if need be by their destruction. The spiritual must be actualized.

And when the ancient state failed, the consequence of this was the transference of the attempt at actualization to a minute legalism and ceremonialism. The Jews hoped that the time would come when their faithfulness in observing the minutiae of their laws would lead to the miracle—the glorification of Israel.
The greatness and the weakness of Hebraism are here together.

Biblical religion is often briefly described as an ethical monotheism. But here Adler was agreeing with those who find it more accurately described as fusing its prophetic ethics with monotheism and a *Jewish epic of history.*

In this same discussion, Adler went on to an even more harsh comment about St. Paul's influence on Christianity.

St. Paul [he said] took a huge sledge-hammer and knocked man's moral ability, even his ability to strive effectively, to pieces. In turn St. Augustine preaches predestination, and Luther insists on fighting free-will as the devil.

This would seem to overlook the moral ability Paul finds to be imparted by grace. And I think it only fair to Adler to quote from him another statement on Paul that I believe is superbly apt.

A tempestuous, volcanic nature, extolling the divine grace. . . . Paul is the prototype of the whole struggling world of Christians after him, who remain immersed in their business and in their passions and lifted their arms up to Christ as the means of raising them above their condition.

But of greatest moment for Adler's relation to Christianity, whose leading exemplars he studied much, is his view of Jesus as portrayed in the Gospels. Rightly or wrongly, more than most Jewish and even than some Christian scholars, he saw in Jesus's counsel to self-purification, to correcting "the beam in one's own eye," an original and epochal contribution to ethical perception. He also accepted the command to do good, not evil, to one's enemies. But he could not adopt this as a policy of nonresistance. The idea of "turning the other cheek," of dwelling in meekness' and humility on self-purity alone, seemed to him to make sense only in an apocalyptic, end-of-the-world context. It is not a workable rule for building a better society on this earth.

Moreover, the turn to a personal Savior and to hero-worship so prevalent in Christianity also clashed with his belief that a transformed social ethic is indispensable.

No single supreme individual [Adler said] can embody the moral ideal. The godhead, instead of being conceived as a perfect individual, is to be symbolized as a perfect society. Worship in the older sense, as homage toward a single being regarded as embodying in himself the totality of excellence, is replaced by the creative endeavor to realize, or approximate to the realization of the infinite organic scheme in terms of actual social progress.

It seems odd that in the passage mentioning Augustine and Luther as predestinationists, Adler did not include Calvin, to whom he had devoted equal attention. Elsewhere he notes that the extreme divine election Calvin grants to his Sovereign God puts mankind in a monstrous tyranny. Yet, despite this, Felix Adler admired in Calvin

the straining after perfect righteousness, the longing for absolute virtue, the refusal to be measured by any but the highest standard. This straining, this longing, was carried too far. It led to fatal errors, but as a desire, as a tendency, it fills us with a certain awe.

The statement is indeed revealing, since not a few people were critical of what they felt to be an excessive awesomeness within Adler's own moral absolutism. On this point I am inclined to add that probably millions of people (most of whom never heard of Adler) would very likely find his religious views too awesome toward some human institutions and not awesome enough toward great aspects of nature apart from man. To me it seems that Adler had reason to find modern men, and perhaps Americans especially, too casual about much of their culture. Yet, did he share in a possible arrogance toward nonhuman nature, which also infects the Judaic and Christian traditions in part, and which may want correction not by a return to ancient paganism but by new ecological wisdom?

Adler's ethical religion said little, if anything, about the world apart from its providence for human betterment. Yet without reviving "natural theology" may it not continue to be a due work of religion to assist imaginative and fruitful regard for nonhuman as well as for human nature? I do not imply that Adler was unresponsive to natural wonders and beauties but ask only whether this bore enough meaning in his religious views. His own expres-

sion of attitude is more than once stated along the lines of a letter
to his wife in 1896.

In 1870 when I was here there was no railroad and I still remember
what an exhilarating ride it was on the top of the diligence. Toward evening we reached Interlaken facing the Jungfrau. The whole valley was
already in shadow, not a gleam of light anywhere. Only the highest sum-
mits of the incomparable mountain were wonderfully illuminated. The
pure white snow of the summit was dipped in gold. It seemed all radi-
ance, etherial beauty, celestial glory.

Then a sad change occurred as the light traveled upward the glow
turned into the whiteness of death, and the vast field of snow and the
gaunt rocks and the glacier with its motionless stream below sent a chill
to the very heart.

Twenty-six years ago! . . . Then I was at the beginning of my career,
a student of nineteen with intense susceptibilities to the influence of natural scenery, the enjoyment of which was a kind of intoxication to me.

Tonight I walked again in the garden of the Kursaal. . . . But my
thoughts were chiefly with you. The susceptibility to natural beauty has
perhaps become less intense, the day-dreams less splendidly colored, the
life purpose looms larger.

And in reflections of later life he adds:

I never was a Pantheist, and therefore never believed that a spiritual
presence actually inhabits the material phenomena. . . . I rise above and
pass beyond the objects of Nature, seeking a truer, yet still imperfect
analogy in the spiritual relations to my fellowmen. I no longer delay to
listen to the accompaniment, and am intent on the burden of the song
itself.

Felix Adler did give a cosmic religious scope to one crucial
idea—that in caring for worthy relations among themselves, men
deserve an ethical regard also from all other beings in the infinite
universe with whom they may prove able to communicate. But by
this human accent of his cosmic reach and by his rejection of
hero-worship, Adler's intensely ethical and social emphasis in religion was in contrast to much emphasis in familiar traditions. Differences of this kind are apt permanently to maintain and produce variety in religion.

In 1923, Felix Adler gave the Hibbert Lectures at Oxford,
which brought to publication a summing up of his main thoughts
under the title *The Reconstruction of the Spiritual Ideal* (1924). Here
he repeated and stressed his idea that religion must meet the spir-

itual "pains" that disturb people. And as characteristic of our times he mentioned a three-fold pain which religious consciousness should strive to overcome:

First, a painful sense of man's insignificance in the vast, physical universe.

Second, the pain due to the fate of those innumerable fellow beings who perish by the wayside, while man slowly and awkwardly tries to achieve progress.

Third, the intolerable strain of twisted relations and of divided conscience . . . especially in regard to standards that should regulate the morality of groups.

Adler's ethical and religious teachings attempted to give relief from all three of these great pains, though especially from the last.

In social ethics, and the "strain of divided conscience over the morality of groups" one can say that there has been a measure of general religious progress, bringing more active conscience to bear upon society's divisions and injustices. But a specific joining of religion with stronger "vocational" ethics was, at most, sought for by individuals, even within Ethical Culture circles, rather than by defined groups. Socialism, which Adler had denigrated as "mass individualism," remained more prevalent among some of his followers in their critique of existing society, especially after the Russian Revolution.

Man's power to pursue understanding and mutual regard was invoked to counteract his sense of "insignificance in the vast, physical universe." From a humanistic position, the pain "due to the fate of those who perish by the wayside" while progress is lagging, seems particularly difficult to overcome. By prizing right effort more than results, it can be met in part. But Adler was not satisfied by this kind of meliorism alone. Instead, he attributed to the "wayside perishers"—indeed to everyone, as we have seen—a distinctive role in the universal society of right. Their distinctive ethical energy contributes, however secretly, to the eternal flow in mankind of the "crystal fountain" of perfection.

A point always to be remembered is that, in accord with the "critical" strain in Kantian thought, Adler never looked upon his religious views as demonstrable "science" but rather as exemplifiable directives of effort. And the persistence of his work put both the direction and the honesty of his interest beyond question. Occasionally, as in the following statement, Adler described the religious attitude in quite familiar terms of "resignation and acceptance."

The religious attitude of the human mind remains thus essentially that which the ancient religious teachers marked out: one of an assurance without knowledge, one of resignation and acceptance of a certain unalterable doom, of crucifixion too in the sense that the divine is revealed to us only as a light piercing through darkness. The unbearable anguish that is nevertheless endured, with the faint margin of triumph at its rim, is the witness of faith now as in the past.

Yet a different spirit of decisive modern change came to the fore in other sayings of Adler's. This is very clear in his reflections on words attributed to Jesus, such as "My yoke is easy, and my burden is light." Not feeling this way about his own yoke, Adler pondered much about how it could be validly said. The answer seemed clear to him in the Gospel words: "Blessed are the meek," and again "Take my yoke upon you, and learn of me, for I am meek and lowly in heart." Your burden will be lightened if you also become meek and lowly. Relax concern for all but inner readiness for the Kingdom of God's approach. This world can then be meekly accepted as a light burden soon to pass away.

Clearly Adler's own ethics, so strongly charged with refashioning this world's society, could not offer these same tidings of relief to the heavy laden. And Christianity indeed, in the long history of its many adaptations, had become much mixed and complicated in its morals. Individuals the world over were universally challenged by a Christlike ideal of self and conduct. But the leadership and policies of the churches brought a great variety of social compromises and conflicting standards. Some imposed rigid and narrow restraints upon humanity. But more prevalent on the whole was accommodation to worldliness and conformism. This, Adler thought, tended consciously and unconsciously, to enervate a vigorous and healthy social upbuilding.

To what degree, he wondered, would his own religious teaching contribute more to such upbuilding? Like other prophetic minds who came to a new inspiration, especially if it is clarified freshly rather late in life, Adler at the end felt he would really need a second life to forward his matured thoughts more effectually. This is how I regard his "finding myself in a relation pitifully anti-climactical to the thing I had ideally conceived."

In 1931, at the age of eighty, he declared himself to have been "a religious seeker, but not the founder of a new religion." As a seeker, he had arrived at a personal vision of belonging in a universal order of divine life. This was no note of "absolute failure!" Indeed, what I have called the message of mutual maturing through active interrelation between all potentially capable of it is, it seems to me, a truly sublime turn of religious purpose. It is also in timely accord with the current forward-looking increase of human caring. Yet Adler was critical enough to say: "I know full well that moral science is still in its beginning, and I feel myself a beginner. . . . Dimly, darkly the great moral problems lift themselves before my view."

In April 1933, Felix Adler met for the last time with his colleagues. About fifteen people were gathered at the Fieldston School in a pleasant lounge into which the spring sunshine filtered. As one of Adler's later colleagues, Algernon Black, recalled it, the occasion was a seminar on internationalism. Adler, now eighty-one, was trying to improve his view of the nature of nations. For the first time in these sessions, Adler's voice faltered, perhaps twice. He seemed unable to continue his thought. Slowly taking his watch from his pocket and looking at it, he quietly said, "I guess my time is up," and left immediately for his nearby home.

His days thereafter in the hospital were few. He died on April 24, 1933, of the cancer that finally took its toll.

On April 27, laurel leaves and a spray of red roses lay on the coffin that stood before the platform from which Felix Adler had addressed his audiences at the Society for Ethical Culture for so many years. Those who spoke at the funeral service were his colleagues, Drs. David Saville Muzzey and John Lovejoy Elliott; and it was my privilege to say a few words for the family at the cemetery. What seemed to me notable was not that he had believed in himself, but that he had believed also in us.

The occasion of death is apt to bring some concentration of insight about the departed, and this was shown at the memorial meeting held by the Ethical Culture Society on May 7, when tributes from the wider public were tendered. The speakers on this occasion from outside of Ethical Culture included Dr. Nicholas Murray Butler, president of Columbia University; Dr. Stephen Wise, founder of the Free Synagogue; the Reverend Henry S. Coffin, president of Union Theological Seminary; and Mrs. Mary Simkhovitch, headworker of the Greenwich House Settlement.

It seemed to me particularly gratifying that Mrs. Simkhovitch expressed an understanding of Adler's "social ethics," not only in specific applications, but also in its leading differences from both socialism and individualism. For she noted that he "refused to be stamped into a greater belief in the mass than in the individual . . . and saw the need of an austere discipline for both the individual and for the social process." Otherwise, she said, "the voluminous selfishness of the mass is arrayed against the selfishness of strong individuals." Above all, she placed Adler's concept of relatedness and predicted "he will remain a living force in our changing world . . . because we live in a world of scattered bits, and this integration for which he stood is the greatest need of our society today."

Besides recognition of his practicality—that he was a teacher who also "sawed wood"—there was emphasis on Felix Adler's more ultimate search for spiritual fellowship. This was stressed not only by his intimate professional companions, like John Elliott, but by others as well. Among these was Henry S. Coffin, who spoke "as a near neighbor during the summer months with the opportunity of seeing much of Adler and of having experienced the surprising effect of sharing his friendship." Besides admiring this friend's intellectual integrity and his perception in religious studies, Dr. Coffin said:

At the core of this prophet of righteousness there was depth of molten lava, which was frequently erupted in golden eloquence; but in conversation his mind relieved itself with the play of words and ideas in a humor that was charming and not oppressive. . . . His wit had an extensive range, from puns, good, bad, and indifferent, to subtle and devastating irony.

Rabbi Stephen Wise also expressed a warm sense of personal indebtedness, saying that Adler had "concerned himself always with the innermost substance of life, beyond all externals. . . . His was an epoch upon which he laid the impress of his massive moral idealism. . . . Life cannot be the same again to those whose lives he touched." And Dr. Nicholas Murray Butler agreed that Adler's "appeal reached the public mind, not merely the public ear." For one found in "Adler a true captain of the soul, who knew what the soul's life was, and taught it, gladly, generously, finely to his fellowmen."

In the last chapter of his most autobiographical book, *An Ethical Philosophy of Life* (1918), Adler near the close makes a rather special comparison of himself with an early Swiss liberator, Arnold Winkelried (d.c. 1386). He stressed that Winkelried gave full way to the spears inflicted upon him by his opponents.

I am like Arnold Winkelried who gathered the sheaf of spears into his breast, and even pressed them inward, to make way for liberty. So do I press the sharp-pointed spears of frustration into my breast to make way for spiritual liberty.

For these cruel spears turn into shafts of light, radiating outward along which my spirit travels, building its final nest—the spiritual universe.

Comparison with Winkelried would certainly be a strained one, if "the spears" in Adler's case were interpreted literally as weapons in the hands of enemies. They should be more broadly seen as all the sharp-pointed differences with which he had to contend throughout his life. They must include the distinct "bests" in other people whose strengths differ from his own. Only so "by pressing them into his breast" do they force him toward finding what is "best" in himself and thus "turn into shafts of light." Spiritual liberty depends on the entire range of relating one's own and other natures.

"Religious" implied for Felix Adler a concern for latent potentials and Ethical Culture was very much future-oriented. Yet his personal life-journey as a religious seeker did not look only to what the future might add for a consummation. His religious consciousness was also crowned by a present sense of partaking in life's infinite linking—life unto life, spirit unto spirit. "A truer vision of the ideal," he said,

can arise only on the basis of persistence and fortitude in grappling with actual circumstances throughout life. The ethical viewpoint, as I see it, means linkage and interrelation for health of soul *now*. To touch the spiritual quick in the life of others, and to have the experience of its effect upon our own life—this is the supreme experience. And the conviction of spiritual community that can grow out of this experience is sufficient to bring man serene peace amid all his battles and torments.

EPILOGUE:
MEMOIR AND PROSPECT

One of Dr. Adler's favorite walks on summer afternoons a few hours before sundown was on a stretch of forest path which he used to call "the cathedral aisles." It lies on the lower, western side of the Adirondack mountain named The Giant, about half an hour's climb from its base at a moderate pace. There is a fairly level trail here amid a splendid stand of great and well-preserved hemlocks. After going up and along this stretch, eastward, and then turning to come back westward, one faces the rays of the declining sun as they slant through the still aisles of the trees, and the play of light and shade makes the walk home a forest communion with symbolic depth.

Taking this walk at times with Dr. Adler in his late years, it was inevitable that I wonder how the light was that he faced in the sundown of his life. An answer can be given only with hesitation. Yet I think that the warm, golden rays that were seen had to break through growing shades and a darkening sky. He could surely feel fortunate in having been able to serve so well, and so nearly to the very end, the commanding and sustaining "idea that had used him." But neither could he avoid a deeper sense of personal frailty and of the uncertainty in man's fate, such as comes to all who have yearned for a great spiritual goal. In the end such idealists are not likely to be sanguine about what they have accomplished.

The archaeologist, Hetty Goldman, a daughter of Adler's sister, remarked that in her experience he showed two quite distinct personalities. She expressed great pleasure in the wit and the easy delightful range of their private talks together. Yet in his public teaching and addresses she felt that a different spirit took over, tending to be austere, charged with formidable demands, and rather highly styled.

Whether viewing him as two personalities or not, I am sure that the presence of each of these manners in Adler was familiar to many people who knew him well enough to have seen both. The fact that I myself found his easy and severe sides present both in his play and in his work, as features of *one* complex human being, may be due to the degree of my association with him in his late years, and perhaps to a temper of my mind as well as of his.

In any case, there are points about Felix Adler which one learns whatever one may read or hear of him. Prominent in such common knowledge is the fact that he sought to promote freer thought and voice in religion and greater justice in human relations. These two dominant concerns were vitally joined in Adler's idea of Ethical Culture. He was a "deliverer" in two senses: he wanted to deliver people *from* conventions and superstitions that seemed to him to impede freedom in religious idea; and he wanted to deliver them *to* better relations and practices in human society.

If one learns anything of Felix Adler it is that he wanted to make ethical development central and dominant through all the human bond. He did not view the distinctive unique "worth" of each individual person as an isolated datum, but as entailed in the perfecting of his relations individually and in groups. Criticism of traditional monotheism was based by Adler not primarily on natural science, but on the sense that interpersonal relations were therein subordinated to a reverence of possibly less ethical character.

An innovating man such as Felix Adler is bound to be viewed and estimated with various emphases and valuations. He was full of energy and entered both gravely and more lightly into an unbounded hodgepodge of current relations. He advised a great many people with special personal care. And he built different kinds of institutions for a more lasting social guidance: religious societies, schools, vocational agencies, and fellowships.

It is inevitable that the experience of individuals among such personal and institutional relations should be strong in the coloring of their views of Dr. Adler. Most of those who have expressed themselves about him, with whatever slant, have been through much or at least a part of the mill—the system of culture—he established. They quite often speak of having "been born into Ethical Culture" as children of their parent members. And even more frequently they are likely to have attended an Ethical Culture school or other connected organization.

My own personal history, however, was not of this type. My forbears had no memberships in Ethical Culture and indeed scarcely any knowledge of it. I myself attended none of its schools, and its Societies only quite irregularly in my early twenties. My first meetings with Dr. Adler were as a graduate philosophy student visiting his seminars at Columbia University. This was in the closing years of World War I and during its early aftermath. Three particular conditions have thus occurred to me as strongly affecting my own response to Felix Adler. First, my coming to hear him as a philosophy teacher; second, that this took place amid the controversies over World War I and its settlement; and lastly, to be sure, my personal familiarity with Adler during the last decade of his life by my marrying his daughter, Ruth, in 1923 after some two to three years' acquaintance.

These facts have deeply accented, I believe, my distinct perspective upon Felix Adler. This book that I have written, if not loosely subjective, is still very strongly personal in what it has selected to stress and to say. In it I have not become occupied in detail with much of Adler in his leadership of Ethical Culture, even though I chose membership in the New York Society in 1926 and served various functions in both School and Society ever since. Yet in this book I have tried to present vital stages in Felix Adler's more general thought and social endeavor as a contemporary man.

In doing so, two achievements of his have impressed me as belonging to his most noteworthy contributions. The first of these has indeed received a very wide acceptance, far beyond Ethical Culture. The second, although also active in general life, is still controversial even within Ethical Culture itself.

The first of these contributions was the aim and content of elementary schooling as worked out in the Ethical Culture School of New York, 1880–95, in what was then called the Workingman's School. Instead of structuring elementary study around a number of chosen subjects ("the three r's") the aim taken was to develop the whole child in his humanity. In pursuit of this each was given regular medical examinations, his nutrition, so often deficient in poverty circles, was improved. He was developed in hands as well as in brain with a diversified program of arts and crafts. He was taken outdoors to play in parks and to see forming agencies of the city. Products and persons of the environment were brought into the school's laboratories and workshops. There was much good singing and dramatic festival. There was emphasis on fruitful steps in men's historical progress with one another. There was a creative emphasis on a *doing*, wherever possible, of the kinds of things being studied.

Dr. Adler at times felt that this program of elementary schooling could be rated his outstanding success. Though very unevenly followed, it has in time tended to become much of a model of elementary schooling in this country—or might we even say the world over? It is the elementary schooling, the first eight grades, *not* including the high school, that is here being noted. Elementary education, since about 1880, began to be made over so as to become experienced as a more complete period of human life.

Of course, in this development many, many others have enhanced what Adler did; so, for example, in reforming the nature of learning—to become a cooperative rather than a dictative relation between teacher and pupil—John Dewey's intelligence and influence have had most consequential effects.

In a second personal view, far less widely shared than the foregoing first one, I find in Adler's rather late expressions on religion another main contribution of his. This in fact is what he mostly talked about in his Adirondack cliff study when I listened to him there in his late seventies. He dwelt on a shift of religion from worship of an individual God to an interrelation of all persons serving to bring one another into a "Divine Life" of mutual maturing. I prefer this last phrase to using the more general "life of love" (not that the latter is excluded) because it more definitely conveys a sense of growth and is, moreover, less emotionally diffuse.

Was there anything more than traditional usage in Adler's keeping the phrase "Divine Life?" Yes; there was a reason why he was not satisfied with sheerly humanistic language—such as, "the ideal of all people forwarding one another at their best," although he used this too. But in his religious outlook he wanted the process of mutual maturing maximized to its uttermost—"infinitized," he more often said. That is, he did not mean to keep religion within the limits of relations between human beings. He believed it quite possible, or even likely, that there existed nonhuman beings capable of an intercommunicating that furthered such a mutual maturing. The totality of all such belonged for him within the divine life, expressed for him his idea, not of God, but of Godhead as implying a society with "infinitely inter-supportive members perfecting one another."

Perhaps at times in his early years Felix Adler put forward an "ethics" and a "religion" that were identical. Throughout life he certainly sought religious views that brought greater centrality and effect to his ethical ideas. Nevertheless, with philosophic growth he realized that other motives would continue to shape a variety of religious attitudes, and that therefore one should not expect the world to adopt any one universal form of faith. Belief in a single infinite God had numerous grounds of appeal—some accented in heroic salvationism, some in pantheistic leanings of unity, and many in still other historic revelations. It would surely involve fanaticism to think of Adler's own view as eliminating the power in these other alternatives.

Yet the magnitude I find in Adler's religious vision I can perhaps register by a comparison with two great and widely held alternatives. In India a religious approach of devout meditation upon the infinitude of being and a care to find terms of one's own part therein has been particularly strong. In the West, whether among Jews, Christians, or Moslems, the predominant religious approach has long been one of reverence for an Infinite Lord, a Creator who searches and loves and judges mankind. Many, both high and low in mind, have claimed that without trust in such divine guidance man's purpose and integrity crumble. But a capital stress is here to be given the claim that Felix Adler conceived still a third religious approach, one of reverence for *an infinity of ethical interrelations* of persons and of groups. In this his view of "the spiritual manifold or universe" included all mankind but also all others with and among whom there could be personal intergrowth. In point of departure this approach was humanistic but it was not so in its inclusive extent.

Among Ethical Culture members in good standing there are not a few who ignore, or even disparage, this religious turn of Adler's thought. At best they perhaps grant its significance for him personally. But in my judgment this was not only a personal consummation but a grandly universal construction as well. He did with this view give his religion a more unmixed and thoroughly *ethical* character. And this should count, I believe, as a main contribution of his that remains to invite a still further development in the future.

It must be granted that there are many who are not troubled by an ethical inadequacy in their religion, but instead are looking for an intensification of some other dimension. It may be widely felt that Adler's "ethical religion" puts virtually all its emphasis on the interpersonal and acknowledges too little the presence and possibilities of grandeur that are not of this kind. Like all radicals, Adler must accept the uncertainty of how far the religious future is going to promote his ethical emphasis or turn away from it. The direction and strength that it gives to one's life efforts and prospects is what counts, I would add. And whether or not the religions of the world are changing at their roots and zenith, they mostly do appear to take fuller interest in the ethical issues of the human bond.

Felix Adler's character was intricate, sufficiently devoted to one's benefit while also marked with tart critical inquiry, so as to evoke a wide range of responses from those who consulted him. Those persons who felt most blessed regarded his association of a caring dearness with his hallowed magnitude as virtually a miracle, which had been their spiritual fortune. But then there were many whose benefit from Adler was accompanied by a rather strong sense, quite often expressed, of having been "scared" by his many-sided and severe concern for "rightness." One can find those who carried this scare to the point of thinking of him as a martinet whose discipline repelled them more than it aided. I venture to add the thought that Adler, in his own sense of human complexity, did not want to be stereotyped as an example of any one such character.

It is a hazardous though provocative moment to engage in prophecy. Since Felix Adler's death so much has happened to raise new issues along with the old. He did not live to witness World War II nor the advent of the nuclear age. People are now wrestling with new dangers that had engaged him hardly at all. There is the unknown course of the world's population; also, the tremendous advance of technology which had not yet spelled for him the possible disasters to environment, the ecological damage which now threatens us. Still more unclear and sensitive are problems on the horizon in further knowledge of genetics and other life-processes. Those too have largely come forward since his death.

Whatever remains unknown about the further applications of Adler's energy and matured thought, there are a number of points about which we incline to have certain feelings. There cannot be doubt, for instance, that his name and work are less well known today than they were at the time of his death. And this obscuration is likely to grow because of the just noted new concerns of mankind. Yet with a comparable assurance Adler's highest hope, as he expressed it in an address of January 1901, at the opening of the century, remains an unchanged, lasting legacy of his.

Above all, the one thought into which all I cherish most, all I most hope for, and aspire to, can be compressed is this: May the humanity that is within every human being be held more and more precious, and be regarded with ever deepening reverence.

The vice that underlies all vices is we are held cheap by others, and far worse, that in our inmost soul we think cheaply of ourselves.

Felix Adler was less averse to cooperative combinations, less wary of "bigness," than was his brother-in-law, Louis Brandeis. Yet one can hardly imagine his influence being diverted to a support of any absolute sovereignty lest it be that of his Ethical Ideal as such. With respect to people's relations and institutions, a distribution of authority, a social pluralism grounded in vocational experience and competence, can hardly be disassociated from him.

"I am grateful for the idea that has used me," he declared. To honor the "worth" in people implied for him not alone a feeling toward them but a way of life. I am confident to conclude that the idea of mutual worth and maturing is profound and capacious enough to draw many others of ability into its continued and further use. Amid the progress of these many others, what Felix Adler was and did in his time will reward frequent careful recall, because most of what he did was of a kind that must be done afresh in every succeeding generation.

ETHICAL CULTURE SINCE
FELIX ADLER: AN AFTERWORD

EDWARD L. ERICSON

When Felix Adler died, Franklin D. Roosevelt had occupied the White House for only seven weeks. Hitler had been in power in Germany for barely three months. The intellectual and social world that had shaped Adler had been irreparably fractured by the events of 1914–1918, and the decade to follow his death would bury much of the civilization he knew under an avalanche of fiery cataclysm and nihilist terror.

Yet the ethical conception of life and the democratic faith have survived. Roosevelt's New Deal would not have satisfied Adler's vision of an ethically directed "organic" social order, but it moved the United States into an era of increased responsibility for the poor and the racially excluded, a policy that mirrored much of the same social conscience that had activated the practical side of Adler's ethical idealism.

The Ethical Culture movement and its schools survived its founder, and in the quarter century that followed, considerably increased the number and geographical range of member societies—thus becoming a singular exception to the short life of several similar experiments to realize Emerson's prophecy of a coming "church of moral science." Yet, despite the spread of societies, the overall number of adherents has remained fairly constant, except for a bulge in the decades following World War II that accompanied a "baby boom" in the Sunday Schools and a sharp increase in organized religious activity in the nation. Despite its uniqueness in other respects, Ethical Culture could serve as a reasonably accurate barometer of the state of vitality of mainline and liberal religious bodies in America.

At the time of his death in 1933, Felix Adler was the uncontested leader of the Ethical Culture movement. He had always had success in drawing to himself colleagues of strong character and intellectual talent. Several were brilliant and won recognition as scholars of considerable accomplishment; others, no doubt, would have achieved equal or greater recognition had they chosen a more conspicuous field. Ethical Culture built solidly; but, following the example of its founder, never compromised its message or method for popular acclaim.

In his lifetime Adler had taken pains to make a distinction between his individual philosophical system and the possible ways of thinking that might yet develop in the Ethical Culture movement. He always insisted that his was *an* ethical philosophy of life—not *the* definitive philosophy. Nevertheless, his prestige and the continuing force of his personality assured that as long as he lived, his views would predominate and that the liberal, experimentalist philosophy that was emerging as the leading challenge to his thought—naturalistic humanism, of which Adler entertained a poor opinion—would not fare well in his shadow.

Yet, in theoretical philosophy as in his political and cultural universe, Adler had outlived his epoch—or so, at least, it seemed for the next forty years, in which Adler's neo-Kantian ethical idealism with its metaphysical underpinnings that twentieth-century humanists found hard to understand, came to be considered an anachronism in his own religious house. Honored as a founder, venerated as an educator, admired and emulated as a social critic and reformer, he was virtually abandoned by his successors as a philosopher. This situation has only recently been partially reversed by a revival of interest in his thought—especially as it applies to his conception of religion and of the value-forming process—by the younger generation of leaders and members. This development brings the wheel full circle, presenting our and future generations with the same question that must be posed with respect to the thought of any thinker whose ideas have a lasting impact: What lives and what is dead in the thought of Felix Adler?

Rather than presuming to answer this question, we might simply record that just as the Ethical Culture movement outlived its founder, so the founder's seminal ideas have outlived earlier prophecies of their obsolescence, his views continuing to challenge and fructify the thought of the Ethical movement.

We may doubt that his ethics and metaphysics, as a systematic philosophy, will ever regain the following it enjoyed during his lifetime. In this respect his system must be a creature of time, sharing the fate of all intellectual constructs. But even as their unity and coherence disintegrate, the best of idealist systems of nineteenth-century philosophy, and Adler's in particular, become depositories of ethical formulations and perceptions that much of this century's philosophizing has assimilated poorly or simply missed. At least as a foil and corrective to our much too indulgent, pragmatic humanism—to say nothing of the subjective relativism that has sapped a generation of ethical thinking—Adler bars the path as an unremitting challenger on the side of an objectively grounded and lastingly valid ethics.

Only the future can tell whether the continuing dialogue between the type of idealist philosophy represented by Adler and the humanistic naturalism exemplified by John Dewey can regenerate and revivify the thought of Ethical Culture—the movement that Adler built and Dewey, through his followers, so quickly inherited.

This much must be said in fairness to both philosophical approaches and their advocates. When Adler died there were no young or even middle-aged successors to carry forward his distinctive philosophy of ethical idealism. Naturalism and humanism held the field. The two most brilliant philosophical leaders in the Ethical movement—V. T. Thayer at the helm of the Ethical Culture schools, and the youthful Jerome Nathanson, soon to rise to prominence in the leadership of the New York Society—were both vigorous and able champions of Dewey. While they admired Adler and were superb builders of the institutions he left behind, their hearts and minds belonged to the still formative American school of pragmatism and naturalism that ran from Pierce and James to Dewey and the large circle of humanistic and progressive philosophers, educators, and democratic social thinkers that Dewey energized.

The social philosophy of Ethical Culture also underwent significant change, at least in emphasis and tenor, after Adler's passing from the scene. John Lovejoy Elliott, already approaching his mid-sixties, succeeded Adler as Senior Leader in New York. While he and Adler had collaborated for nearly half a century on the settlement house movement, race and labor relations, and other social issues, Elliott's bent was far less theoretical than Adler's. Elliott had no pretensions as a philosopher and his warm, practical nature turned instinctively to the immediate tasks of the Depression years and the approaching test of democracy in World War II.

Adler's right hand in helping to meet the needs of the poor had been Elliott, who had earned a national reputation as a social reformer and community worker. His distinctive labor, as he turned increasingly in his final years to the organizational and global responsibilities of the Senior Leader, fell on Algernon D. Black, who became an Ethical Culture Leader the very year after Adler's death. Articulate, energetic, and magnetic in personality, Black was well suited to voice Ethical Culture's social conscience.

What Nathanson provided in philosophical reformulation and exposition, Black gave in capturing the attention of a generation of social activists who had to make sense of a world gripped in hard times, facing palpably unjust extremes of poverty and wealth, a state of affairs exacerbated by pervasive racism and religious bigotry—the Ku Klux Klan parading in masses that would not be seen again until the demonstrations of Civil Rights advocates and peace activists a third of a century later. Black, Nathanson's senior by seven years, shared the humanist outlook of Thayer and Nathanson, providing it with his own strong emphasis on social criticism and community action.

Less interested than his colleagues in metaphysical issues, Black put his own stamp on Ethical Culture through his work as a teacher, and later, Head of Ethics of the Ethical Culture Schools—combined with his effective activity at large in the anti-Fascist, racial justice, labor, civil liberties, peace and other causes from the 1930s to the present. Without doubt, through his involvement in many national committees and coalitions, and as a forceful speaker at rallies and through the media, he became the most widely recognized Ethical Culture Leader in the fifty years following Adler, except perhaps for David S. Muzzey (Elliott's successor as Senior Leader in New York) who had made his reputation as a Columbia University professor and whose textbooks on American history were studied for a generation by millions of American high school and college students.

In the intellectual life of Ethical Culture during this half century, no one played a more constructive and harmonizing role than Horace Friess himself—Adler's son-in-law by marriage to the youngest of the children, Ruth, and an Ethical Culture Leader over and above his distinguished career in philosophy at Columbia. A naturalistic humanist in his own religious philosophy, he retained a strong sympathy and appreciation for Adler's older philosophical style, which he tirelessly interpreted to new generations. His colleagues were always impressed with the clarity and balance of his mind, and his intellectual devotion to his lifelong task of completing this study of his late mentor and family patriarch.

This brief afterword cannot trace the thought and careers of many other distinguished leaders and laymen who served during this half century the movement Adler had built. (Howard Radest's excellent history of the Ethical Societies in the United States, *Toward Common Ground,* is the most available source for detailing this story.) What emerges from this glimpse at the course of Ethical Culture during the half century since Adler is a vital movement of Societies and schools, still small in number (twenty-one societies and fellowships at present, with schools in New York City and Washington, D.C.), still occupied with forefront ethical issues in education, government, social and business practice, intergroups and international relations, family and personal values, as well as providing a distinctive ethical and religious approach to the larger spiritual question of life's meaning and ultimate worth.

What Felix Adler began still lives; after fifty years of exploration beyond his lifetime, his movement finds itself seeking a better understanding of the thought and work of its founder and inspirer. This careful, masterful study by Horace Friess is an invaluable resource in the recovery of Adler's essential character and contribution.

As a living faith today, Ethical Culture reveals the interplay of many minds, hearts, and hands. Nevertheless, Felix Adler would find its major premises consonant with the "common ground" of the centrality of ethics and the affirmation of human worth that underlay his reformulation of religion and moral philosophy.

Ethical Culture has never been reduced to a formal creed, but in its one hundred years of continuing self-definition certain cardinal principles have emerged which may be said to describe its essentials, both as an ethical religion and as an educational and social methodology.

The present writer believes these essentials can be summarized in the following four points, which should be read not as dogma, but as the distillation of a century of experience in the faith and practice of Ethical Culture:

1. Ethical Culture affirms the supreme worth of the person. Every human individual must be treated as a unique and irreplaceable moral being. No human being should be considered primarily as a means but as an end in himself; that is, no individual can truly be said to fulfill his moral potential if he or she does so at the expense of others.

2. Ethical Culture asserts the centrality of the ethical factor in human relationships. We develop and define our character as human beings through the moral quality of our relationships with others. The greatest creative and redemptive force in life and history is released by the shared moral concern of human beings for each other and the community and world. Commitment to ethical development requires us to express our faith and moral courage in practical deeds to raise the level of human relationships and to strive for social justice.

3. Ethical Culture requires and upholds the democratic process and community. A corollary of our belief in the worth of the person and the centrality of ethics is our belief that only democratic methods and principles are consistent with human dignity and needs. We are unconditionally loyal to democracy as affirming the inalienable right of human beings to enjoy individual dignity and to participate responsibly in society.

4. Ethical Culture has faith in the free exercise of the mind in community and the open contest of ideas. Human dignity requires that there be freedom to explore and to publish conflicting

ideas and beliefs, to question and to test both accepted and disputed beliefs, and to search freely for new truths and understandings. No social system, political or ideological theory, or religious or philosophical belief can ever be exempt from vigorous criticism and dissent except at the cost of freedom and social morality.

These fundamental beliefs, expressed in varying forms over the past century, have constituted the undergirding moral and intellectual discipline of Ethical Culture. If we profess these values as the driving commitment of our religion, we may yet achieve the historic mission that the young Adler took as his life's work when he brought together that fledgling body of seekers who became the Society for Ethical Culture.

Edward L. Ericson
Chairman, Board of Leaders
New York Society for Ethical Culture
New York City

May 1980

PRINCIPAL WRITINGS

Collected Papers

The Papers of Felix Adler, numbering approximately 17,000 items, are housed in the Rare Book and Manuscript Library of Columbia University. The collection has been boxed and listed and is described by the Library as follows:

COLLECTIONS OF CORRESPONDENCE AND MANUSCRIPT DOCUMENTS

NAME OF COLLECTION: ADLER, Felix, 1851–1933—Papers

SOURCE: Gift of Mr. & Mrs. Horace L. Friess, 1974

SUBJECT: ethics; morality; religion

DATES COVERED: ca. 1870–1933   NUMBER OF ITEMS: ca. 17,000

STATUS: (check appropriate description)
Cataloged:___ Listed:_X_ Arranged:___ Not organized:_____

CONDITION: (give number of vols., boxes, or shelves)
Bound:_____ Boxed:__57__ Stored:_____

LOCATION: (Library) Rare Book and Manuscript Library

CALL-NUMBER: Ms. Coll/Adler

RESTRICTIONS ON USE

DESCRIPTION: The manuscripts, typescripts, notes and correspondence of Felix Adler, 1851–1933, (Columbia College, A.B.,

1870) religious leader and educator. Included are published and unpublished manuscripts of his lectures, essays, articles, books and random jottings on a wide range of topics, such as, ethics, morality, philosophy, Bible, theology, Judaism, politics and art. Many of the lectures were given at the New York Society for Ethical Culture, founded by Adler in 1870. Also included are his lectures at Columbia University, where he was professor of social and political ethics from 1902 to 1933. There are manuscript notes of an autobiographical nature, including diary entries for the years 1902 to 1924. Of interest are his notes of Conversations on Religion and Ethics with various individuals, including Woodrow Wilson and Tagore. The collection is classified by subject and arranged in numbered folders. There is an index of personal names referred to in the collection.

Books and Pamphlets

1880 *Creed and Deed: A Series of Discourses by Felix Adler.* New York: Putnam (copyright 1877). 5th ed., 1894.

1884 *The Ethics of the Political Situation.* An address delivered before the Society for Ethical Culture, Sunday, October 19. [New York, 1884?]

1892 *The Moral Instruction of Children.* New York: Appleton. 5th ed., 1909.

1903 *Life and Destiny: or Thoughts from the Ethical Lectures of Felix Adler.* New York: McClure, Phillips. London: Watts, 1913.

1905 *The Essentials of Spirituality.* New York: James Pott, 1905.

1905 *Marriage and Divorce.* New York: McClure, Phillips. Amplified 2d ed., New York and London: Appleton, 1915, 1926.

1905 *The Religion of Duty.* New York: McClure, Phillips. New York: Doubleday, Page, 1909.

1910 *What the Ethical Culture School Stands For.* New York: American Ethical Union.

1915 *The World Crisis and Its Meaning.* New York and London: Appleton.

1918 *An Ethical Philosophy of Life Presented in Its Main Outlines.* New York: Appleton. Further editions, 1923, 1925.

1919 *National Self-Determination and Its Limits.* New York: American Ethical Union.

1919 *Nationalism and Zionism.* New York: American Ethical Union.

1919 *Punishment of Individuals and of Peoples.* New York: American Ethical Union.

1919 *Religion and the Joy of Life.* New York: American Ethical Union.

1921 *Disarmament—Its Ideals and Possibilities.* New York: American Ethical Union.

1923 *The Reconstruction of the Spiritual Ideal.* Hibbert Lectures, delivered in Manchester College, Oxford, May 1923. New York and London: Appleton, 1924. Reprint ed., New York: AMS Press, 1978.

1926 *Some Characteristics of the American Ethical Movement.* New York: American Ethical Union.

1926 *Personality—How to Develop It in Family, School, and Society.* New York: American Ethical Union.

1930 *Incompatibility in Marriage.* New York and London: Appleton.

1946 *Our Part in This World: Interpretations by Felix Adler, Selections by Horace Friess.* New York: King's Crown Press.

INDEX

Abbot, Francis E., 75, 76
Abenheim, Max, 56
Adler, Abraham (uncle), 17, 18
Adler, Eleanor (daughter), 111
Adler, Felix: appearance of, 2, 57; appointed chairman of Council on Conciliation, 156-58; assumes presidency of American Philosophical Association, 220; assumes presidency of Free Religious Association, 75-77; calls for "Religion of the Ideal," 3, 53, 63, 91; develops educational model, 95-100, 121-37; develops ethical leadership in U.S., 81-90; develops ethical movement in Europe, 111-20; education of, 19, 21-25, 27; ethical theory of society, 2, 8, 69-72, 220-23; forms Union of Religion, 43; interest in German thinkers, 2, 12, 31, 32-35, 209-12; joins movement for "good government," 103-6; oratorical style, 40-41, 57-58; works with Tenement House Commission, 100-3
—— *views on:* divorce, 168-70; ethics teaching, 124-28; family life, 159-73; imperialism, 184-208; Jewish nationality and Zionism, 197-98; the "labor question," 35, 60-61, 71, 73, 139-50, 154-58; League of Nations, 203-6; Marxism and Socialism, 146; moral law, 35; "organized democracy," 150-53; pacifism, 201; Populism, 147-48; racial issues, 193-97; Reform Judaism, 36-37, 51; religious faith, 3, 9-10, 91; social justice, 23, 71-72, 222, 224-45; Vocationalism, 148-50, 154, 164
—— *writings mentioned:* "American Ideals," 191; "Anti-democratic Tendencies in American Life," 189; *Creed and Deed,* 52, 55, 58, 59, 226; "Critique of Kant's Ethics," 217*n;* "The Distinctive Part of Woman in Creating the Civilization of the Future," 173; "The Divorce Law," 166; "The Duty of Civilized Nations to the Uncivilized," 187; "The Effect of Modern Industrial Development on the Family," 169; "The Enlightenment of the Masses," 51; *Ethical Addresses,* 48*n;* "The Ethical Element in Religion," 114; *An Ethical Philosophy of Life,* 1, 34, 41, 142, 153, 162, 181*n,* 211*n,* 220, 231, 232, 247; *Ethical Problems,* 50; "Ethical Standards Applied to Economics," 114; "The Ethics of the Labor Struggle," 106; "The Ethics of the Social Question," 65; "The Fall of Jerusalem," 39; "The Form of the New Ideal," 52, 53; "The Function of Teleology," 213; "The Good and Evil Results of War," 187; "The Highest Hopes for Humanity," 150; "The Illusion and the Ideal of Marriage," 170; "The Judaism of the Future," 36, "Just Measures of Social Reform," 70, 72, "Marriage," 166, 167; *Marriage and Divorce,* 170; "The Matter and Method of Moral Education," 114; *The Moral Instruction of Children,* 112, 125, 126; "Moral Questions Involved in the Proposed League of Nations," 203; "The National Crisis," 201; "The New Ideal," 51, 52, 54; "Organization," 217*n;* "Our National Shortcomings and Our National Greatness," 191-92; *Our Part in This World,* 14*n;* "The Priesthood of the Ideal," 56;